Success!

How to Succeed in
Leaving Certificate English Paper 1
Higher Level

Jim Lusby

Gill & Macmillan Ltd
Hume Avenue
Park West
Dublin 12
with associated companies throughout the world
www.gillmacmillan.ie

978 07171 4605 5

Design and page make-up by Mike Connor Design & Illustration

The paper used in this book is made from the wood pulp of managed forests. For every tree felled, at least one tree is planted, thereby renewing natural resources.

Picture Credits

For permission to reproduce photographs the author and publisher gratefully acknowledge the following:

ALAMY: 17, 22, 25, 28, 29, 36, 38, 44, 56, 57, 64, 71, 87CR, 93, 98, 109, 112, 114BL, 120, 132, 134, 140, 143, 156, 169, 173, 176; COLLINS PHOTOS: 101; CORBIS: 32, 87BL, 96, 172; GETTY: 10, 107, 114CR, 114TR, 125, 167, 181; IMAGEFILE: 14; PA PHOTOS: 87TR, 114BR, 166, 174, 178; PANOS: 69TL, 69TR, 69BL, 69BR, 103; THE KOBAL COLLECTION: 11; PHOTOCALL: 19; REPORT DIGITAL: 87TL; REUTERS: 87CL, 105; SEVENTEEN: 82; THE SUN ARCHIVE/ NI SYNDICATION: 4B, 4T.

The author and publisher have made every effort to trace all copyright holders, but if any has been inadvertently overlooked we would be pleased to make the necessary arrangement at the first opportunity.

Contents

Guide to using *Success*

This book prepares candidates for the Leaving Certificate Higher Level English Paper I, Comprehending and Composing and is intended for day-to-day classroom use in both fifth year and sixth year. Its starting point is the examination requirements, and it therefore makes extensive use of texts from past Leaving Certificate papers, but it also insists that preparing properly for the examination improves, rather than damages, our appreciation of the English language.

Part One explores how to *read* for the examination, with the emphasis on preparation. **Part Two** explores how to *write* for the examination, with the emphasis on performance.

Given a two-year cycle of preparation, teachers may find Part One more suited to fifth year students and Part Two more appropriate to sixth years, although the chapters on Composing in Part Two will probably be used for both years.

A guide to using Chapters One – Three

Each of **the three chapters in Part One** deals with a separate language category: **Information**, **Argument** (including *Persuasion*) and **Narrative** (including *Descriptive Writing,* the term that often appears on the examination paper, and *The Aesthetic Use of Language*, the term that is used in the Department of Education syllabus).

Each chapter consists of:

- a brief **introduction** to the language category
- two preliminary **samples** offered for critical reading in class and designed to introduce the student to the basic requirements of the language category in question
- a more advanced text, **an example from past Leaving Certificate papers**, offered for critical reading in class and designed to acquaint the student with all the requirements of the relevant language category
- a text offered as a **class assignment**, which can be treated either as a full-scale test paper for later assessment by the teacher or as a class exercise in which each student reads and notes their critical responses for the first part of the session and then contributes to a general discussion and analysis for the second part
- a selection of short-term **homework** options and long-term **tasks**, which the teacher can use or ignore as desired, but which can also work as helpful suggestions if the teacher wants to research further appropriate material to use in additional teaching sessions.

A guide to using Chapter Four, Answering Question A

Chapter Four, Answering Question A, is divided into four sections, one for each type of question set in Comprehension on Paper I.

Each section consists of:

- a **sample text** from a past Leaving Certificate paper
- a **sample answer** to the relevant question set on that text

- a **detailed guide**, based on this sample answer, to **interpreting the question**, **locating the material in the text** and **organising the written answer**
- a **key tip**

The three **class assignments with assessment sheets** that conclude this chapter are intended to reinforce the material already introduced, to allow the student to put into practice what has been learned, and to allow the teacher to assess the progress of individual students and identify where errors are made and marks lost.

A guide to using Chapter Five, Answering Question B

Chapter Five, Answering Question B, is divided into three sections, mirroring the chapter divisions in Part One: **Informative Question B**, **Argumentative Question B**, **Narrative Question B**.

Each section consists of:

- a general **description** of the Question B type
- a list of the **formats** the student may be asked to write in
- a reminder (from Part One) of the **key elements** of each type
- a **sample answer 1** to a past Leaving Certificate task, with plan and assessment
- a **sample answer 2** to a past Leaving Certificate task, with plan and assessment
- a relevant **assignment with assessment sheets** that can be used as homework or as a class exercise

A guide to using Chapters Six – Eight

Chapters Six, Seven and Eight deal with writing the three types of composition set in the examination, the **short story**, **personal essay** and **discussion essay** respectively.

Each chapter consists of:

- a brief **introduction** to the composition type
- a **sample 1**, with a detailed critical reading
- the **key elements** of a successful short story, personal essay or discussion
- further **samples**, with detailed critical readings
- a **sample without critical comments** for the student's assessment
- a section on **tips and potential problems**
- an **assessment sheet**

The marking scheme for English

This book prepares you for Higher Level English Paper I, and since all your work is assessed with reference to the Department of Education's PCLM Marking Scheme, it is essential that you understand what this scheme asks of you and how it works. The following guide will therefore be a constant reference point for you.

P = Clarity of Purpose, which is explained as *engagement with the set task*; it evaluates the relevance of your material, and is worth 30 per cent of the available marks. In other words, have you clearly understood the task that you were given, have you clearly understood the precise question that you were asked, do you know enough about the given topic, and have you a clear grasp of the genre that you are either using or discussing? In the simplest English, this asks: *Do you know what you're talking about?* Throughout this book, the term most widely used for this is *content*. Is the *content* you introduce relevant to the task?

C = Coherence of Delivery, which is explained as *ability to sustain the response over the entire answer*; it evaluates the structure of your essay, and is worth 30 per cent of the available marks. In other words, have you properly structured your answer, is it properly organised, have you sustained your discussion in a consistent manner, using appropriate illustrations and examples? In plain English: *Does your answer hang together?* Throughout this book, the term most widely used for this is *structure*. Is the *structure* of your composition sound?

L = Efficiency of Language Use, which is explained as *management and control of language to achieve clear communication*; it evaluates the appropriateness of your written expression and is worth 30 per cent of the available marks. In other words, how good are your writing skills, how accomplished is your written expression, how familiar and comfortable are you with the relevant technical terms and how aptly can you use them in discussion? In plain English: *Can you express yourself?* Throughout this book, the term most widely used for this is *style*. Is the *style* of your writing appropriate to the task?

M = Accuracy of Mechanics, which evaluates your *spelling and grammar* and is worth 10 per cent of the available marks.

Part One:

How to Read for Leaving Certificate Higher Level English Paper 1

Chapter One:

The Key Elements of an Effective Informative Text

Introduction

This may seem a little obvious, but the purpose of an informative text is to inform; to increase the knowledge and understanding of a reader. Everything else is of secondary importance.

The following comparison of two reports of the one incident should leave you with a keener awareness of how to evaluate informative writing. This skill is essential in answering such questions as 'Jan Stevens sets out to inform the reader on the topic of ghost writing. What features make this an interesting piece of informative writing?' (LC Paper I 2006, Text 2). It will also help you in writing an informative text of your own – essential for managing such tasks as 'A Journey through Time: Imagine that you have discovered a time capsule containing a number of items from the distant or more recent past. Write a letter to a local or national newspaper announcing your find and describing the items contained in the capsule.' (LC Paper I 2003, Question B, Text 1).

The samples

The following material provides two accounts of a shooting at the Harvey Nichols store in London.

The first is from the English tabloid the *Sun*. The second is from the English Berliner the *Guardian*. (A Berliner is a newspaper format between the sizes of the tabloid and the broadsheet.)

CRITICAL QUESTIONS

1. The word 'carnage' means 'extensive slaughter'. When you have read the whole article, come back and decide how appropriate the headline is.

2. What's the difference between being shot by a 'handsome' man and being shot by an ugly man?

3. The word 'crazed' means 'driven insane'; 'pumped' means 'to deliver shots repeatedly with great force' and 'blowing your own brains out' would leave them rather detached from the rest of you.

Sample 1 from the *Sun* newspaper

Carnage at Harvey Nicks

By RICHARD WHITE and TONY BONNICI

TERRIFIED shop girls at Harvey Nichols told last night how a handsome man began chatting to a colleague – then shot her dead.

The crazed ex-lover pumped five bullets into his victim's head before blowing his own brains out.

4. Does the photograph here add to our understanding of the event? Does it make an effective visual impact? Is it attractive, or distracting?

Sealed-off ... Harvey Nichols

5. When was the last time you heard of 'two hysterical *men*' running from anywhere?

Two hysterical girls from the posh store ran into a nearby H&M shop, screaming: 'Oh my God, she's just been shot — we saw it all.'

6. Someone said that someone else told them?

A 25-year-old H&M worker said: 'They told me a smart young man had walked in and was chatting to the girl. They assumed it was her boyfriend.

7. Another photograph. Is it there to provide information or to arouse interest?

Horror . . . killer's body on floor of store

Then he went round behind her counter. That was when they heard the shots.'

Last night the killer's body could be seen 15 metres from the sealed-off front entrance of the famous store in Knightsbridge, central London – where he had once worked as a guard.

8. A '26-year-old sales girl'? Have you ever heard of a '26-year-old sales boy?' And 'believed to be called Claire' and 'it was thought' and 'said to be' and 'it was understood'. Anything wrong with these?

A co-worker said the 26-year-old sales girl – believed to be called Claire – had recently dumped him and it was thought she had taken out a restraining order on him.

The killer, said to be in his 30s, was known to police and it was understood there had been a history of domestic violence reported by his victim.

9. Would the killing be less interesting if the pot of moisturiser cost £9.65? That's a serious question.

He entered at 7.45pm, 15 minutes before closing time, and made his way to her post, the ground floor's La Prairie skincare counter – where a pot of the exclusive range's basic moisturiser costs £96.50.

10. But surely he 'pumped five bullets' and didn't really 'let rip'?

Terrified staff and customers dived for cover as he let rip with a handgun.

One Harvey Nichols worker said: 'It was about 7.45pm. I was looking at my watch, ready to go home, then I heard six gunshots.'

A witness said last night: 'He pulled the trigger time and time again. Then he put the gun to his head and pulled the trigger.'

11. Didn't they also 'dive for cover'?

Another said: 'Everyone stared in horror and then ran to the exit.'

12. The word 'haunt' means 'to visit in the form of a ghost'. Good choice of word in this context?

Armed police raced to the store – a favourite haunt of Princess Diana and of TV characters Patsy and Edina in sitcom *Absolutely Fabulous*.

Later murder squad detectives questioned weeping members of staff and customers.

One police source said: 'People were in a state of shock.

'There was a domestic history of violence between the man who carried out the shooting and the victim.

'They had been in a relationship and when it ended there had been threats of violence.

'But nobody could have foreseen such a horrific ending.'

Sample 2 from the *Guardian* newspaper

Store gunman 'had stalked victim'

A former Harvey Nichols security guard who gunned down a beauty counter worker in the store after she ended their relationship had been 'stalking' and 'pestering' her.

Clare Bernal, 22, was shot several times by 30-year-old Michael Pech, a former security guard at the exclusive store, who had pleaded guilty to harassing her only two weeks ago.

Despite having threatened to kill her as long ago as March, Pech was out on bail on condition that he did not contact her or enter Dulwich Village, the upmarket area of south London where she lived.

But last night, he walked into Harvey Nichols just 20 minutes before closing time, strode calmly up to the La Prairie cosmetics counter and shot her several times with a handgun in front of terrified customers and staff.

The Czech national, who lived in a shared terraced house in Tottenham, north London, then shot himself in the head.

Miss Bernal's mother, Patricia, who lives in Tunbridge Wells, Kent, was said to be 'absolutely distraught'. She is being offered police family liaison support.

Her daughter's close colleagues at the department store in Knightsbridge, central London, were similarly distressed. Some openly embraced each other and burst into tears as they arrived at work.

They described Miss Bernal as a popular, well-liked member of staff, who was quiet and well-spoken, while a former next door neighbour said she was 'extremely attractive' but quite shy.

Miss Bernal split up with Pech following a brief relationship earlier this year, deciding she 'didn't want any more to do with him'.

But he began to stalk her, following her in the street, pestering her with phone calls, standing around outside her house and bombarding her with text messages.

CRITICAL QUESTIONS

1. Why is the phrase in quotation marks? Does this headline have a greater or lesser impact than the one in the *Sun*? Is 'impact' the most important consideration?

2. Purely from the point of view of providing the reader with information and context, which opening paragraph is superior? And why?

3. Hang on. Didn't the *Sun* claim that Ms Bernal was 26? Which newspaper is correct? Think very carefully before answering.

4. The word 'upmarket' means 'relating to products that are relatively expensive and of superior quality'. Do you think that the word 'posh', used by the *Sun*, means the same? Which is better?

5. The phrase 'shot her several times' seems terribly dull by comparison with 'pumped five bullets into her'. But are we more concerned with dramatic effect than with accuracy in a news report?

6. Similarly, 'shot himself in the head' is pretty tame beside 'blew his own brains out'. Which is closer to the actual event?

7. 'Distraught' here and 'distressed' in the next paragraph are polite alternatives to 'weeping members of staff'. Are they more, or less, appropriate?

8. Is it good to know that the unfortunate young woman had been 'extremely attractive'?

A closer look

Sample 1 from the *Sun* newspaper

Carnage at Harvey Nicks

1. The word 'carnage' is an example of sensationalism – deliberately heightened or exaggerated language, for the purposes of arousing excitement, horror and curiosity. Since the purpose of an informative text is to provide all the relevant facts as clearly as possible, the word is not only inaccurate, but inappropriate.

2. Firstly, it should be noted that the use of strong photographs always adds to the visual impact of a text. They attract the eye and therefore the interest. But the primary purpose of an informative text is not impact, and so this photograph really serves the glamour of the headline rather than providing any further clarification.

3. The adjective 'handsome' is irrelevant. Its intention is to titillate – mildly excite – rather than inform. It is also a subjective judgment, since beauty is notoriously in the eye of the beholder, and as such, has no place is what is supposed to be an objective reporting of fact.

4. 'The crazed ex-lover pumped five bullets into his victim's head before blowing his own brains out' offers more examples of sensationalist language. The word 'crazed' means 'driven crazy by', which suggests that someone other than himself must be responsible for his condition.

5. 'Two hysterical girls from the posh store ran into a nearby H&M shop, screaming.' Of course you've never heard of 'hysterical men' or 'hysterical boys'. In the tabloids, only girls and women are 'hysterical'.

6. 'A 25-year-old H&M worker said: "They told me a smart young man . . ."' Reporting what somebody said that somebody else said is an example of employing hearsay instead of testimony; very, very poor in a supposedly objective report.

7. The second photograph is as powerful as the first, but again, its effect is to heighten the drama rather than to inform.

8. 'A co-worker said the 26-year-old sales girl – believed to be called Claire – had recently dumped him.' More sexism here, employed out of sloppiness rather than prejudice. It is not possible to get away with using the expression 'a 26-year-old boy' – it simply sounds absurd – but 'a 26-year-old girl' is somehow acceptable. The verb 'dumped' is also worthy of close attention. It suggests a brutal rejection, and it therefore implies a motive, perhaps even a justification for his violence. There is further sloppiness, of course. Neither reporter could be bothered to find out the facts, and so they gratuitously insult the memory of the victim in their awfully insensitive 'believed to be called Claire'.

9. '. . . a pot of the exclusive range's basic moisturiser costs £96.50.' The cost of the product is utterly irrelevant, of course. What is it doing here? Again, it is meant to titillate.

10–11. '. . . as he let rip with a handgun.' The short report contradicts itself throughout.

The earlier expression 'pumped five bullets' indicated focus, whereas 'let rip with a handgun' suggests indiscriminate shooting.

12. 'Armed police raced to the store – a favourite haunt of Princess Diana and of TV characters Patsy and Edina in sitcom *Absolutely Fabulous*.' We might observe that in tabloid land, armed police never 'go' anywhere, they always 'race', and we might note that fictional characters cannot shop at a real store, but the far more insensitive use of language is the verb 'haunt' to describe the dead Princess of Wales. No insult was intended, but that's precisely the point – the article's careless use of language throughout manages to hurt almost everyone concerned, including the victim's family.

Sample 2 from the *Guardian* newspaper

Store gunman 'had stalked victim'

1. In the headline, the phrase 'had stalked victim' is in quotation marks because it is taken from testimony and not necessarily an objective fact – an early indication of this article's concern for accuracy.

2. 'A former Harvey Nichols security guard who gunned down a beauty counter worker in the store after she ended their relationship had been "stalking" and "pestering" her.' The language used here is neutral; that is, devoid of any distracting emotional content. Because of that, it exhibits clarity – the noun is derived from the adjective 'clear' – which is an essential feature of good informative writing.

3. 'Clare Bernal, 22 . . .'. The *Sun* reports the victim's age as 26; the *Guardian* as 22. Which is right? The correct answer is that you don't know. But you *trust* the *Guardian* more than the *Sun*, don't you? Why? Precisely because the *Guardian*'s use of language is more restrained. You believe that its motive is to reveal the facts as much as possible.

4. 'Dulwich Village, the upmarket area of south London where she lived . . .'. 'Upmarket' is a neutral description of a commercial reality; but 'posh' is a slightly mocking judgment. The two words reveal the difference between objective and subjective use of language.

5,6,7. 'But last night, he walked into Harvey Nichols just 20 minutes before closing time . . .'. The language throughout this report is restrained, unemotional, accurate. In an informative text, precision is much more important than colour; and so this report is superior to the other.

8. '. . . a former next door neighbour said she was "extremely attractive" but quite shy.' Probably the one false note in the entire report is this reported description, 'extremely attractive'. Although it is identified as a subjective judgment by being placed in quotation marks, it is still irrelevant and verging on being guilty of adding colour to make the event slightly more titillating.

Introducing the key elements of an effective informative text

You have just engaged in a critical reading of two informative texts. You can read for many good reasons – pleasure, knowledge, distraction – but in an English language class you always read critically; that is, with the intention of appreciating *why* the author selected the words.

The next stage is to apply that appreciation. Use *specific* readings to establish basic *general* rules. What makes *any* text successful? In this case, what makes it work as an informative document? What *are* the key elements of an effective informative text?

Based entirely on the analysis of the two news reports, here are the essential ingredients of informative writing:

- It should contain all relevant factual and explanatory material. This refers to *content*, the aspect of a text that is broadly covered in the marking scheme for Leaving Certificate English under the heading *Clarity of purpose (P)*.
- It should organise this material into a logical, user-friendly sequence, so that it is both easy to follow and increasingly instructive. This refers to *structure*, the aspect of a text that is broadly covered in the marking scheme for Leaving Certificate English under the heading *Coherence of delivery (C)*.
- It should communicate this material in a clear, straightforward manner, employing clarity in the language and avoiding sensationalism, exaggeration, distortion, obscurity, jargon, and other features that draw attention to themselves rather than to the subject matter. This refers to *style*, the aspect of a text that is broadly covered in the marking scheme for Leaving Certificate English under the heading *Efficiency of language use (L)*.

An example from past Leaving Certificate papers

If you take one of the informative texts from past Leaving Certificate papers and apply the basic key elements of effective informative writing to it, you are obviously preparing yourself for answering Question A on English Paper I. But you can achieve much more than this. A critical reading of such a text can expand the basic list to a comprehensive list, covering everything you need to know about the content, style and structure of informative writing.

Here is a critical reading of Text 1 from 2007.

Films to change your life

CRITICAL QUESTIONS

The following text is based on extracts from the recent publication, 1000 Films to Change Your Life, *edited by Simon Cropper.*

1. The opening paragraph provides a personal context for the material that is to follow.

I never went to the cinema as a child. As a bookish teenager I loved reading and going to the theatre. I felt film could not rival the blood-and-sweat physicality of live drama. It seemed impossible that film could ever give voice to the idealism and tangled passions that raged in my teenage heart.

2. This paragraph synopsises effectively.

3. Clarity and simplicity are essential when explaining. Here, hardly any of the words is longer than two syllables.

And then, luckily, I happened to see Vittorio De Sica's *Bicycle Thieves*. A simple story at heart, it charts the struggles of proud but unemployed father, Antonio Ricci, to find a job in post-war Italy that will let him feed his wife and child. He is finally offered work – pasting film posters across the city – but he has to lie and pretend he has a bicycle. His wife pawns their bed sheets so he can get one, but it is stolen almost immediately. For the rest of the film he wanders up and down the city, often with his young son in tow, trying to track down the thief. The anger he reveals, both in the words that he yells as well as in every eloquent close-up of his face, underlines his frustration. Ricci's defiance demonstrates that this is not the way society should be. That simple idea is the first and most important stage in encouraging viewers to imagine what a better society would look like.

4. This paragraph explores a single category or genre. Multiple examples are provided to illustrate a single point.

Documentaries can achieve the same effect. Among the most well known are those of journalist-turned-film-maker Michael Moore. Whether taking on the chairman of General Motors in *Roger and Me,* the powerful gun industry in *Bowling for Columbine,* or the Bush administration in *Fahrenheit 9/11,* he concocts an old-fashioned tale of good versus evil and casts himself as the underdog yapping away at the heels of political and corporate giants.

5. The opening sentence in every paragraph establishes a link by referring back before moving forward.

Political films also set out to make us see the world in a new and clearer light. Without explicit commentary they dramatise issues like the oil-industry drama, *Syriana,* or *Erin Brokovich,* the true story of a single mother's exposé of an industry water poisoning case. These films make an impact because you reflect on the issues raised and this strengthens your own views and understanding.

6. Comedy is the category here. Notice how each paragraph deals with a separate category.

But cinema doesn't just make us think. It makes us laugh too. Humour is impossible to define but it's about something that's in us all. It's about the mistakes we make and the craziness of the world we live in. Ben Stiller's fashion spoof, *Zoolander*, is a wonderful satire on the vanity and corruption of the fashion industry. Comedy has always been best at mocking pretensions and can say quite as much as drama and documentary while reaching a bigger audience. Group laughter in a darkened movie-theatre is also a comforting, confidence-building mode of social bonding.

7. The opening sentence uses repetition through variation, a very important technique to notice and learn.

Then there are, of course, the great positive movie moments that can and do take you out of yourself, lift your mood, crack a smile, raise your spirits. Classic Hollywood films continue to exert a glamorous spell over our imaginations. Taking the regular television schedules as an indicator of our taste in cinema, we see *The Wizard of Oz, It's a Wonderful Life, The Sound of Music,* to name only the most obvious titles. All underline our need for the guaranteed joy that these endlessly repeatable movies provide.

8. The final paragraph offers an overall assessment.

Nothing entertains us like the movies but they also have the power to ignite strong passions. A film can make us laugh, make us sad, frighten or reassure us, make us angry – and even sometimes make us want to change the world.

Expanded notes

Completing the key elements of an effective informative text

Content: The primary purpose of a book called *1,000 Films to Change Your Life* is to offer the reader information about the selected films. Of course, there are personal judgments involved in the choice and descriptions of the films, but apart from such strictly factual texts as schedules and user manuals, informative writing cannot escape the author's perspective. The very words we decide on reveal our preferences and our prejudices, even – as was demonstrated above – when we're writing such apparently objective reports as news items. Here, the personal perspective is an essential part of the information being provided.

Other important things to note in relation to content include the range and comprehensiveness of the material, which is organised into categories or genres – Italian neo-realist films, documentaries, political films, comedies, classics – and the use of multiple interesting and relevant examples –

Syriana, Zoolander, The Wizard of Oz – to illustrate points. Essentially, an informative text groups or categorises its content, and it's almost impossible to think of an effective example that does not do this. A school timetable, for instance, is organised around subjects and a mobile phone manual is organised around the device's features.

Structure: The shape or layout of this text is really worth close attention, because you will be expected to produce something similar if you are writing an informative Question B in the examination. Here is the skeleton:

- **An Introduction**, consisting of one paragraph, which provides a context or background for the material that is to follow.
- **A Development**, consisting of five paragraphs, which groups the material into separate categories.
- **A Conclusion**, consisting of one paragraph, that offers an assessment or recommendation on the basis of the material already supplied.

Style: The text offers a fascinating exploration of writing style for the interested student. It opens, as observed above, on a personal note. Poorly presented information can be dry, dull, factual and unappealing. Where appropriate, a personalised approach can make the material more accessible, warmer, more intimate and colourful; as can the use of humour. It certainly achieves that here. Notice the use of suggestive metaphors: 'blood-and-sweat physicality' is a metaphor because nobody is *literally* bleeding; the intense verbs: 'I loved reading', 'raged'; and the heightened adjectives: 'tangled passions'.

But please also note that in the second paragraph, when factual information needs to be conveyed, clarity becomes more important than suggestion. The adjectives become neutral and factual: 'proud but unemployed father'; and the verbs: 'pretends', 'pawns', 'wanders', are strictly literal. This does not reduce the interest of the piece; it simply means that precision has replaced impact as a priority.

Another important technique that is repeatedly used here is the establishment of links between one paragraph and the next by the very simple device (which you must learn) of referring back before moving forward.

When you are discussing a writer's style, you should look for recurring features. For instance, if you notice one metaphor, such as 'blood-and-sweat', in the opening paragraph, then there are surely others, such as the description of Michael Moore as 'the underdog yapping away at the heels of . . . giants'.

Finally, the use of repetition is vital in conveying and reinforcing information. Without variation in the expression, however, repetition can be counter-productive; boring instead of enlightening. In paragraph six, the phrases 'take you out of yourself', 'lift your mood', 'crack a smile', 'raise your spirits' all mean much the same thing, but because the expression is varied the cumulative effect is stronger than if the sentence had simply read 'the great positive movie moments that can and do take you out of yourself'.

Class assignment

This is Text 2 from the 2006 Leaving Certificate paper. Using the key elements, techniques and vocabulary introduced above, assess it as an effective piece of informative writing.

Ghost writing

Jan Stevens

Jan Stevens is a ghost writer; that is, someone who writes books that are published as the work of someone else.

On ghost writing

I am a ghost writer. I write books that other people take credit for – people more famous than me, or busier, or who simply can't be trusted with a pen.

I have written for well-known authors, celebrities, and even for other ghost writers who found themselves over-worked. I have written legal thrillers, historical non-fiction, mysteries, and even ghost stories. However, my name doesn't appear on the covers of any of these books, or on their copyright page.

My anonymity is complete. Sometimes, even the publishers don't know I exist. My name, of course, does appear on my contracts. To prevent confusion, the language of these contracts calls me the ghost writer and the other party is referred to as the author. Under the terms of my contracts, I'm forbidden from revealing the identity of my authors. Ghost writers have to keep their secrets, or face lawsuits.

Ghost writing can be challenging. For one thing, ghost writers have to write very quickly. We are often given work that has a looming deadline. I once wrote a 120,000-word novel in twelve weeks. That's 2,000 words every day for five days a week. Maintaining this sprinter's pace at marathon length was painful, requiring much solitude and coffee. However, I made my 2,000-word count every single day without fail. One of the advantages of ghost writing is that the almost-right word will serve as well as the right word.

Some ghost writers I know are haunted by the loss of recognition and go to great lengths to put secret codes into their ghost novels. They concoct sentence-length acronyms or give minor characters anagrams of their own names, so that future historians will decipher the work's true author. Others enjoy private jokes: inserting the names of cats, roommates, or favourite restaurants into their ghosted books as a kind of petty claim to ownership.

A common question asked of ghost writers is, 'So, what do the authors actually do?' The answer covers a considerable range. I once wrote a novel from a fifty-page outline that provided specific adjectives and images for each chapter. Other authors provide only a paragraph or two. Some offer little guidance, but attack the finished work in minute detail. This ghost writer cares little because, by then, I'm busy haunting somewhere else.

As a rule, the most 'prolific' authors are the most detached. I've written five books for one man whom I've never met or spoken to, or even e-mailed. His editors, however, assure me that he has actually read the books, and that he rather enjoyed them.

A good ghost writer is expected to pick up an author's style by reading the author's other books. I often wonder if these were, in fact, written by yet another ghost writer. Am I a copy of a copy?

So, what of the ethics of ghost writing? Is ghost writing a case of false advertising? Is it simply bad manners? It can be argued that a book is simply a product; you either enjoy it or you don't, and the author's name is no more a personal signature than the Nike logo or any other well-known trademark. Moreover, publishing is a business like any other. As in every business in a market economy, the aim is to make profit from someone else's labour. I don't object to this. Indeed, someday I hope to come up with a get-rich idea, a detective or adventure series that will be hugely successful with the reading public. I'll write the first few books in the series, and then let some other poor ghost writer follow my instructions for a while.

After all, I've got to know quite a few ghost writers in the last decade. Between us, I could author twenty books a year without too much effort. Indeed, when I mentioned I was going to write this essay, one of them volunteered to write it for me!

(And how do you know she didn't?)

Homework and tasks

1. Locate two newspaper reports of a similar incident, such as a natural disaster or outbreak of war, but from different historical periods or different countries, and compare them as informative texts.
2. Locate two travel guides to the same location and compare them as informative documents.
3. Locate a user manual for a mobile phone, a television, a computer or any other device, and assess it as an informative document.
4. Locate the obituary of an individual you find interesting and assess it as an informative text.
5. Locate an informative profile of a performer or artist or politician known to you and assess it. Compare it with the profile of the fictional rock star Eva Maguire offered as Text 3, 'Public Lives', on the 2005 Leaving Certificate English Paper I.
6. Locate a review of a concert, a CD, a play, a film, a car, a restaurant or any other event or product, and assess it as an informative text.

Chapter Two:

The Key Elements of an Effective Argumentative or Persuasive Text

Introduction

At its simplest, argument is the expression of a point of view. Persuasion is the attempt to convince others to share that point of view. There are far more similarities than differences between the two, although it should be noted that while an argument is weakened by unreliable evidence, persuasion can thrive on lies.

An argumentative text can take many forms, from an exchange of personal opinions in conversation, through a letter to a newspaper, an analytical article, a radio or television talk, a public speech, and on to a passionate defence of a cause. The most common form of persuasion in our society, on the other hand, is advertising.

The following comparison of two opinion pieces should leave you with a keener awareness of how to evaluate argumentative writing – essential in answering such questions as 'Do you think the writer is justified in the conclusions drawn in the final paragraph? Explain your view.' (LC Paper I 2006, Text 3). It will also help you in writing an argumentative text of your own – essential in managing such tasks as 'Students in your school have been invited to contribute articles to the school website on issues relevant to young people. This week's issue is "We are what we wear". Write an article for the website expressing your views on the topic.' (LC Paper I 2008, Question B, Text 3).

The samples

The following material provides two opinion pieces relating to gender issues.

The first is a speech delivered by a fictional character who is outraged by the fact that young Irish people are increasingly finding partners from other cultures and other races. The second is an article from the *Irish Times* of 24 August 2005, by the journalist Kevin Myers.

Sample 1

An Irishman's speech

Romantic entanglements between immature boys and girls from different cultures are not only always extremely dangerous, they are also morally wrong.

CRITICAL QUESTIONS

1. Many advise opening an argument with a clear expression of your opinion. But should you? Is this the best way to begin?

2. What do you think is achieved by the speaker's inclusion of the audience here?

3. How effective is the speaker's use of statistics here?

4. The language is very colourful, even extreme. Is this a good or a bad thing in an argument?

We all know that the breakdown in marriages is causing serious problems in our society. There isn't anyone listening to me here who hasn't suffered, directly or indirectly, as a result. What we're not as aware of, though, is that statistically marriages between people of different races or nationalities are the greatest casualties. The reasons must be blindingly obvious to anyone who thinks about it. Let's take, for example, a black African boy who has grown up being waited on hand and foot by females in his own culture. Nothing wrong with that, you might say. It's their way. But of course, it's not our way. Swept off her feet by the exotic, by the attractive differences in colour and attitudes, an Irish girl might not, initially, consider it a bit much that her new boy friend expects to have his bottle of beer opened and poured for him, but not consumed, expects to have his breakfast cooked for him every morning and maybe his bed warmed for him every night. Love is blind, as we all know. But to do these duties voluntarily, even if under the influence of Cupid, is one thing; to be forced into them, after an ill-considered marriage, is nothing short of slavery. I'm not saying there is wrong on either side, but there is lack of understanding on both. And where there is ignorance, there is always suffering.

5. The speaker illustrates his point with an example, as you should do. But how good is the illustration here?

6. Repetition is employed deliberately. A good or a bad technique in debate?

7. The speech closes with a specific example designed to clinch the argument. But how convincing is it?

If there were only the practical consequences to consider, the problem might be manageable. But there is also the far more serious moral dimension. Today, young people are encouraged by advertisers to enter thoughtlessly into contracts, without any sense of responsibility and without considering the effects on their own lives and the lives of others. Live life to the max, as the slogan has it. Do whatever you want. Do it impulsively. And do it now. But while this may not have serious consequences if only a soft drink is involved, it certainly can be fatal if there are more serious concerns involved. Young people should be taught to take responsibility for their own actions. A kiss may seem like a harmless gift. A kiss is only an expression of friendship, of attachment, you say. Yes, for us it is. But what if the kiss, as it is in some cultures, is a binding contract, a solemn promise of marriage? Useless to regret it all and say afterwards, I didn't understand that your customs were different.

We never have any idea what we're doing when we close our eyes. We stumble about and cause injury to ourselves and to others. And you have to remember that a young girl always closes her eyes for her first kiss.

CRITICAL QUESTIONS

1. Rather than opening with an abstract point, this writer begins with something specific; a news item and his reaction to it. Which method do you think is more popular with professional writers?

2. I'd consider the language very provocative in places and at times quite derisive. Is this good or bad in an argument?

3. Having made his point, the writer provides an example to support it. How strong is the illustration?

Sample 2

An Irishman's diary

God, I hate this time of year, when the Leaving Cert results emerge and feminists start preening and sneering, while complaining about the relatively lower incomes of mature women, as if the adult world were decided by the exam results of 18-year-olds. The debate – such as it is, though the na-na-na-naa superiority competition that we are obliged to witness every August hardly merits the term – is bad enough, but it usually passes in time. All that is needed is for us chaps to keep our noses below the parapet, and our powder dry, and all should be well.

Michael Buerk, the BBC newsreader, did neither, and now he's allowed the 'debate' to turn nastier than usual. I was hoping it would stay on the British side of the Irish Sea, but this being August, and almost nothing to write about other than the patent academic superiority of girls over boys, Brenda Power

weighed into Michael Buerk last weekend in the *Sunday Times* with the usual combination of personal abuse and withering sarcasm that any man who does not accept the party line on feminism can faithfully expect.

The last well-known British journalist to attack the role of women and feminism in the media was Neil Lydon 10 years ago. It was, in fact, a poor piece of journalism, both simplistic and exaggerated in its judgements, and poorly researched. It was but one article, just one, and we are all entitled to have a bad day at the office. However, he was not given such indulgence; instead, he was promptly lynched in the media. Editors boycotted him, one by one his columns were dropped, and his income simply vanished. He had to sell his house, and he almost went bankrupt – all on the strength of one article.

4. Here is a question that is designed to make a point rather than to elicit a response. Any idea what the technical term for such questions is?

Who would bother doing that again? Well, actually the BBC newsreader Michael Buerk did: only sort of. He didn't actually write an article on the power of women in the media, but was being interviewed in the *Radio Times* and as anyone who has done an interview knows, in print journalism, the interviewer is the one who decides what appears on the page. Moreover, few of us (especially journalists, who are usually on the other side of the process) are clever enough to construct sentences as we talk which are not open to misconstruction, or which fully convey what we are trying to say.

Even allowing for that, his arguments were weak. 'All the big jobs in broadcasting were held by women – the controllers of BBC1 television and Radio4 for example,' he is quoted as saying. Good. So what about BBC2, BBC3 and BBC5, or the various ITV networks, or Chanel 4, or Radios One, Two and Three? Who controls them? Martians? And then there was his attempt at humour – always a way of leaving open a flank for attack by the sisters. 'What are the men left with? All they are is sperm donors, and most women aren't going to want an unemployable sperm donor loafing around and making the house look untidy. They are choosing not to have a male in the household.' Instead of this being taken for what it was, a piece of fun at men's expense, it was taken as a literal statement of what he believes. And so of course, he has been torn limb from limb, though his observations about the traditional qualities of maleness – reticence, stoicism, single-mindedness – are surely worth more than the shrieks of derision and misrepresentation which they have earned to date.

5. The article is aggressive, but is it also uncontrolled?

'Look at the changes in the workplace,' he added. 'There is no manufacturing industry any more, there are no mines, few vital jobs require physical strength. We have lots of jobs that require people skills and multi-tasking – which women are a lot better at.' Brenda Power reduced that to: 'Buerk believes that women are stealthily and callously manipulating a society where physical force is being replaced by communication, empathy, initiative and tact.' Yet he didn't say this: is it any wonder a feminist can win an argument using such intellectually worthless rhetorical methods? And what can one say to her argument, which actually cited the stoning to death of women in certain countries as ammunition against poor Michael Buerk? Moreover, we have often seen feminists employing the kind of language which is denied the rest of us. 'If men didn't want us to guess that they were useless, they should have made themselves more useful. Now they've been rumbled, all they can do is whinge,' is the observation of that intellectual she-bear of feminism, Germaine Greer. And maybe boys do whinge these days, but girls sneer, as in Brenda Power's description of Michael Buerk as 'a crotchety-looking newsreader'.

6. Repetition is employed deliberately. A good or a bad technique in debate?

Does she want to know what I feel about her appearance? Does it matter? Does the look on her face make any difference to the argument she's making? Would a male writer be allowed refer to the nature of a woman's face if he was disagreeing with what she was saying? And if he did, would he not be lynched for doing so? Last weekend the *Sunday Times* illustrated the issue of female power in the media today by showing a picture of a confident young woman crushing two world globes, like testicles, in her hand.

7. The article closes with a specific image designed to clinch the argument. How convincing is it?

No doubt it was thought to be amusing. But what newspaper would dare to present the opposite imagery, in which male power is – rather 'entertainingly' – visually represented by a man violently and triumphantly abusing female genitalia?

Courtesy of The Irish Times

A closer look

Sample 1: An Irishman's speech

1. 'Romantic entanglements between immature boys and girls from different cultures are not only always extremely dangerous, they are also morally wrong.' Opening an opinion piece with a bald *statement* of your position is certainly appropriate and can be effective, but it's not the best approach. It immediately splits your audience into two: those who agree with you and those who disagree with you. It's also less interesting for the audience, since there's nothing at all intriguing about an abstract point.

2. 'We all know that the breakdown in marriages is causing serious problems in our society.' When you're addressing a live audience, it's essential to *consistently address and include your listeners*. The technique is good here, since the speaker establishes common ground between himself and his audience. However, he then fails to build on the agreeable relationship, as he should do.

3. '. . . statistically marriages between people of different races or nationalities are the greatest casualties.' This is not a *statistic* at all. Merely putting the adverb statistically in front of a claim does not turn it into a statistic. The speaker is presenting an invention as evidence. Overall, this text is much stronger on *personal opinion* and *unsubstantiated claims* than on *evidence*.

4. 'Romantic entanglements', 'immature boys and girls', 'extremely dangerous', 'ill-considered marriage', 'nothing short of slavery'. The speaker's *language* is certainly *colourful* and at times *extreme*. In itself, there is nothing wrong with this. Opinions should be expressed forcefully, with conviction. However, an author should always be in control of the words and always aware of their potential impact. In a speech using 'a black African boy' as a central example, the careless use of the term 'slavery' is extremely sloppy and counter-productive.

5. '. . . an African boy who has grown up being waited on hand and foot by females in his own culture' and 'young people are encouraged by advertisers to enter thoughtlessly into contracts, without any sense of responsibility' and 'what if the kiss, as it is in some cultures, is a binding contract, a solemn promise of marriage?' Throughout the speech, the *illustrations* used to support the points are no more than convenient inventions. They are therefore extremely weak and not at all convincing.

6. 'Live life to the max, as the slogan has it. Do whatever you want. Do it impulsively. And do it now . . .'. In an argumentative text, *repetition* is an essential technique for emphasising a point, clarifying a point, making a repeated impact on an audience and building up momentum in the delivery. As with any form of writing, though, the repetition becomes boring if the expression is not *varied.*

7. 'And you have to remember that a young girl always closes her eyes for her first kiss.' The speaker tries to end with an *image* that will clinch his argument about the blindness and ignorance of young Irish women who become involved with men from other cultures. Unfortunately, the chosen image is both absurd and lacking in relevance. How does he know that every girl closes her eyes for her first kiss? And even if girls do close their eyes for their first kiss, what could it possibly prove about the potential difficulties of inter-cultural romances?

Sample 2: An Irishman's diary

1. 'God, I hate this time of year, when the Leaving Cert results emerge . . .'. The author doesn't start with the statement of any point of view, but rather with *an item in the news*: the reaction to the Leaving Cert results in August 2005. This is what is known as an *anecdotal opening*, the description of some specific incident or event relevant to the general point that the writer wants to make. It is only towards the end of the second paragraph that Myers even approaches the general issue he is addressing. It's important for you to note the sequence here: anecdote, development of anecdote, statement of point. Among professional writers, this is by far the most popular style of opening an opinion piece.

. . . Lynched in the media.

2. '. . . feminists start preening and sneering . . .'. The terms 'preening' and 'sneering' are *exaggerated*, offensive and *provocative*. This is just the sort of *controlled, vigorous*

language that should be used in argument. And an essential ingredient of any successful argument is the effective use of *humour*, and particularly of humour that criticises, such as *sarcasm, irony* and *satire*. Examples here include the mocking 'na-na-na-naa superiority competition', the ironic 'All that is needed is for us chaps to keep our noses below the parapet, and our powder dry, and all should be well', and the derisive 'any man who does not accept the party line on feminism'. While on the subject of exaggeration for effect, we might also note the phrase 'was promptly lynched in the media'. Actually, Neil Lydon wasn't lynched at all, so this is an example of an exaggerated metaphor.

3. 'The last well-known British journalist to attack the role of women and feminism in the media was Neil Lydon 10 years ago.' A point has been made – that feminists overreact to any perceived criticism of women – and immediately *evidence* is introduced to support that point, in this case a rather similar event which happened a decade ago. In an argument, *factual evidence*, which is objective, is always superior to *anecdotal evidence*, such as personal experience, which is subjective and cannot be either proved or disproved.

4. 'Who would bother doing that again?' This is the first of many *rhetorical questions* in the article, that is, a question designed to make a point rather than to elicit an answer. Again, this is a device that is essential to argumentative writing. The rhetorical question makes a point with great clarity and force. It also invites the audience or the reader to share the author's reflections and feelings.

5. 'And so of course, he has been torn limb from limb, though his observations about the traditional qualities of maleness – reticence, stoicism, single-mindedness – are surely worth more than the shrieks of derision and misrepresentation which they have earned to date.' The article is *aggressive*, but the language is *never uncontrolled*. An example of such controlled aggression is provided by the contrasting terms here – 'reticence, stoicism and single-mindedness' which you are obliged to deliver in a slow, appreciative manner, and 'shrieks of derision' with its hissing 's' sounds, which you cannot help but spit out.

6. 'Does she want to know what I feel about her appearance? Does it matter? Does the look on her face make any difference to the argument she's making? Would a male writer be allowed refer to the nature of a woman's face if he was disagreeing with what she was saying? And if he did, would he not be lynched for doing do?' This is a powerful example of the *combined use of rhetorical questions, repetition and emphasis* to drive a point home.

7. '. . . what newspaper would dare to present the opposite imagery, in which male power is – rather "entertainingly" – visually represented by a man violently and triumphantly abusing female genitalia?' Note how the author concludes his argument, not with a general restatement of his opinion, but with a *powerful image*, something specific that carries his message more powerfully than bland statement, supported once more by the rhetorical question and the heightened language.

Introducing the key elements of an effective argumentative or persuasive text

You have just engaged in a critical reading of two argumentative texts.

The next stage is to apply that appreciation. Use *specific* readings to establish basic *general* rules. What makes *any* text successful? In this case, what makes it work as an argumentative document? What *are* the key elements of an effective argumentative text?

Based on the above analysis of the two opinion pieces, here are the essential ingredients of argumentative writing:

- It should have a sharply defined and clearly expressed point of view on the given topic, supported by relevant and effective factual evidence and anecdotal evidence. This refers to *content*, the aspect of a text that is broadly covered in the marking scheme for Leaving Certificate English under the heading *Clarity of purpose (P).*
- It should organise the material so that the central point is effectively developed from a specific example, then applied to two or three situations and finally illustrated by a clinching example. This refers to *structure*, the aspect of a text that is broadly covered in the marking scheme for Leaving Certificate English under the heading *Coherence of delivery (C).*
- It should communicate the central point by means of a variety of rhetorical techniques, such as rhetorical questions, sarcasm, irony, satire, exaggeration, repetition, emphasis, colourfully described examples and illustrations and vivid images. This refers to *style*, the aspect of a text that is broadly covered in the marking scheme for Leaving Certificate English under the heading *Efficiency of language use (L).*

An example from past Leaving Certificate papers

If you take one of the argumentative texts from past Leaving Certificate papers and apply the basic key elements of effective argumentative writing to it, you are obviously preparing yourself for answering Question A on English Paper I. But you can achieve much more than this. A critical reading of such a text can expand the basic list to a comprehensive list, covering everything you need to know about the content, style and structure of argumentative writing.

Here is a critical reading of Text 1 from 2004.

The importance of play

CRITICAL QUESTIONS

The following text is adapted from the writings of Vivian Paley, a teacher who has written over many years about the importance of play in the lives of small children. Paley's books include descriptions of how children play and the stories they tell. The extracts used in this text are taken from her books, The Boy Who Would Be a Helicopter *(1990) and* You Can't Say You Can't Play *(1992).*

1. The opening is anecdotal, a description of relevant personal experiences.

1. In my early teaching years I paid scant attention to the children's play and did not hear their stories, though once upon a time I too must have invented such wondrous stories. Indeed, my strongest childhood memories are of the daily chase of good and bad guys on the playground. Nothing else mattered, only the play. We acted out fear and friendship and called into being characters who would speak the lines. Luckily, life cannot erase this storytelling instinct; it is always there, waiting to be resurrected.

2. The central point is developed from the opening anecdote.

3. An example is immediately provided to support and illustrate the central point.

2. Play is the primary reality of the young school child. Imagine two dozen children in self-selected acting companies, each group performing a different drama, moving through one another's settings, proclaiming separate visions of life and death, inventing new purposes and plots, and no one ever inquires, 'What's going on?'

'Y'wanna play tiger? Sabre tooth?'

'Superman! I shotted you.'

'Wah, wah, mommy, mommy!'

'Ghostbusters! Green Slimer!'

'Meow, meow, nice kitty.'

'Are you the dad, Simon? Here's our cave for good bears.'

Not one child asks, 'What is everyone doing? Who are these crawling, crouching, climbing people?' There is no confusion, only the desire to fit into someone's story or convince a classmate to enter yours.

4. The central point is repeated, though the expression of it is varied, and again supported and illustrated by detailed examples.

3. The deep importance of shared play is clearly evident in the reaction of a child who is told that he or she 'can't play', can't be a part of someone else's story. Lately I have become more aware of these voices of exclusion in the classroom. 'You can't play' suddenly seems too overbearing and harsh, resounding like a slap from wall to wall. So I propose to my class group that we try out a new rule: You can't say, 'you can't play'. The children who find the idea appealing are the children most often rejected; the loudest in opposition are those who do the most rejecting. 'But then what's the whole point of playing?' Lisa wails.

4. Later, shy Clara speaks for herself. 'Cynthia and Lisa builded a house for their puppies and I said can I play and they said no because I don't have a puppy only I have a kitty.' This is the longest sentence she has spoken in school to date. 'They said I'm not their friend.' Clara hugs her tattered kitty and sniffs back her tears.

'We said if she brings in a puppy she can play,' Lisa explains. Even the victim does not know how to react. 'I'll ask my mommy if she could get me that kind of puppy like they have,' Clara offers.

'They has to let her play,' Sheila insists, 'unless they really don't want to.'

'But it was my game!' Lisa cries. 'It's up to me!' She is red-faced and tearful. 'Okay, I won't play then, ever!'

5. Once more, the piece closes on a specific image designed to clarify the central point, which is then given a final expression.

5. Being told you can't play is a serious matter. It hurts more than anything else that happens in school. Everyone knows the sounds of rejection: You can't play; don't sit by me; stop following us; I don't want you for a partner; you're not going to be on our team.

6. The children I teach are just emerging from life's deep wells of babyhood and family. Then along comes school. It is their first real exposure to the public arena in which everything is to be shared and everyone is meant to be equal. And free acceptance in play, partnerships and teams is what matters most to any child.

Expanded notes

Content: The *central point* is *clearly put* and strategically placed at the beginning of the second section: 'Play is the primary reality of the young school child.' Note how *short and precise* this vital sentence is. There is no attempt to explain, expand on or illustrate the point within the same sentence. Such overloading always leads to confusion and lack of clarity. Note also that there is *only a single point* to be made. Everything else is *elaboration* and *illustration*. Throughout this text, the same point – that play is the primary reality of the child – is repeated at intervals, although the expression of it varies from location to location, from 'the deep importance of shared play' at the beginning of section 3 through to 'free acceptance in play . . . is what matters most' in the final paragraph.

No point, no matter how attractive, can sustain itself, however. Interestingly, the material introduced to support the central point in this text is either entirely *personal*, such as the author's reported recollections of her professional experiences as a teacher, or entirely *invented*, as in 'imagine two dozen children in self-selected acting companies'. None of this material can be independently verified. It is therefore anecdotal evidence and not *factual evidence*. It's a matter for the individual reader to decide whether or not this weakens Vivian Paley's case, but the issue is certainly directly relevant to one of the comprehension questions set on this text: 'Would you agree or disagree with the view that the writer has made a convincing case for the "deep importance of shared play" in the lives of children?'

Structure: The shape of this text is worth close attention, because you will be expected to produce something similar if you are writing an argumentative Question B in the examination. Here is the skeleton:

- **An Introduction**, consisting of one section, which offers a *personal anecdote* recalling the author's inadequacies as a young teacher and which provides a *lead-in* to the author's *central point*, that play is the most important activity for a child.

- **A Development**, consisting of four sections, in which the *central point is expanded on and applied* to a number of situations involving children at play.
- **A Conclusion**, consisting of one section, in which the material is *summarised* and the *central point is re-stated.*

Style: The author is more interested in making a *passionate personal plea* for the importance of children's play than in delivering a persuasive public speech. Many of the debater's techniques are therefore not relevant here, particularly the use of *rhetorical questions, cutting humour* and *exaggeration for effect.* In the absence of rhetoric and humour, the *personalised approach* makes the material more accessible, warmer, more intimate and more colourful. The author's mild self-criticism – 'In my early teaching years I paid scant attention to the children's play' – is appealing and her obvious affection for the children and dedication to her job – 'Clara hugs her tattered kitty and sniffs back her tears' and 'Lately I have become more aware of these voices of exclusion' – are also attractive.

Although the *language* is not as intense as it might be in public debate, it is still *robust* and *forceful*, as for example in the *adjectives* '*deep* importance' and '*wondrous* stories' and the verbs *wails, sniffs, offers, insists* and *cries* to capture the different reactions of the various children. The *detailed descriptions* of classroom and playground scenes are particularly effective, most notably the touching profile of shy Clara as she *hugs her tattered kitty and sniffs back her tears*, which conveys both the child's vulnerability and her bravery. All in all, the author successfully brings the techniques of descriptive writing – the *creation of character* through dialogue, behaviour and appearance, and the *creation of dramatic scenes* through detail – to a personal opinion piece.

Class assignment

Here are two short opinion pieces, the first from the *Observer* and the second from the *Guardian*. Both are English newspapers. Using the key elements, techniques and vocabulary introduced above, assess them as effective examples of argumentative writing.

Headscarves – they're the new afros

Catherine Johnson

I'm a Londoner, my father came from Jamaica and my mother spoke only Welsh until she was 12. When I went to school 30 years ago, the majority of my classmates were Jewish. I remember some Yiddish and can sing 'Hava Nagila' all the way through. My son goes to our local comprehensive. It's around 70 per cent London Bangladeshi; he knows some great swear words and has a love of Indian sweets.

I write for teenagers and about two years ago, I began a book with a protagonist like the girls at my son's school, clever and feisty with a variety of strategies for walking the narrow path between ambition and expectation. I did some research at the sixth form of a local girls' school. They were fantastic young women, with places lined up to study medicine, engineering and law at top London universities. They were articulate and confident. They loved their families and relished the opportunities open to them. Some wore too much make-up, some wore none; some wore impossibly high heels, others flats; and although all were Muslim, only about a third wore headscarves.

Last week, I went in again. My sixth formers had flown and there was a new crop. One thing had changed. Nearly every girl wore a headscarf. Should society be worried? Absolutely not. For most of these girls, it's about proclaiming allegiances. A headscarf says I am more devout than my cardigan-wearing mother and beardless father. It says I am serious and I am proud of my heritage and my ethnicity in exactly the same way that an Angela Davis T-shirt or, in my brother's case, his sizeable afro, might have 30 years ago. It says I am other. Even better, it says I am proud of my otherness.

For those of us who are children of immigrants, London is the best place in the world. Everywhere else, we are outsiders. In the places our parents call home, we are exotic. Being a teenager is hard for everyone, more so if you are struggling with two cultures. Who can blame these girls for making a statement with their clothes, something London teenagers have been leading the world in for decades?

Baby, this just isn't working for me

Madeleine Bunting

Women with young children suffer more discrimination at work than any other group, a government-commissioned report concluded yesterday. It was not a finding that would have surprised any working mother. Take a very personal example: I was rung at 11.10 am yesterday by a G2 commissioning editor asking me to write this piece. 'Ye. . .es,' I said, and she heard my hesitation. What was going through my mind was that rapid, computer-like calculation as to whether the assignment would make me late home and leave any of my three children stranded. One was at the childminder – who could work late. Another was at a friend's and had insisted I pick him up at a certain time – he could lump it if necessary. The third, aged 12, might have to hang on 'home alone' with a jam sandwich until I could get back.

Tedious personal detail? Perhaps, but it's exactly the kind of tedious detail of which motherhood is generally made. At the same time, to most employers, my hesitation would be marked down as not-so eager, not-so flexible. In so many professional worlds, where such characteristics are the essential engine oil of career development, women – and it is still largely women – who have to make such calculations end up being imperceptibly sidelined, shunted on to well-defined 'mummy tracks' (if you're lucky) or eased out of the company altogether. Imagine the lawyer who hesitates about taking on a big case because it will require 60-hour weeks or frequent travel; the supermarket supervisor who decides not to become a manager because it involves working long hours; the teacher unsure about stepping up to a headship because of a sick child at home. This is how careers are destroyed.

These kinds of working women will still find paid employment, but for the vast majority, the pram in the hall marks, at best, a plateau in their career – treading water – at worst, its abrupt end. And in today's labour market, you don't get a second chance: very few women who take a break manage to pick up their careers after a family.

Homework and tasks

1. Go to the American site **www.teenink.com**, locate an opinion piece on a topic of interest to you and assess its merits as an argumentative text.
2. Go to **www.guardian.co.uk**, locate an opinion piece from the current edition of the newspaper and assess its merits as an argumentative text.
3. Find a copy of any daily Irish newspaper, for example the *Irish Times*, the *Irish Independent* or the *Examiner*, select an opinion piece from its central pages and assess its merits as an argumentative text.
4. Locate a famous speech, for instance on **www.famousquotes.me.uk/speeches** or from *The World's Greatest Speeches*, edited by Vijaya Kumar, and do an analysis of the argumentative and persuasive techniques employed by the speaker.
5. Using the weekly schedules published in newspapers and magazines, locate, listen to and record a radio talk on a topic of interest to you and take notes on its merits as an argumentative text.
6. Listen to any public speech, perhaps in a school debate, and take notes on its merits as an argumentative text.

Chapter Three:

The Key Elements of an Effective Descriptive or Narrative Text

Introduction

Put simply, a narrative is a description of a sequence of events. Interestingly, advertisers have discovered that it is a far more powerful means of communication than information, which was the format advertisements used in the distant past.

Words not only describe events, obviously; they can also describe people, places, feelings, thoughts and many other things and experiences. The term 'descriptive writing' often appears on Leaving Certificate English papers and as well as the language of information, of argument, persuasion and narration, students are encouraged to study 'the aesthetic use of language'. What does the phrase mean? The dictionary definition of 'aesthetic' is *relating to pure beauty rather than to other considerations, artistic*. I don't think that anyone has successfully used language exclusively to create 'pure beauty'. Words can't shake off the meanings we attach to them. So I think that this final category is well named as the aesthetic *use* of language. It's a guide to appreciating the many artistic uses of language, but without neglecting the meaning.

Two texts follow, one strictly narrative and one more generally descriptive. A critical reading of both pieces should leave you with a keener awareness of how to evaluate narrative and descriptive writing – essential for answering such questions as 'One reviewer of the novel *Tenderwire* described it as "a compelling and well-written thriller". From your reading of the extract, do you agree with this view?' (LC Paper I 2008, Text 2). It will also help you in writing a narrative or descriptive text of your own – essential for managing such tasks as '"Hours later . . . the boy's soul raged. . ." Imagine that, in an attempt to control his feelings, the boy writes into his diary an account of the incident and his reactions to it. Write out his diary entry.' (LC Paper I 2006, Question B Text 1).

The samples

The following material provides two examples of narrative and descriptive writing.

The first, 'Black Dog appears and disappears', is Chapter Two of Robert Louis Stevenson's famous adventure novel, *Treasure Island*. The second is an extract from Chapter Twenty-seven of *The Lost Continent: Travels in Small Town America*, by Bill Bryson, in which the author describes his one-night stop-over in the town of Sundance.

CRITICAL QUESTIONS

1. A story has to interest its audience from the beginning. How well does Stevenson succeed?

2. A good deal of attention is given to the weather here. Why?

Sample 1

Black Dog appears and disappears

It was not very long after this that there occurred the first of the mysterious events that rid us at last of the captain, though not, as you will see, of his affairs. It was a bitter cold winter, with long, hard frosts and heavy gales; and it was plain from the first that my poor father was little likely to see the spring. He sank daily, and my mother and I had all the inn upon our hands, and were kept busy enough without paying much regard to our unpleasant guest.

It was one January morning, very early – a pinching, frosty morning – the cove all grey with hoar-frost, the ripple lapping softly on the stones, the sun still low and only touching the hilltops and shining far to seaward. The captain had risen earlier than usual and set out down the beach, his cutlass swinging under the broad skirts of the old blue coat, his brass telescope under his arm, his hat tilted back upon his head. I remember his breath hanging like smoke in his wake as he strode off, and the last sound I heard of him as he turned the big rock was a loud snort of indignation, as though his mind was still running upon Dr. Livesey.

Well, mother was upstairs with father and I was laying the breakfast-table against the captain's return when the parlour door opened and a man stepped in on whom I had never set

3. Identify some of the techniques used to bring this new character alive on the page.

my eyes before. He was a pale, tallowy creature, wanting two fingers of the left hand, and though he wore a cutlass, he did not look much like a fighter. I had always my eye open for seafaring men, with one leg or two, and I remember this one puzzled me. He was not sailorly, and yet he had a smack of the sea about him too.

I asked him what was for his service, and he said he would take rum; but as I was going out of the room to fetch it, he sat down upon a table and motioned me to draw near. I paused where I was, with my napkin in my hand.

'Come here, sonny,' says he. 'Come nearer here.'

I took a step nearer.

'Is this here table for my mate Bill?' he asked with a kind of leer.

I told him I did not know his mate Bill, and this was for a person who stayed in our house whom we called the captain.

'Well,' said he, 'my mate Bill would be called the captain, as like as not. He has a cut on one cheek and a mighty pleasant way with him, particularly in drink, has my mate Bill. We'll put it, for argument like, that your captain has a cut on one cheek – and we'll put it, if you like, that that cheek's the right one. Ah, well! I told you. Now, is my mate Bill in this here house?'

I told him he was out walking.

'Which way, sonny? Which way is he gone?'

And when I had pointed out the rock and told him how the captain was likely to return, and how soon, and answered a few other questions, 'Ah,' said he, 'this'll be as good as drink to my mate Bill.'

The expression of his face as he said these words was not at all pleasant, and I had my own reasons for thinking that the stranger was mistaken, even supposing he meant what he said. But it was no affair of mine, I thought; and besides, it was difficult to know what to do. The stranger kept hanging about just inside the inn door, peering round the corner like a cat waiting for a mouse. Once I stepped out myself into the road, but he immediately called me back, and as I did not obey quick enough for his fancy, a most horrible change came over

4. A man is compared to a cat here. Do you know the technical terms for such comparisons? Can you find other examples of such comparisons in the text?

his tallowy face, and he ordered me in with an oath that made me jump. As soon as I was back again he returned to his former manner, half fawning, half sneering, patted me on the shoulder, told me I was a good boy and he had taken quite a fancy to me. 'I have a son of my own,' said he, 'as like you as two blocks, and he's all the pride of my 'art. But the great thing for boys is discipline, sonny – discipline. Now, if you had sailed along of Bill, you wouldn't have stood there to be spoke to twice – not you. That was never Bill's way, nor the way of sich as sailed with him. And here, sure enough, is my mate Bill, with a spy-glass under his arm, bless his old 'art, to be sure. You and me'll just go back into the parlour, sonny, and get behind the door, and we'll give Bill a little surprise – bless his 'art, I say again.'

So saying, the stranger backed along with me into the parlour and put me behind him in the corner so that we were both hidden by the open door. I was very uneasy and alarmed, as you may fancy, and it rather added to my fears to observe that the stranger was certainly frightened himself. He cleared the hilt of his cutlass and loosened the blade in the sheath; and all the time we were waiting there he kept swallowing as if he felt what we used to call a lump in the throat.

5. This is a first-person narrative, in which one character tells the entire story from their perspective. What do you think are the advantages and disadvantages of this approach by comparison with the third-person narrative?

At last in strode the captain, slammed the door behind him, without looking to the right or left, and marched straight across the room to where his breakfast awaited him.

'Bill,' said the stranger in a voice that I thought he had tried to make bold and big.

The captain spun round on his heel and fronted us; all the brown had gone out of his face, and even his nose was blue; he had the look of a man who sees a ghost, or the evil one, or something worse, if anything can be; and upon my word, I felt sorry to see him all in a moment turn so old and sick.

'Come, Bill, you know me; you know an old shipmate, Bill, surely,' said the stranger.

The captain made a sort of gasp.

'Black Dog!' said he.

'And who else?' returned the other, getting more at his ease.

'Black Dog as ever was, come for to see his old shipmate Billy, at the Admiral Benbow inn. Ah, Bill, Bill, we have seen a sight of times, us two, since I lost them two talons,' holding up his mutilated hand.

'Now, look here,' said the captain; 'you've run me down; here I am; well, then, speak up; what is it?'

'That's you, Bill,' returned Black Dog, 'you're in the right of it, Billy. I'll have a glass of rum from this dear child here, as I've took such a liking to; and we'll sit down, if you please, and talk square, like old shipmates.'

When I returned with the rum, they were already seated on either side of the captain's breakfast-table – Black Dog next to the door and sitting sideways so as to have one eye on his old shipmate and one, as I thought, on his retreat.

He bade me go and leave the door wide open. 'None of your keyholes for me, sonny,' he said; and I left them together and retired into the bar.

For a long time, though I certainly did my best to listen, I could hear nothing but a low gattling; but at last the voices began to grow higher, and I could pick up a word or two, mostly oaths, from the captain.

'No, no, no, no; and an end of it!' he cried once. And again, 'If it comes to swinging, swing all, say I.'

6. The action is about to hot up. Identify the part of speech that becomes increasingly important at this stage.

Then all of a sudden there was a tremendous explosion of oaths and other noises – the chair and table went over in a lump, a clash of steel followed, and then a cry of pain, and the next instant I saw Black Dog in full flight, and the captain hotly pursuing, both with drawn cutlasses, and the former streaming blood from the left shoulder. Just at the door the captain aimed at the fugitive one last tremendous cut, which would certainly have split him to the chine had it not been intercepted by our big signboard of Admiral Benbow. You may see the notch on the lower side of the frame to this day.

That blow was the last of the battle. Once out upon the road, Black Dog, in spite of his wound, showed a wonderful clean pair of heels and disappeared over the edge of the hill in half a minute. The captain, for his part, stood staring at the signboard like a bewildered man. Then he passed his hand over his eyes several times and at last turned back into the house.

'Jim,' says he, 'rum'; and as he spoke, he reeled a little, and caught himself with one hand against the wall.

'Are you hurt?' cried I.

'Rum,' he repeated. 'I must get away from here. Rum! Rum!'

7. Certain expectations were aroused in the reader by the opening of this chapter. Have they been fulfilled? Go back to the opening sentence of this text. What are the connections between that and this final paragraph?

A closer look

1. 'It was not very long after this that there occurred the first of the mysterious events that rid us at last of the captain, though not, as you will see, of his affairs.' The opening few sentences of a narrative have a great deal of work to do. Ideally, they should simultaneously introduce *character, situation* and *theme*, while at the same time stimulating the reader's interest in what is about to happen. The situation described must be full of promise, full of potential tension or conflict or danger. Stevenson's masterly story-telling style promises everything, but gives nothing away.

2. 'It was one January morning, very early – a pinching, frosty morning – the cove all grey with hoar-frost, the ripple lapping softly on the stones, the sun still low and only touching the hilltops and shining far to seaward.' The creation of *atmosphere* is vital in narrative and descriptive writing. In fact, atmosphere and theme are inseparable, since an optimistic tale can't have a gloomy feel to it and a sad story can't be bright and cheerful. Here, the weather is used to create a tense, crackling atmosphere, sharp and cold and potentially explosive. It communicates the sense that something dark and violent is about to happen.

3. 'He was a pale, tallowy creature, wanting two fingers of the left hand, and though he wore a cutlass, he did not look much like a fighter.' Almost all stories concern themselves with human *characters*. It is essential, therefore, that you learn how to bring such characters alive on the page. There are four aspects that you should pay close attention to: *appearance, behaviour, dialogue* and *reflections*.

   Appearance covers all visible features, including body language, facial expressions, gestures, clothes and physique. Here, the most intriguing little detail, beautifully expressed, is 'wanting two fingers of the left hand', which suggests a man prone to starting fights, and losing them. A good writer will select the most significant and most revealing details and discard the rest. That a man sits down on a chair is hardly worth reporting, but such descriptions as 'The stranger kept hanging about just inside the inn door, peering round the corner' tell us a great deal about a restless, anxious, nervous individual. What a character says and how they say it are equally important, of course. Here, the stranger's oily repetition of 'my mate Bill' and his pretend affection for the boy narrator – 'I have a son of my own' – mark him immediately as dangerous and treacherous.

4. '. . . like a cat waiting for a mouse.' *Comparisons* are the basic material of all descriptions.

   If the comparison is direct, using 'like' or 'as' – 'as solid as a rock', 'like a cat waiting for a mouse', then the technical term for this is a *simile*. If the comparison is not direct – 'taking things with a pinch of salt', for instance, or 'not looking a gift horse in the mouth' – then the technical term is *metaphor*.

5. 'I was very uneasy and alarmed, as you may fancy, and it rather added to my fears to observe that the stranger was certainly frightened himself.' There are two basic methods of telling a story: as a *first-person narrative*, in which one character tells the entire story from their perspective, or as a *third-person narrative*, in which the author has a detached, god-like perspective and is able to see into the hearts and minds of all the characters.

   The advantage of the first-person narrative is that it is easier to control. The major advantage of the third-person narrative is access to every character's thoughts and feelings.

6. 'Then all of a sudden there was a tremendous explosion of oaths and other noises – the chair and table went over in a

lump, a clash of steel followed, and then a cry of pain, and the next instant I saw Black Dog in full flight, and the captain hotly pursuing, both with drawn cutlasses, and the former streaming blood from the left shoulder.' *Treasure Island* is an adventure story and it shares with the thriller, the saga, the blockbuster, the crime story and the horror story an emphasis on action. And the part of speech that mainly carries the action is the *verb*. The colourful *adjectives* here – 'a *tremendous* explosion' – and the onomatopoeic *nouns* that imitate the sounds of the struggle – 'explosion', 'lump', 'crash', 'cry' – all contribute to the overall effect, but they are dependant on the vigorous verbs – 'pursuing', 'streaming' – and the intensifying *adverbs* – 'hotly pursuing'.

7. '"Rum," he repeated. "I must get away from here."' If the opening of a good narrative introduces a situation full of potential *conflict* or tension, then that promise has to be delivered on. The situation has to be brought to the point of *crisis* in the development of the story and this crisis has to be *resolved* in one way or another.

The opening sentence promised us 'the first of the mysterious events that rid us at last of the captain.' Notice how the suspense is gradually built up and how the tension is increased from this point onwards, until it all finally explodes in the violent fight between the two men, which is resolved by the flight of one and the exhaustion of the other.

CRITICAL QUESTIONS

Sample 2

A night in Sundance

Thus it was that I ended up in Sundance, thirty miles further down the road. Sundance is the town from which the Sundance Kid took his name, and from all appearances that was the only thing in town worth taking. He wasn't born in Sundance; he

1. As might be expected from a travel book, the writing here is dedicated to descriptions of places. Identify the part of speech that is most important to the author.

2. Humour can serve many purposes. What is it being used for here? Locate other examples in the text.

3. What distinguishes one place from another is atmosphere. How is it created here?

just spent some time in jail there. It was a small, charmless place, with just one road in and one road out. I got a room in the Bear Lodge Motel on Main Street and it was pleasant in a basic sort of way. The bed was soft, the television was hooked up to HBO, the cable movie network, and the toilet had a 'Sanitized For Your Protection' banner across the seat. On the far side of the street was a restaurant that looked acceptable. Clearly I was not about to have the Saturday night of a lifetime here, but things could have been worse. And indeed very soon they were.

I had a shower and afterwards as I dressed I switched on the television and watched the Reverend Jimmy Swaggart, a TV evangelist who had recently been caught dallying with a prostitute, the old rascal. Naturally this had put a certain strain on his credibility and he had taken to the airwaves, more or less continuously as far as I could tell, to beg for mercy. Here he was once again appealing for money and forgiveness, in that order. Tears rolled from his eyes and glistened on his cheeks. He told me he was a miserable sinner. 'No argument there, Jimbo,' I said, and switched off.

I stepped out on to Main Street. It was ten of seven, as they say in this part of the world. The evening was warm and in the still air the aroma of charbroiled steaks floated over from the restaurant across the street and berthed in my nostrils. I hadn't eaten all day and the whiff of sirloin made me realise just how hungry I was. I smoothed down my wet hair, needlessly looked both ways before stepping off the sidewalk – there was nothing moving on the road for at least 100 miles in either direction – and went over. I opened the door and was taken aback to discover that the place was packed with Shriners.

The Shriners, if you are not familiar with them, are a social organisation composed of middle-aged men of a certain disposition and mentality – the sort of men who like to engage in practical jokes and pinch the bottoms of passing waitresses. They get drunk a lot and drop water balloons out of hotel windows. Their idea of advanced wit is to stick a cupped hand under their armpit and make farting noises. You can always tell a Shriner because he's wearing a red fez and his socks don't match. Ostensibly, Shriners get together to raise money for charities. This is what they tell their wives. However, here's an interesting fact that may help you to put this claim into perspective. In 1984, according to *Harper's Magazine*, the amount of money raised by the Shriners was $17.5 million; of this sum, the amount they donated to charities was $182,000. In short, what Shriners do is get together and be assholes. So you can perhaps conceive of my disquiet at the prospect of eating dinner amid a group of fifty bald-headed men who are throwing pats of butter around the room and setting fire to one another's menus.

4. Places are almost invariably populated by people. Identify some of the techniques used here to bring the characters alive on the page.

The hostess came over. She was chewing gum and didn't look overfriendly. 'Help you?' she said.

'I'd like a table for one, please.'

She clicked her chewing gum in an unattractive fashion. 'We're closed.'

I was taken aback once more. 'You look pretty open to me.'

'It's a private party. They've reserved the restaurant for the evening.'

I sighed. 'I'm a stranger in town. Can you tell me where else I can get something to eat?'

She grinned, clearly pleased to be able to give me some bad news. 'We're the only restaurant in Sundance,' she said. Some beaming Shriners at a nearby table watched my unfolding discomfort with simple-minded merriment. 'You might try the gas station down the street,' the lady added.

'The gas station serves food?' I responded in a tone of quiet amazement.

'No, but they've got potato chips and candy bars.'

'I don't believe this is happening,' I muttered.

'Or else you can go about a mile out of town on Highway 24 and you'll come to a Tastee-Freez drive-in.'

This was great. This was just too outstanding for words. The woman was telling me that on a Saturday night in Sundance, Wyoming, all I could have for dinner was potato chips and ice-cream.

'What about another town?' I asked.

'You can try Spearfish. That's thirty-one miles down Route 14 over the state line in South Dakota. But you won't find much there either.' She grinned again, and clicked her gum, as if proud to be living in such a turdy place.

'Well, thank you so much for your help,' I said with elaborate insincerity and departed.

And there you have the difference between the Midwest and the West, ladies and gentlemen. People in the Midwest are nice. In the Midwest the hostess would have felt bad about my going hungry. She would have found me a table at the back of the room or at least fixed me up with a couple of roast beef sandwiches and a slab of apple pie to take back to the motel. And the Shriners, sub-imbecile assholes that they may be, would have been happy to make room for me at one of their tables, and probably would even have given me some pats of butter to throw. People in the Midwest are good and they are kind to strangers. But here in Sundance the milk of human kindness was exceeded in tininess only by the size of the Shriners' brains.

5. Kindness is presented as milk here. Do you know the technical term for such odd comparisons? Can you find other examples of such comparisons in the text?

I trudged up the road in the direction of the Tastee-Freez. I walked for some way, out past the last of the houses and on to an empty highway that appeared to stretch off into the distance for miles, but there was no sign of a Tastee-Freez, so I turned around and trudged back into town. I intended to get the car, but then I couldn't be bothered. There was something about the way they can't even spell 'freeze' right that's always put me off these places. How much faith can you place in a company that can't even spell a monosyllable? So instead I went to the gas station and bought about six dollars' worth of potato chips and candy bars, which I took back to my room and dumped on the bed. I lay there and pushed candy bars into my face, like logs into a sawmill, and watched some plotless piece of violent Hollywood excrescence on HBO, and then slept another fitful night, lying in the dark, full and yet unsatisfied, staring at the ceiling and listening to the Shriners across the street and to the ceaseless bleating of my stomach.

6. Even this little account of a night spent in a dull town has a narrative shape. How does the ending relate to the opening?

And so the night passed.

A closer look

1. 'It was a small, charmless place, with just one road in and one road out. I got a room in the Bear Lodge Motel on Main Street and it was pleasant in a basic sort of way.' Just as vigorous, suggestive *verbs* are essential when describing action, so precise, suggestive *adjectives* are needed when capturing the essence of a place. In this initial description of Sundance, the adjectives are 'small', 'charmless' and 'basic'. Taken together, they give the impression of a dull, unattractive location. Note that the author is not relying on a single adjective, but on a cluster or group, all supporting each other to provide a more powerful effect. Note also how the initial impression is consistently maintained throughout by adding further appropriate adjectives to the list.

2. 'Clearly I was not about to have the Saturday night of a lifetime here, but things could have been worse. And indeed very soon they were.' Throughout this piece, the *humour* is derogatory, derisive, critical, sarcastic. It's a matter for the individual reader to decide whether this reflects poorly on the town or on the author, but clearly the intention is to use comedy to ridicule and make fun of Sundance and its inhabitants.

3. 'I stepped out on to Main Street . . .'. The place's distinctive *atmosphere* is created here through the use of sensory detail, the impressions made on the author's senses. The details are very cleverly chosen, because the 'aroma of charbroiled steaks' seems to promise satisfaction, while the sight of the empty road – 'nothing moving . . . for at least 100 miles in either direction' – captures the empty reality.

4. 'The hostess came over. She was chewing gum and didn't look overfriendly. "Help you?" she said.' As already noted, there are four aspects that you should play close attention to in the creation of *character: appearance, behaviour, dialogue* and *reflections*. This applies to every form of descriptive writing. Here, the waitress's behaviour is off-putting – she chews and clicks gum in the author's face – her body language communicates indifference and her speech – 'Help you?', 'We're closed' – is abrupt and uncaring. The overall portrait is of an unpleasant person.

5. '. . . the milk of human kindness was exceeded in tininess only by the size of the Shriners' brains.' Also as already noted, *comparisons* are the basic material of all descriptions. If the comparison is direct and explicit, using 'like' or 'as', as in 'pushed candy bars into my face, like logs into a sawmill', then the technical term for this is a *simile*. If the comparison is not direct, but is implied, as in 'the aroma . . . berthed in my nostrils', then the technical term is *metaphor*. Here, Bryson uses a metaphor from Shakespeare's *Macbeth*, in which Lady Macbeth worries that her husband may be 'too full of the milk of human kindness' to kill the old king and grab power in his stead. The image used, of milk, suggests softness, smoothness, tenderness, maternity, care.

6. 'And so the night passed.' Every successful text has a *coherent structure*; an

introduction, development and conclusion that relate to each other and work together. Here, the opening paragraph makes two claims, that the only thing worth taking from Sundance is its name and that what it had to offer was worse than acceptable. Everything that follows must relate to and support these claims. Otherwise, the piece will lack consistency in the material and coherence in the organisation.

Bryson delivers on the promise of the opening, since he doesn't even take away a good impression and the town's facilities and inhabitants are repeatedly exposed as unappealing.

Introducing the key elements of an effective narrative or descriptive text

You have just engaged in a critical reading of two texts, one narrative and one descriptive.

The next stage is to apply that appreciation. Use *specific* readings to establish basic *general* rules. What makes *any* text successful? In this case, what makes it work as a narrative or descriptive text? What *are* the key elements of an effective narrative or descriptive text?

Based on the above analysis of the two opinion pieces, here are the essential ingredients of narrative and descriptive writing:

- It should have credible *characters*, credible *situations*, credible *locations* and credible *events*, all brought to life by the careful use of effective detail. This refers to *content*, the aspect of a text that is broadly covered in the marking scheme for Leaving Certificate English under the heading *Clarity of purpose (P)*.
- It should shape the material so that a potentially problematic *situation* is established, then brought to the point of *crisis*, and finally *resolved*. This refers to *structure*, the aspect of a text that is broadly covered in the marking scheme for Leaving Certificate English under the heading *Coherence of delivery (C)*.
- It should employ all the resources of aesthetic language in its creation of characters, places and events, most notably *comparisons*, either as *metaphors* or *similes*, realistic *dialogue*, vivid *adjectives*, expressive *verbs*, *colour* and *atmosphere*. This refers to *style*, the aspect of a text that is broadly covered in the marking scheme for Leaving Certificate English under the heading *Efficiency of language use (L)*.

An example from past Leaving Certificate papers

If you take one of the narrative or descriptive texts from past Leaving Certificate papers and apply the basic key elements of effective narrative or descriptive writing to it, you are obviously preparing yourself for answering Question A on English Paper I. But you can achieve much more than this. A critical reading of such a text can expand the basic list to a comprehensive list, covering everything you need to know about the content, style and structure of narrative and descriptive writing.

Here is a critical reading of Text 1 from 2006.

'What seems to be the problem, Lady Sarah?'

CRITICAL QUESTIONS

In this extract (adapted from A Border Station, *by Shane Connaughton) a father and son are cutting down a tree. The father, a garda sergeant, has been given permission by Lady Sarah, a member of the landed gentry, to cut down a small tree on her lands. However, he decides to ignore her wishes and cut down a magnificent beech tree on the avenue leading to the Great House. We join the story as the tree falls . . .*

1. The central comparison throughout this text is that between a tree and a human being. The technical term for attributing human qualities to things is personification.

'She's going,' said his father. Branches quaking, the huge tree tilted, twisted and, fighting to stay upright, grabbed at a neighbouring tree but, bowing to its fate, keeled over and with a creaking goodbye-sigh rushed to the earth with a thunderous hurricane crash. The boy felt the shock waves in his feet and saw the light flood in to the space where the tree had stood. It was mad, he thought. Ridiculous. Lady Sarah was bound to find out. His father grinned.

'It'll see us in firewood for the winter, thank God.'

Tired out he sat on the tree-stump beside his father and had alternate swigs at the bottle of cold tea.

2. A situation full of potential conflict or danger.

Hearing a noise he turned his head and instantly his body and blood went cold. Approaching along at the wheel of her antiquated Rolls Royce was Lady Sarah. Time stopped dead. His father gave a strangled groan and his face iced over in hatred. They were caught like rats in a trap.

3. Three characters, each brought to life through appearance, dialogue and behaviour. Although a third-person narrative, it is told exclusively from the boy's perspective and so we also have access to his thoughts and feelings.

The car crunched to a halt. He was terrified in case his father did something desperate and was all the more amazed when he saw him smiling and in high good nature waving to Lady Sarah as she, horror-stricken, stepped onto the drive. Wearing a peculiar 1920s hat and a flapping plastic mack she dismissed his father's greeting and staggered towards the tree.

'What have you done, Sergeant, what have you done!' she wailed. 'You have killed one of my beauties!'

Grabbing and clutching the stricken branches she buried herself in the copper coloured leaves.

'Oh Beatrice, Beatrice, my beauty, how has this occurred?'

His father winked.

'What's wrong, what seems to be the problem, Lady Sarah?'

'The problem,' she replied, stepping from the tree, 'is that you have murdered the wrong tree.' Behind the thick lenses of her spectacles her eyes were tiny red dots of dismay.

'Oh no, we haven't, have we?' howled his father, his face a dancing mask of pantomime surprise. 'Good Lord, I can't believe it. Are you sure Lady Sarah?'

'Oh yes I'm sure alright. I gave you a weakling ash, not this!'

Suddenly he turned on the boy and made as if to strike him.

'Didn't I tell you it wasn't this one? I told you all along.'

The boy hung his head in shame and didn't dare look at Lady Sarah because he knew she knew his father lied.

'I'll do anything I can by way of reparation, anything.
I remember you saying the tree's name is Andy. I think that's what confused me. That and the boy. Beech wood is no good to me anyway. It's a poor burner. A weakling ash is just what I wanted, Lady Sarah.'

4. The conflict is brought to the point of crisis.

Once more he blamed the boy and made a run at him as if to hit him. Darting out of his way he went close to Lady Sarah and looked into her eyes.

She knew.

Turning away she faced the dead Beatrice and with her frail hand plucked a copper leaf.

Resting on her fingers like a clot of blood, she held it to her mouth and nose and sighed as if kissing goodbye to a loved one.

Tears welled in the boy's eyes. Lady Sarah looked very old, very sad, and a little frightened. She owned the great demesne, employed many people, but up against his father she knew the truth. He was the Garda Sergeant and she was just a lonely spinster, powerless to command. She needed him to protect her property. The law was hers but it was on his word that it was carried out.

Getting into her car, she spoke softly, her pride hurt, her spirit shocked.

'You may as well finish what you so cruelly started.'

'Well that's the only damn thing we can do now, Lady Sarah.'

5. The crisis is resolved by the father's victory, but, as always in good stories, the resolution has consequences for the future.

Hours later as they drove home, though his body ached, the boy's soul raged rampant at the conquering smirk on his father's face.

Expanded notes

Completing the key elements of an effective descriptive or narrative text

Content: Essentially, fiction is the creation of *characters* and significant *situations*.

Here we have three characters caught in a situation that gives rise to some very complex and very significant conflicts. Much to his young son's embarrassment and resentment, a garda sergeant is deliberately destroying a beautiful tree on the grounds of a local member of the gentry. See how rich in *themes* this situation is? You have the vast complications of the emotional relationship between father and son, a major theme in all literature. You have the struggle between two forms of social and political power, the old aristocracy represented by Lady Sarah and the new regime represented by the garda. And since the sergeant destroys something alive and beautiful and turns it into something dead and functional, you also have an aesthetic and practical question: is firewood more important than natural beauty?

Note that none of these themes is imposed on the story by the author. They all grow organically out of the situation and the characters. Each character is brought alive through description, dialogue and behaviour. Lady Sarah's odd, outdated personality is expressed through her 'peculiar 1920's hat and a flapping plastic mack', her gentleness and sentimentality in her anguished cry, 'Oh Beatrice, Beatrice, my beauty, how has this occurred?' and in her desperate embrace of the dying tree.

Structure: The shape of this story is worth close attention, because you will be expected to produce something similar if you are writing a narrative Question B in the examination. Here is the skeleton:

- **An Introduction,** consisting of four paragraphs, which immediately plunges us, without background explanation, into a situation full of potential conflict and into the lives of the characters caught in it.
- **A Development,** consisting of sixteen paragraphs, in which the conflict between the characters is brought to the point of crisis.
- **A Conclusion,** consisting of four paragraphs, in which this crisis is resolved, but with obvious consequences for the future, which is left undefined.

Style: Although it is very short, the opening paragraph here is also very powerful. The writing effectively captures a scene in which there is action, movement, and human reaction, and it manages to move fluidly between the various aspects. Opening with a brief, dramatic piece of *dialogue* – 'She's going.' – immediately creates a sense of *tension* and *expectation*.

Over the next sentence, the tension is held and increased, as the slow, reluctant descent of the falling tree is captured in the evocative *verbs* – 'quaking', 'tilted', 'twisted', 'fighting' and 'grabbed' – which take us slowly through the various stages of the tree's almost heroic resistance. The end approaches with a couple of words evoking painful sounds – 'creaking' suggests discomfort and 'goodbye-sigh' suggests regret – and then finally arrives with a triple assault on the ear, when 'thunderous', 'hurricane' and 'crash' all imitate the *cacophony* of the tree smashing against the earth.

As the noise subsides, the *imagery* moves from reverberating in the ear to touching the other *senses*, as the boy feels the 'shock waves' along the ground where he stands and catches the 'light' pouring through the gap created by the felling of the tree. The verb 'flood' is particularly effective to describe the burst of light, because it suggests the onrushing of a tidal wave in the wake of the 'shock waves' of the earthquake. *Verbs*, *adjectives* and *images* combine here to suggest that something truly momentous has occurred.

The use of *personification* throughout – the trees even have individual names, Beatrice and Andy – and the role of *appearance*, *dialogue* and *depiction of action* in the creation of *character* have already been noted.

Class assignment

This is Text 2 from the 2008 Leaving Certificate paper. Using the key elements, techniques and vocabulary introduced above, assess it as an effective piece of narrative writing.

False identity?

This text is taken from Clare Kilroy's novel, Tenderwire, *narrated in the voice of Eva Tyne, an Irish violinist living and working in New York. The story involves Alexander who has offered Eva the opportunity to buy a rare violin, a Stradivarius, at a fraction of its market value. However, this violin comes without documents of identity or rightful ownership.*

Nobody believed the real story of how I found the Magdalena (all old violins have names and Magdalena is this one's name). Her origins are suspicious at best. I got her from a Russian. At least I thought he was Russian. He was a giant of a man and blond as a child. His name, he told me, was Alexander. I encountered him in a bar done up like a KGB office, or a New York bar owner's impression of one: red lights, black walls, yellow scythes. I couldn't say at what point Alexander started telling me about violins, about a very special one, about a Stradivarius.

That name was all it took and I was in the passenger seat of a battered car driving at speed over the East River to Alexander's apartment, a few blocks away. Here he produced the violin, holding it out like a cushion on which a crown is placed. 'It is the real thing, I promise you,' he said. By agreeing there and then to pay him 600,000 dollars, I confirmed that this violin was no ordinary instrument. As a musician you instinctively sense when something is special and I heard something special when I put bow to string and began to play. I heard something that unveiled an Aladdin's cave of possibilities.

This is not what Zach, manager of the orchestra I played in, thought, when I related the encounter to him: 'The more I hear, the worse it gets,' he said. 'It's either fake, or worse – it's the real thing and the Russian doesn't have a rightful claim on it; it'll be seized within days of your first performance. Have you considered what that will do to your career? Being linked with a stolen violin? You might be arrested? You'll be deported from the States at least.' The absoluteness of

his voice, the surety of his manner: everything Zach said was right. Logical, reasonable and right! And yet I couldn't allow myself to agree with him.

When Zach left, I organised the money that I had managed to get together. Everything my father had left me and more for a violin! The cash formed an unwieldy bulk. How was I to transport it to Tompkins Square Park where I had arranged to meet Alexander? What was to stop him from grabbing it and making off? I swept the money into one large pile and made a big pyramid of it, a drift of autumn leaves, then shoved it into a plastic bag. Now it had no separate identity. It was just counters in a game. A game of high risk!

Saturday night's blizzard had deposited an icing of snow. New York has a way of seeming brand-new sometimes. I put on my runners in case I had to run and stepped out onto the street. The faces around me looked fresh in the bracing whiteness. I tried not to look in their eyes lest they detect the alarm in mine. It was natural to feel jittery as the pressure of walking around with such a large sum was breathtaking. I took out my inhaler and wheezed piteously. There was a faint warmth in the January sun that shone on my face.

I wiped snow off a bench and sat on it. My hands in my lap were like two dead puppies. Between them was the plastic bag. I was happy, that was the odd thing. It was like sitting in a darkened cinema waiting for a horror movie to begin.

Then I saw Alexander as he trudged doggedly through the snow. Shafts of sunlight spilled through the trees onto his ash-blond hair, causing it to flicker like fire. He cut through the centre of the park, sat down beside me and let out a companionable sigh as he placed the violin case by my feet. 'Open it,' he grinned, as if it were a carefully chosen gift.

I put the plastic bag on the ground and wedged it securely between my ankles, then lifted the lid of the case. It looked like the same violin. My hands unstrapped it, finetuned the strings and then hesitantly sounded the high notes. How ethereal they were on the icy air!

It was the first time since childhood that I'd played outdoors and in the frozen world of Tompkins Square Park, the sound was startlingly pure. I was almost laughing, almost crying in wonder at the loveliness of the sound. I listened to the laughter of the children in the playground, the cooing of the woodpigeons, the barking in the dog run.

If I was about to make the biggest mistake of my life, then so be it.

Homework and tasks

1. Write down the best narrative joke that you have ever heard and assess its merits as a story, with reference to its shape or structure, its ability to describe situations and characters, and its language. A narrative joke is a reasonably lengthy tale with a punch-line.
2. Write down the best holiday story you have ever heard and assess its merits, with reference to its structure, its ability to create interesting characters and situations and its descriptive language.
3. Select a chapter from a travel narrative, taken from an account of the author's journeys through another country, and assess its merits as a descriptive text.
4. Select a chapter from a biographical narrative, taken from an account of an individual's life, and assess its merits as a descriptive text.
5. Select a chapter from a historical narrative, taken from an account of a previous age, and assess its merits as a descriptive text.
6. Select a chapter from a popular fictional narrative, such as a thriller, a crime novel, an adventure novel or a romantic novel, and assess its merits as a descriptive text.

Part Two:

How to Write for Leaving Certificate Higher Level English Paper 1

Chapter Four: Answering Question A

Introduction

For 50 marks, you are set three specific questions on your selected text. Most of these are simple comprehension questions, asking you to discuss the content. A few may request a short passage ranging beyond, but still related to, the content. Others require an appreciation of the author's style. The remainder, attached to the visual text, ask for your response to an image or a group of images.

And that's it. There are only four types of question: **Assessing a Point Made by the Author**, **Developing a Topic Beyond the Text**, **Analysing Language and Style** and **Reading an Image**.

The best way of learning how to deal with each type of question is by starting with a detailed appreciation of a sample answer and building an understanding from that of how to prepare, shape and express your response. If you know how to drive one make of car, you know how to drive all cars. If you know how to answer each type of question from the four that are set, then it doesn't matter what text is put in front of you.

Assessing a point made by the author

The sample

The following question was set on the 2006 Leaving Certificate paper, Text 2, 'Ghost writing', which is reproduced on page 14. You should read the question several times, then the text and then the following sample answer.

(i) On the evidence of this passage, what is the attitude of Jan Stevens to ghost writing?

Sample answer

The first two paragraphs of the text concentrate on providing the reader with basic information about ghost writing and it is only in the opening sentence of the third paragraph – 'Ghost writing can be challenging' – that Jan Stevens begins to reveal her personal attitudes to the activity. The use of the word 'challenging' is very interesting here. Usually when used in such a context, it suggests a task that is demanding but enjoyable, a job that is difficult but fulfilling. On the one hand, then, Stevens finds ghost writing onerous at times, confirmed by her use of the word 'painful' to describe working at it at full stretch, churning out 2,000 words a day. On the other hand, she also undoubtedly finds it satisfying, indicated by her obvious pleasure in meeting her demanding deadlines 'without fail'. The word 'challenging' then comes to mean something demanding that is executed with skill and with pride.

Nevertheless, Stevens hardly considers the occupation *worthy*, no matter how 'challenging' it might be. The fact that it contents itself with the second-rate obviously disappoints her a little, as indicated by her confession that 'the *almost* right word' is usually good enough. Now, the limitations of finding *almost* the right word can be understood by applying the phrase to other areas of life – finding *almost* the right partner, for instance, or *almost* getting across the road safely.

She has come to terms, personally, with the job's limitations, though. Her revelation that some ghost writers are 'haunted' by its inadequacies seems to exclude herself. Her attitude is one of self-deprecating resignation, obvious enough from the modesty and the good humour of the passage.

Stevens, then, is happy to make a good living from challenging work, but not too eager to claim public credit for it. I get the impression that she's mostly glad that her 'name doesn't appear' on the books.

Key elements when assessing a point made by the author

Interpreting the question. Since you are awarded marks only for answering the set question, your grade in Question A will be determined more by your understanding of the question than by your understanding of the text. What distinguishes the A student from the C student is a perceptive reading of the question. What's the difference, for instance, between an author's attitude to something and an author's opinion on something? Well, an 'attitude' very clearly includes feelings as well as views, doesn't it? As language students, you are expected to appreciate the differences in meaning and suggestiveness between words. Consider some other questions from recent years asking for an assessment of a point made by the author. In question (i), Text 1, 2007 – 'In what way, according to the author of this text, do films change the way we think and/or feel about life?' – the single most important word is 'change'. You should mark it as such. It defines what you're looking for in the text. In answering question (i), Text 2, 2007 – 'Virginia Woolf described London in 1930 as a "city alive". In your own words, outline the aspects of the city that impressed her most' – you need to concentrate on those aspects that capture the sense of 'a city alive'. In answering question (iii), Text 1, 2008 – 'Do you think the writer of this text is sympathetic to the modern teenager?' – you must offer some understanding of what 'sympathetic' means.

Locating the material in the text. Once you have identified the central features of the question, critically read the text, marking the relevant words and phrases. In responding to 2007, Text 1, (i), for instance, you are searching for words and phrases that indicate 'change'; in response to 2007, Text 2, (i), words and phrases that suggest 'a city alive'; in response to 2008, Text 1, (iii), words and phrases that express 'sympathy'; and in response to 2006, Text 2, (i), for my sample answer, words and phrases that reveal the author's 'attitude'. You will notice that I have selected 'challenging' and 'painful', among others, because these are the type of words that contain feelings and value judgments rather than neutral description, and so express the writer's 'attitude'.

Organising the answer. You have reflected on the question, you have gathered the appropriate material, and now you need to write your response. So . . .

1. Answer the question as quickly and as directly as possible. In the sample answer, I state clearly that Jan Stevens finds ghost writing 'demanding but enjoyable, a job that is difficult but fulfilling'. I have something else to add, that she 'hardly considers the occupation *worthy*', but I leave this to a later paragraph.

2. Use quotations or detailed references to support the points you make. Here, I use 'challenging' to illustrate my initial point and '*almost* the right word' to support my second.

3. Explain why your chosen quotations or references are so relevant and effective. I conclude that 'the word "challenging" . . . comes to mean something demanding that is executed with skill and with pride' and that 'the limitations of finding *almost* the right word can be understood by applying the phrase to other areas of life'.

4. Briefly summarise your points in a short final paragraph.

Key tip

Many students lose a considerable number of marks because of the brevity of their answers, which may be perfectly accurate, but not detailed enough to gain full marks. Ensure that you have enough material for a comprehensive response by considering each of the following when assessing a point made by the author:
(1) Where is the author's point first introduced?
(2) How is the author's point developed; in other words, how is it clarified, expanded on and applied to a number of situations?
(3) What examples does the author offer to illustrate the point and how interesting and effective are they? (4) At what stage is the point re-emphasised? (usually the final paragraph).

For further guidance in this area, refer back to Part One, Chapter Two, page 24 and pages 27–28, where the techniques of introducing, developing and supporting a point are discussed.

Developing a topic beyond the text

The sample

The following question was set on the 2005 Leaving Certificate paper, Text 3, 'Public lives'. You should read the question several times, then the text and then the sample answer that follows it.

(iii) Does the kind of superstar lifestyle described in this passage appeal to you? Give reasons for your answer, supporting the points you make by reference to the text.

Public lives

Some people's lives seem far from ordinary. Modelled on articles from a number of celebrity magazines, the text below was written by a Leaving Certificate student. It offers a glimpse into the lifestyle of imaginary rock star, Eva Maguire.

World exclusive! Irish rock diva speaks to readers from her Italian villa.

Hi, my name is Jerry Philips. I interview sport stars, superstars, rock stars, divas, celebrities. My targets are the super wealthy, the faces of the moment, the famous; extraordinary lives that excite the curiosity and interest of ordinary people. I cover film premieres, music awards, Oscar ceremonies and star-studded parties; the significant global events of the world of entertainment.

This evening, I am in Florence, ensconced in a huge leather armchair in the waterfront palazzo home of Eva Maguire. In a rare, exclusive and candid interview, the 24-year-old rock superstar reveals where she sees her destiny and for the first time shares with *Celebrity* readers some of the secrets of her forthcoming wedding plans.

Our photo shoot shows her posing with one of her pet miniature greyhounds, wearing her favourite Jacqui Getty jewellery and chic designer labels. As we discuss her plans for the future, personal and professional, candles light up her sun-baked, marble terrace with its glorious views over the Arno River, far from the terrace house of her childhood in a small

Irish town. It has been a roller-coaster 18 months for this Irish-born music queen originally from the midlands. Discovered on Christmas Eve, busking in Covent Garden, her rise to fame has been meteoric. She has achieved head-spinning global success, winning international music awards, packing concert venues and seeing her albums topping charts all over the world. Her first CD was the fastest-selling debut album to hit the UK charts and she is fast becoming a rock icon. Her life for the past year has been about L.A., London, New York and Monte Carlo. Some reviewers have criticised her ruthless quest for fame but she is certainly professional, hard-working and determined to succeed in a tough industry. She has been constantly under the media spotlight, (and indeed, some would suggest that today's celebrity culture has gone too far), but says that her stable Irish family background has helped her to cope with the pressures of fame and with the world's press constantly on her doorstep.

'I'm a very reserved person,' she says, 'but this business is no place to be shrinking and insecure, it takes a certain attitude,' she stops and grins. 'The point is, I deal with projection all of the time. With a few smart changes, anyone can become a style goddess. Doors have opened for me and I am not afraid to take risks,' she says bluntly.

She is extraordinarily beautiful and astonishingly tough, steely and ambitious. Her golden hair frames features dominated by huge blue eyes. She wears a diamond and sapphire-studded ring on her left hand, reminding us that she is about to marry and share her future with Irish music promoter, Ross Kennedy. 300 Irish friends packjammed the luxurious K-Club last weekend in a pre-wedding bash.

International paparazzi are already gathering in the little Italian village where the ceremony will be held. It is expected that a galaxy of Hollywood celebrities, musicians and film producers will attend. It is even rumoured that some surprise politicians will be represented at the wedding. Limousines and helicopters have been arriving at the village for the past 48 hours. About 400 close friends of the couple are flying in from all over the world this weekend.

This spectacular event promises to knock off in style. Expect six hundred doves to flock the Italian sky at the moment when the wedding vows are made and a church filled with tiny rosebuds, orchids and lily of the valley. Pink, lilac and white are the colours chosen to predominate this glittering extravaganza. The couple intend to settle on the Italian Riviera. Welcome to their high-octane world of glitz, glamour, sleek yachts and private jets. The honeymoon will begin with a train journey on the Eastern and Oriental express but the ultimate destination is a closely guarded secret. It is expected that the couple will party their way through the coming winter season in Italy.

Sample answer

Let's examine the features of Eva Maguire's life as revealed in the article. She lives in Florence, in a private villa, surrounded by fashionable, expensive accessories. She has already tasted considerable success in her chosen art form, although she clearly works very hard to sustain this. She is 'constantly under the media's spotlight', and the paparazzi are camped on her doorstep, if such fashionable accommodation is allowed to have a doorstep. For as long as she is famous, she will live her life in public, trading celebrity exposure against the risk of someone with a very long lens snatching an embarrassing shot of her using the toilet on her honeymoon train.

For me, the most attractive feature of her lifestyle is her professional success. Since she began as a busker, 'in Covent Garden', it's obvious that she sang and played primarily because she loved performing and only partly to scratch a living from her talents. She was not a wide-eyed dreamer, in other words. Nobody who longs to be a 'rock diva' exposes themselves to the indignity of busking; they cut a CD in their bedroom or garage and hawk it around the music and radio studios. That popular success, in itself, is of little value to her is indicated by her unwillingness to indulge her own ego, her determination to be 'professional, hardworking'. Talent, combined with energy and application, is a recipe not only for success, but also for personal satisfaction. This area of her life, taken by itself, is the most appealing. But there's the rub. It cannot be taken by itself, in isolation. There's a balance to everything, and Maguire must pay a price for her fame. For me, that price is too high.

Of what value is an Italian villa if it becomes a prison, surrounded not by walls and fences, but by reporters and photographers? At least walls have no eyes, and in that respect are kinder jailers. What pleasure can be gained from fashionable jewellery and 'chic designer labels' when you are forced to wear them all the time or run the risk of being derided as dowdy or sloppy? What comfort is there in an intimate kiss when you must keep both eyes open for intruders?

Eva Maguire has sold her privacy. It is too heavy a price to pay for a public life.

Key elements when developing a topic beyond the text

Interpreting the question. Since you are awarded marks only for answering the set question, your grade in Question A will be determined more by your understanding of the question than by your understanding of the text. What distinguishes the A student from the C student is a perceptive reading of the question. What's the difference, for instance, between 'rewarding' and 'appealing' in question (ii), Text 1, 2007, 'As a teenager the writer found reading books more rewarding and appealing than watching films. Has this been your experience?' Well, you might enjoy watching a film more than reading a book, but you might also find reading the same book more beneficial in many ways than watching the same film. As language students, you are expected to appreciate the differences in meaning and suggestiveness between words, and yet, many candidates in 2007 confined their answers to their preference for films and completely ignored the second aspect, thereby severely damaging their grades.

Consider some other questions from recent years asking you to develop a topic beyond the text. In question (iii), Text 2, 2007 – 'If given the choice, in which of the two Londons, (the one described by Virginia Woolf in 1930 or the modern city experienced by Monica Ali) would you choose to live? Give reasons for your choice with reference to the text' – the most important phrases are 'described by' and 'experienced by', since they indicate that it's not modern London and 1930s London you must choose between, but two different perceptions, at different periods, of the same city. Again, many candidates made the mistake of writing about *their* experience of contemporary London. In answering question (iii), Text 2, 2004 – 'What advice would you give to the management of Jordan's factory about how they might improve working conditions for new employees like Paul?' – you must be aware that you are asked to identify the deficiencies in inducting new employees noted or implied by the text and to make suggestions *only* with reference to these. In answering our current sample, question (iii), Text 3, 2005 – 'Does the kind of superstar lifestyle described in this passage appeal to you? Give reasons for your answer, supporting the points you make by reference to the text' – you are confined to the specific lifestyle features mentioned in relation to the star.

Locating the material in the text. Once you have identified the central features of the question, critically read the text, marking the relevant words and phrases. In responding to 2007, Text 1, (ii), for instance, you are searching for words and phrases that indicate precisely what the author means by the distinction between 'rewarding' and 'appealing'; in response to 2007, Text 2, (iii), words and phrases that capture either Virginia Woolf's or Monica Ali's description of their impressions of London; in response to 2004, Text 2, (iii), words and phrases that identify deficiencies in the treatment of new employees; and in response to 2005, Text 3, (iii), for my sample answer, words and phrases that reveal the details of Eva Maguire's lifestyle. You will notice that I have extracted from the text all the relevant features – from the good, such as her success, to the bad, such as her lack of privacy – before proceeding with my assessment of her lifestyle.

Organising the answer. You have reflected on the question, you have gathered the appropriate material, and now you need to write your response. So . . .

1. Answer the question as quickly and as directly as possible. When developing a topic beyond the text, it is absolutely crucial that you don't wander off, self-indulgently expressing your own, largely irrelevant, opinions. Although your views are invited, it is only to those aspects treated in the text that the invitation extends. I recommend, therefore, that you begin with something similar to my own opening sentence – 'Let's examine the features of Eva Maguire's life as revealed in the article' – since this ties you to the text for the remainder of your answer. After that, you can examine the merits or otherwise of each feature separately.

2. Use quotations or detailed references to support the points you make. Here, I incorporate 'professional, hardworking' and 'chic designer labels' into my comments and I use very detailed references to specific aspects of Maguire's lifestyle throughout.

3. Explain why your chosen quotations or references are so relevant and effective. I conclude that 'professional, hardworking' suggests talent combined with energy and application and that 'chic designer labels' is an image of what is desirable, but fundamentally unimportant.

4. Briefly summarise your points in a short final paragraph.

Key tip

Many students lose a considerable number of marks because of the brevity of their answers, which may be perfectly accurate, but not detailed enough to gain full marks. Ensure that you have enough material for a comprehensive development of a topic beyond the text by having at least three points to make in relation to the topic. For example, in answering question (iii), Text 2, 2004 – 'What advice would you give to the management of Jordan's factory about how they might improve working conditions for new employees like Paul?' – you might have noted that (1) there was no one to greet the employee on his first day; (2) there was no one to properly explain his duties; (3) there was no one to accompany him on lunch break; (4) the working environment was oppressive; and (5) the canteen was like a dungeon.

Analysing language and style

The samples

Sample A, informative writing

The following question was set on the 2006 Leaving Certificate paper, Text 2, 'Ghost writing', which is reproduced on page 14. You should read the question several times, then the text and then the following sample answer.

(iii) Jan Stevens sets out to inform the reader on the topic of ghost writing. What features make this an interesting piece of informative writing?

Sample answer A

The primary purpose of an informative piece is to inform, really – without which it cannot be interesting, since it is off the point – so I was particularly impressed by both the insights offered in 'Ghost writing' and the clear manner in which everything was explained. The crisp opening sentence – 'I am a ghost writer' – is a perfect example. Not only is it simple and straightforward in itself, but it is immediately followed by a beautifully clear explanation of the term – 'I write books that other people take credit for.' The piece never descends into obscurity, never gets bogged down in difficulties.

As with the opening, each subsequent major statement – 'Ghost writing can be challenging', for instance – is followed by straightforward clarification and illustration. This is combined with helpful little questions that might occur to the reader – 'What do the *authors* actually do?' and 'What of the ethics of ghost writing?' – so that the reader is skilfully guided through the various stages of the topic. This awareness, on Stevens' part, that the reader's interest needs to be maintained and addressed accounts for much of the success of the text.

As well as this, Stevens provides us throughout with interesting illustrations of the informative points she shares with us. For instance, the details about the number of words involved in the daily routine of completing a novel in twelve weeks are fascinating, as are the examples of the 'dissatisfied' ghost writers and the peculiar lengths they go to in order to stamp their personal mark on a book, and the examples of the various types of 'authors' and their varying instructions. As with any successful informative piece, the colour and variety of the illustrations add considerably to the interest.

Finally, although some informative writing can be very dry and dull – rule books, for instance, or user manuals – Stevens' writing has a lightness of touch that makes it highly enjoyable. She has a wry, self-deprecating humour throughout that is very appealing. It opens with her description of certain 'authors' as people 'who simply can't be trusted with a pen', continues with mischievous use of 'haunted' in relation to ghost writers, and ends with the teasing challenge that she may have had the entire text ghost written and the reader wouldn't know the difference. The humour is never intrusive, never there just for its own sake, but, when well done, it is always immeasurably helpful in communicating information.

So, Stevens' strengths as an informative writer, and the qualities that make the passage an enjoyable as well as an instructive read, are a sensitive awareness of the reader's needs, clarity of language, straightforward explanation, interesting illustrations and examples, and a light, humorous style.

Sample B, argumentative and persuasive writing

The following question was set on the 2006 Leaving Certificate paper, Text 3, 'Pretence'. You should read the question several times, then the text and then the sample answer that follows it.

(iii) Do you think the writer is justified in the conclusions drawn in the final paragraph? Explain your view.

Pretence – everybody's doing it!

Psychologists tell us that the habit of pretending is unique to the human species and begins in very early childhood. From about two years of age children engage in imaginary conversations with make-believe characters (talking to a doll, inventing an imaginary companion) or pretending to engage in a variety of adult activities (talking into a banana as if it were a telephone, pretending to cook and eat mud pies, pretending to be a teacher, a soldier, a Garda). The young of no other creature on earth behave like this.

It seems that this childhood role-playing is just training for later life where pretence is widespread. From the actor on stage shedding tears as he plays a tragic role for the hundredth time, to Ronaldo diving in the penalty area (again!), we are the masters of pretence.

Indeed, pretence often soothes the friction between people and promotes smoother relationships. Without it our world would be a crueller place.

Can you imagine if everyone said, 'Let's stop all this pretence! Let's tell each other the unvarnished truth for a change!'

Imagine it's St. Valentine's Day and the young not so gallant lover comes to his tender lady's door. She twirls in her new dress and utters the invitation to praise. 'Well? How do I look?' And he replies truthfully, 'Well, let me see, dear. Hm . . . You know . . . I'd prefer you in something else!' In this case the absence of pretence might lead to a shorter than expected lifespan!

So why do we have this fascination with pretence?

Well, it is an expression of the two great gifts which make human beings unique: the gift of imagination and the ability to make one another happy.

Sample answer B

In his final paragraph, the writer makes a number of related claims. He suggests, I think, that pretence emerges naturally from our ability to invent things that are not literally true – 'the gift of imagination' – and he believes that we deliberately employ pretence as a means of expressing our care for others – 'the ability to make one another happy'. The question is, how much evidence, factual and/or anecdotal, has the writer already presented us with to justify such claims.

Let's take each in turn.

The suggestion that pretence comes naturally to humans has already been well prepared for. In the opening paragraph, the author refers to the general agreement among psychologists that pretending 'begins in very early childhood'. The next sentence identifies 'about two years of age' as the period when this activity starts. Clearly, any behaviour that begins so early, long before the child is instructed in it in any formal way, can loosely be accepted as natural. The author then supports the point with a number of recognisable and convincing examples, such as a child talking to someone not actually present and a child playing at being an important adult. As the author remarks, and echoes in the final paragraph, no other creature that we know of does this. We are 'unique' in this respect.

I'm not convinced, however, that the author's second claim in the last paragraph – pretence expresses 'the ability to make one another happy' – is at all a conclusion of what has preceded it. In the third, fourth and fifth paragraphs, the author imagines a 'crueller' world in which everybody told the stark truth about everything, but the anecdote used to illustrate this really demonstrates that we lie more out of self-interest than concern for others. The young man tells his girl that she looks wonderful in her new dress because . . . well, he wants a bit of peace and happiness, for himself. A lie in the circumstances 'might lead to a shorter than expected lifespan', which is a joke, obviously, but nonetheless reveals that the young man is avoiding danger, not being sensitive, motivated more by anxiety than concern, although both sensitivity and concern are also present. Anybody who has even been on a date will recognise this mixture of motives.

So, much of the final paragraph is a justifiable conclusion based on the material already presented, but, even in the context of the writer's own article, the claim that we pretend 'to make one another happy', seems very naïve.

Sample C, narrative and descriptive writing

The following question was set on the 2005 Leaving Certificate paper, Text 1, 'An ordinary life'. You should read the question several times, then the text and then the sample answer that follows it.

(iii) Did the description of the market bring it to life for you as a reader? Support your answer by reference to the text.

An ordinary life

Margaret Forster

Margaret Forster writes about her grandmother, Margaret Ann Hind, a domestic servant in Carlisle, a town in the north of England, in the 1890s. Her book is called Hidden Lives – a Family Memoir.

The life of Margaret Ann, my grandmother, was narrow. The physical hardship, the sheer energy and strength needed to get through each day, was commonplace. She expected to be down on her knees scrubbing, up to her elbows in boiling or freezing water, washing and rinsing dishes, rocking on her feet with weariness after hours of running up and down stairs. When she reminisced in later life, it was always without any trace of resentment. Her expectations were low. She was expected to carry on as she was until she dropped. Or married.

Marriage was always an option. Marriage was possibly, but not definitely, or even probably, an escape from servitude. If she married, she knew she'd still have to cook and clean and wash and mend, and without the help of the kind of servant she was to the Stephensons unless she married a rich man. The chances of this happening were nil. Who, in Carlisle, among the servant class, married rich men? Rich, eligible men were few and far between, and girls like Annie Stephenson from good families ever on the lookout for them. But there was rich and rich after all. Plenty of tradesmen around who did quite well for themselves, who could afford to rent or even to buy decent houses and to lead comfortable enough lives. The market was full of them. Plenty of money there, especially among the butchers, with Carlisle being such a big meat-eating place. On Saturday afternoons Margaret Ann would go to the market to buy the meat for Sunday. She went through the glass doors and down the little cobbled hill where the butchers' stalls now were. Some butchers had more than one stall. They had three or four together, positive empires. The meat hung from the ceiling on hooks, whole carcasses of pig and lamb and beef, and on the tiled counters below lay the cut-up portions; the bright red stewing steak, the dark slabs of liver, the great coils of pale, putty-coloured sausage, the crimson mounds of mince, the stiff rows of chops.

Thomas Hind was proprietor of stall number 4. This stall was clean. The carcasses didn't drip blood, the meat on the counter did not lie in puddles of it, the bin for fat wasn't nauseatingly visible. The floor always seemed freshly sawdusted, the aprons of the assistants were spotless. Even though his prices were not the cheapest, there was always a queue at Thomas Hind's. Margaret was a patient queuer. She never attempted to push herself forward but waited her turn calmly. She engaged in none of the banter that other customers seemed to like. She stated her requirement and that was that beyond a please and thank you. These were exactly the qualities which aroused Thomas Hind's interest. He noticed her precisely because of her curious quality of stillness. In 1893, when she first began buying meat from him, he was thirty-five years old and unmarried.

His father had been a butcher and so had his grandfather, and as the only son he was always expected to take over the family business. His father had died when Thomas was a child and his mother, Jane, had become a butcher herself in order to keep the business going for Thomas to inherit. His debt to her was strong and he acknowledged it by now supporting not just her but two of his three sisters (the third had married). He was prosperous enough by then to marry. He was notoriously hard to satisfy and was teased about his high standards by his sisters who despaired of him ever approving of any girl. For four years he observed Margaret Ann quite contentedly, and then, when his mother died in 1897, decided the time had come for him to court her very seriously. Nothing impetuous about Tom.

So it was a slow affair, this courtship, three years of best boned and rolled sirloin, shoulder of lamb, leg of pork, three years of pounds of sausage, best back bacon, ham on the bone. A lot of meat, a lot of pleasantries, a lot of cap-doffing on Tom's part and head-inclining on Margaret Ann's. One Saturday, towards the end of the afternoon, when there were no assistants to hear and smirk, no customer other than Margaret Ann to hear and speculate, he asked her if she would care to go with him and his sisters out to Burgh Marsh for a breath of sea air. He was very much afraid she would refuse, even be offended, but no, she smiled and said she knew his sisters from church and would be glad to accompany them if she could get time off.

Sample answer C

On a first reading, the most striking thing about the description of the market is the author's rich display of colour and effective use of detail. The meat is not just 'meat'; it is 'pig and lamb and beef', it is 'carcasses', originally whole, then butchered into 'steak', 'liver', 'sausage', 'mince', 'chops'. The variety is impressive, but what really whets the appetite is the author's painterly use of vibrant colours: 'bright red', 'dark', 'pale, putty coloured', 'crimson'. The scene is evoked so exactly that it is impossible not to have a visual image of it. The contrast between 'bright red' and 'dark', side by side, is stark and effective, but I particularly enjoy the more subtle shift from 'bright red' to 'crimson', between the appearance of beef cut as steak and beef that is minced.

But the question asks if the description brought the market 'to life', and so far all we have is a very evocative portrait, an impressive *still* life. Re-reading the passage, I became more conscious of how the author subtly captures the activity of the market, the human characters and their movements. The description of Margaret Ann entering the market is again impressively detailed – the quiet little adjectives in '*glass* doors' and '*cobbled* hill' are particularly good – but it is the thriving world inside, suggested by that single metaphor in 'positive *empires*' – wealth, riches, vast expanses of land, strange countries – that is then opened up to us. We join the 'queue' at Thomas Hind's stall. We overhear the 'banter' of other customers. We eavesdrop on the commonplace exchanges between butcher and customer – 'please and thank you' – and then we are drawn back again to observe the same characters at a distance.

To sum up, effective use of visual detail, and of sound and movement, all combine, over a short section of the text, to give a very lively impression of the market.

Key elements when analysing language and style

Interpreting the question. Since you are awarded marks only for answering the set question, your grade in Question A will be determined more by your understanding of the question than by your understanding of the text. What distinguishes the A student from the C student is a perceptive reading of the question. When analysing language and style, it is absolutely essential to know which *type* of text – informative, argumentative, descriptive – the question is asking you to assess. Mostly, since no one is trying to catch you out, the question itself informs you, but occasionally a little interpretation is required. While 'Comment on three features of the style of writing which contribute to making this an interesting and informative text' (2008) and 'One reviewer of the novel *Tenderwire* described it as "a compelling and well-written thriller". From your reading of the extract, do you agree with this view?' (2008) are both self-explanatory, 'What features of the writer's style help to make this an interesting piece to read?' (2007) doesn't actually tell you that the text is primarily informative and 'Monica Ali uses a number of vivid images to portray the modern city of London. Select three that you consider particularly effective and explain why' (2007) doesn't make it *too* obvious that a descriptive piece on London is in question.

Locating the material in the text. Once you have identified the central features of the question, critically read the text, marking the relevant words and phrases. As always, it is essential to know what you're looking for. Use the sections from Part One, Chapters One, Two and Three of this book to learn the key elements of effective informative, argumentative and descriptive writing. These define what you are looking for when analysing language and style within the various categories. In the sample answers, note how I find clarity, effective use of examples and humour in the informative text from 2006, how I assess an opinion on the basis of the supporting evidence in the argumentative piece from 2006, and how I look for adjectives, colour, atmosphere and metaphor in the depiction of a place in the descriptive piece from 2005.

Organising the answer. You have reflected on the question, you have gathered the appropriate material, and now you need to write your response. So . . .

1. Answer the question as quickly and as directly as possible. In Sample A, I immediately stress that I'm impressed by both the insights and the clear style. In Sample B, I quickly ask how much evidence the author has provided to support his claims. And in Sample C, I list the most striking features in my opening sentence.
2. Use quotations or detailed references to support the points you make. This is particularly important when analysing language and style, because the style is *in* the detail, so note carefully the wealth of material taken from the texts and employed in all the sample answers.
3. Explain why your chosen quotations or references are so relevant and effective. Again, this is vitally important when analysing language and style. It is not enough to select an effective metaphor, an impressive piece of evidence, an appropriate use of humour. You must explain *why* this metaphor is so effective, *why* the evidence convinces, *why* the light-hearted touch is appropriate in the context.
4. Briefly summarise your points in a short final paragraph.

Key tip

Many students lose a considerable number of marks because of the brevity of their answers, which may be perfectly accurate, but not detailed enough to gain full marks. If you are discussing an *informative* text, devote a paragraph to each of the following: (i) the clarity of the language; (ii) the helpfulness of the presentation; (iii) the comprehensiveness of the material. If you are discussing an *argumentative* piece, devote a paragraph to each of the following: (i) the weight of the factual evidence; (ii) the colour of the anecdotal evidence in the form of personal experience; (iii) the persuasiveness of the rhetorical techniques. If you are discussing a *descriptive* piece, devote a paragraph to each of the following: (i) the rich suggestiveness of the similes, metaphors and images; (ii) the effectiveness of the adjectives and verbs; (iii) the use of colour, humour, sound or emotion.

Reading an image or a set of images

The samples

Sample A, reading an individual image

The following question was set on the 2006 Leaving Certificate paper, Text 3, 'Pretence'. You should read the question several times, then the text and then the sample answer that follows it.

(i) In your opinion which of the visual images best expresses the theme of pretence?

Masters of pretence

Make-believe

Diving?!

Sample answer A

Although the serious-looking boy is obviously only *pretending* to be a professional fireman and the swordsman is clearly *not* the fictional character Zorro, neither strikes me as the most effective expression of pretence. Worst of all in this respect is the shot of Jürgen Klinsmann, who may or may not be diving, since only what is happening outside the frame of the photograph can indicate whether or not he is pretending. For me, therefore, the image that best expresses the theme of pretence is that of the painted young woman.

Firstly, it is a close-up of the human face, which fills the entire frame, and nothing is more expressive, and more deceptive, than the human face. In the other three images, the face is a minor aspect, and the body and its clothing – black costume, fireman outfit, sports gear – have to carry most of the impact. The whole body is a cruder communicator, relying on broad gestures, as with 'Diving', or on artificial postures, as with the other two images. By contrast, the expressions on the young woman's face are subtle – a sideways glance at the viewer, a hint of a smile on the closed lips – and because of this she seems to be teasing the spectator. Her detailed expression draws the viewer in, whereas the largely studied poses of the other three are less intimate. Pretence here, because of the photograph's exploration of the human face, becomes an exercise in seduction, an invitation to wonder, a *collusion* between subject and spectator. This, I think, is a far more effective representation of pretence than the others' posing.

Technically, the photograph of the young woman is also the most impressive. It is the most powerfully framed of the images, since both Zorro and 'Make-believe' drift about unattached and the squashed shape of 'Diving?' diminishes its impact. Finally, the clarity of the colours, and in particular the blue and white face paint against the green background of the foliage, gives a far sharper impression than in the other photographs.

In terms of both its content and its style, therefore, the photograph of the painted young woman is by far the most impressive expression of the theme of pretence.

Sample B, reading a set of images and combining images and text

The following question was set on the 2005 Leaving Certificate paper, Text 2, 'Ordinary lives in war time'. You should read the question several times, then the text and then the sample answer that follows it.

(iii) 'I learned about war . . . [but] I was more interested in what was going on behind the scenes.' From your reading of the introduction and the photographs, what impression do you have of how people's lives are touched by war?

Ordinary lives in war time

Introduction by Jenny Matthews

The following text consists of a written and visual element. The written text is adapted from an introduction by documentary photographer, Jenny Matthews, to her book of photographs entitled Women and War.

1. Mozambique 1986. Soldier with his baby son just before he returns to the front next morning.

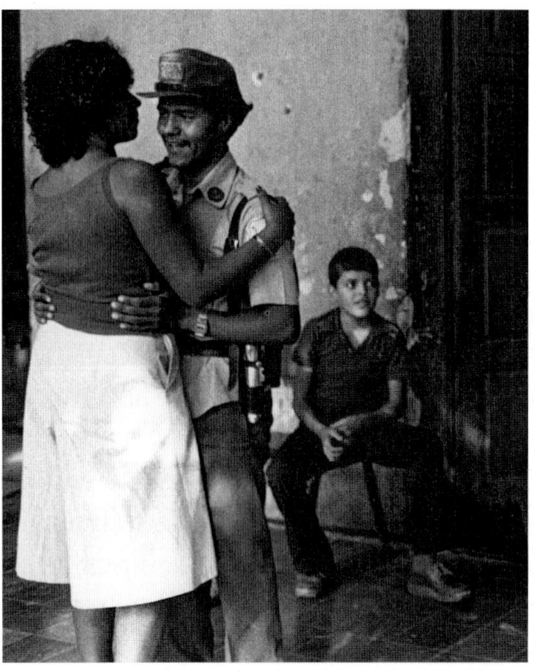

2. El Salvador 1986. An afternoon dance.

3. Bosnia 1994. 21-year-old Spanish soldier serving with UN waving Red Cross convoy over narrow bridge.

4. Eritrea 1988. Fighter back at base after battle.

From the beginning I was interested in covering foreign stories – starting with Central America in the early eighties, a bit off the map for the British media but an exciting place with revolutionary groups fighting guerrilla wars in the mountains. One visit led to another and I learned about war. Although I have often worked where pictures in the news were of the frontline confrontation, I was more interested in what was going on behind the scenes, and that usually involved looking at how women were holding everything together. Some of the wars that I've tiptoed around have been major international conflicts – the Balkans, Middle East, Rwanda, Afghanistan – but others have been practically invisible. I have not been everywhere and this is not a complete record of world conflict; it is my take on recent history, recognising the lives of remarkable women, ordinary people surviving as best they can. As I've travelled I've kept diaries, and the notes from these accompany the photos. All my work has been done in co-operation with a network of people, journalists, friends, fixers, drivers, translators, development workers. Without them it would be hard even to leave home. It has been a great privilege for me to be a photographer, to wander into other people's lives, often uninvited, but usually made embarrassingly welcome. I have lurked around some nasty corners of the world and come across the raw edges of life and death; an infinity of sorrow and fear, but more often than not, tempered with the hope that things will be better for the next generation.

Sample answer B

I think Jenny Matthews's photographs are far more eloquent than her words. Although the selection is small and they feature a bewildering variety of locations, the pictures do offer us some distinct impressions of lives affected by war. The written text does not.

Á la Jenny herself, I could claim that 'one sentence led to another and I learned about how people's lives are touched by war', but this would be so obvious an evasion of the question that I wouldn't get away with it. This vagueness, however, is the main failing of Matthews's prose style, and *she* clearly expects to get away with it. Everything is generalised, leaving us with no distinct impressions at all. Instead of individuals, we are introduced to 'women'. Instead of being told what precisely they were doing and how precisely conflict had impacted on their lives, we are blithely informed that they were 'holding everything together'. *Everything*, if you don't mind. Instead of specific events, we are offered 'recent history' and instead of *demonstrating* what a 'remarkable' woman might look like, we are simply told that Matthews magically recognises them. The written text is a vague glob, leaving no impression other than a faint stickiness from the gluey sentimentality.

The photographs are different, mainly because the subjects are individualised, giving us an impression of how war touched the lives of *this* man, *this* woman, *this* couple. The young Spanish soldier, for instance, although far from home and in a war-torn region, is quite clearly *enjoying* her adventure. And so she should, as a professional soldier on peace-keeping duties, offered opportunities that civilian life at home couldn't possibly provide. The dancing Salvadorian couple are also enjoying their moment of respite, but there is a tension to this photograph which makes it very powerful, giving the impression of lives that are lived contingently, always under the threat of disruption. In fact, all four photographs seem to me to dwell on the intervals, the lulls in fighting, when ordinary life, for a while at least, is reclaimed. The soldier from Mozambique, with a resigned expression on his face, holds his child, perhaps for the last time; the soldier from Eritrea returns to rest and recuperate, also perhaps for the last time. The overall impression of the photographs is of the fragility of ordinary life in times of war.

Key elements when reading an image or a set of images

Although we live in a culture that is saturated and dominated by the image, Leaving Certificate students are sometimes very poor at assessing and analysing photographs and other 'visual texts'. For a start, you must realise that a photograph is merely an expression of an individual's point of view, just as a written text is quite clearly an expression of an individual's point of view. A photograph no more reliably captures the 'truth' than a paragraph in a newspaper does. A photographer selects his subject, his perspective, his background, with the same care and calculation as a writer selects words and phrases.

Here are some of the things you must look out for in assessing a photograph.

The composition of the subjects. The 'subjects' refers to the content of a photograph, whether human figures, objects or landscape, and 'composition' means how these elements relate to each other within the image. A good photographer will arrange the subjects so that the composition controls your view, encouraging your eye to come to rest on the most significant feature.

In image 3, 'Natural disaster', in Text 3, 2007, the eye of the viewer is drawn to the left, to the collapsed roof of the house and downwards from there, to the wrecked fishing boats in the

foreground. The shattered boats indicate that this is a human tragedy as well as a natural disaster. What we are viewing is the destruction of a community and its livelihood. And we notice then that there are no humans at all in the photograph.

In image 2, 'El Salvador 1986', in Text 2, 2005, (page 69) the arrangement of the figures creates a sense of tension where the relaxation of 'an afternoon dance' might be expected. The couple dance stiffly with each other and the boy, awkwardly positioned, looks away from them at some unknown distraction.

In 2008, question (iii) on Text 3 was 'Select one of the other two images of the writers' rooms and write a detailed description of it. You might consider the use of colour, light, details or objects in the image.' With Nicola Barker's room you might notice the worrying number of eyes looking back at you as you look in – the dog, the robot, the religious figure, the masks, the photographs, the figurines – and the fact that the arrangement of the furniture is not very accommodating. The composition of the photograph makes the room seem intimidating rather than inviting.

As demonstrated in Sample answer A above, when the photograph is of a single individual, composition considers body language, posture, facial expression. For example, in image 4, 'Eritrea 1988', in Text 2, 2005 (page 69) the young woman soldier adopts a confident, challenging stance, with her shoulders thrown back, her right hand dangling casually by her side, her automatic weapon slung across her left shoulder.

Framing. Inside the frame of a photograph is everything the photographer decides to include. This is always a conscious decision, and with accomplished photographs, always with specific effects in mind, because quite clearly no photograph can contain everything in the world. If a person is photographed, what body parts are in the frame? Just the head, the torso, the entire body? What are the reasons for this choice? Is the subject shot in profile or frontal? Why, in each case? What else, if anything, is in the frame – a work environment, a landscape, a kitchen, a football pitch? What is the photographer suggesting by including this environment?

In image 1, 'Mozambique 1986', in Text 2, 2005 (page 69) the fact that the image of the soldier is cropped slightly below the waist makes the shot more intimate, more touching, since the framing allows us to clearly see the expressions on both his face and the baby's. This intimacy would be diminished if the soldier was shown full-length and it would be lost if the photograph was taken from a greater distance and the two humans were only tiny figures inside a frame dominated by the landscape.

Actually, widening or reducing the frame of any photograph will lead to a better understanding of the photographer's choices. In 'El Salvador 1986', for instance, if the frame was widened to reveal what the boy is distracted by, then much of the photograph's mystery and tension would disappear. And part of the powerful effect of 'Eritrea 1988' is the fact that the young woman fills almost the entire frame and dominates the photograph.

Going back to question (iii), Text 3, 2008, you might notice that the framing of John Banville's room includes a door, an alcove and sections of the room not directly related to the work desk, while the framing of Nicola Barker's room excludes everything except the work desk, which is hemmed in, almost patrolled, on each side by the life-size figures of robot and saint. The former therefore gives an impression of freedom, the latter an impression of confinement.

In Sample answer A, the most important point made about the framing is that the photograph is a close-up of the human face. In Sample answer B, the most significant point is that the threat of war exists somewhere outside the frame of each of the four photographs.

Colour and lighting. Just as the use of colour, and particularly of light and darkness, provides rich metaphors for a written text, so they are equally expressive and important in photographs. What colours dominate? Are they vivid and vibrant, or are they subdued? How is the photograph lit? Bright artificial interior? Dark interior? Sunlight? Gloom? What is the effect in each case? Why did the photographer select this lighting? The use of colour and lighting in 'Natural disaster' actually suggest that this is the wrong caption, since nature seems quite content, with its brilliant sky, bright trees and calm, clear water, and that what we mean by such an expression is the toll taken by nature on a vulnerable human community.

In all three monochrome photographs from 2005, 'Mozambique', 'El Salvador' and 'Eritrea', the photographer displays a very striking use of white. In 'Mozambique', the child's white blanket suggests innocence and tenderness and vulnerability. It attracts our eye from the first glance and becomes the visual centre of the shot, thereby defining the themes of the photograph. In 'Eritrea', the white wall used as background and the white T-shirt of the soldier combine to create a three-dimensional effect that projects the figure outwards and contributes to the sense of confidence she communicates.

And going back again to question (iii), Text 3, 2008, notice how the clear whites, bright natural wood and splashes of vibrant reds and blues all combine to create the positive effect of John Banville's room, while the dark-stained wood, the deeply coloured rug and walls and the absence of both natural light and vibrant colours all contribute to the much heavier feel of Nicola Barker's room.

Interpreting the question. There are four types of question.

A. You may be asked to assess an individual image, as in 2007, Text 3, (i) 'Select one of the visual images in this collection for the front cover of a book entitled *Forces for Change in Our World*. Give reasons why you consider your chosen image to be the most effective and/or suitable.'

B. You may be asked to assess a set of images, as in 2007, Text 3, (ii) 'Does this set of images represent a balanced view of our changing world? Support your view by reference to the images.'

C. You may be asked to develop a topic beyond the text, with reference to images, as in 2007, Text 3, (iii) 'If asked to select another image to expand this group of images depicting forces for change, what image would you suggest? Give reasons for your choice.'

D. You may be asked if the written and visual elements of a text go well together, as in 2004, Text 3, (iii) 'Do you think that the written and visual elements of the text go well together?'

Locating the material in the text. For all four types of question, you search the text for the key elements of good photography, under *composition, framing* and *colour and lighting,* as discussed above. For **D** you also critically read the written text to assess the points made by the author, as demonstrated in the pages above.

Organising the answer. You have reflected on the question, you have gathered the appropriate material, and now you need to write your response. So . . .

1. Answer the question as quickly and as directly as possible. In Sample A, after a brief overview of the images, I conclude at the end of the first paragraph, 'For me, therefore, the image that best expresses the theme of pretence is that of the painted young woman.' In Sample B, I immediately state, 'the pictures do offer us some distinct impressions of lives affected by war. The written text does not.' The thing to understand when considering whether or not the visual and written elements go well together is that, in answering the previous two questions, you have already answered the third, and it's really only a matter of being consistent. Question (i) usually asks you for the main point of the written element and question (ii) asks you to discuss the impact of the images on you. Question (iii), therefore, simply asks if the images accurately illustrate the main point that you have already discussed. If they do, then the written and visual elements go well together. If they don't, then the elements are unsuited to each other.

2. Use quotations or detailed references to support the points you make. In both sample answers, such references involve details from the images and in Sample B quotations from the written text are selected in the usual way.

3. Explain why your chosen quotations or references are so relevant and effective. As always, it's not enough to select an effective visual detail. You must explain

why this detail is so effective, *why* the composition works so well, *why* the framing influences the viewer's response, *why* the lighting is so suggestive.

4. Briefly summarise your points in a short final paragraph.

Key tip

Many students lose a considerable number of marks because of the brevity of their answers, which may be perfectly accurate, but not detailed enough to gain full marks. When dealing with an image or a group of images, devote a paragraph to each of two of the technical aspects listed above – *composition, framing* and *colour and lighting* – and a third paragraph to a personal response to the subject matter of the photograph. When assessing whether or not the visual and written texts go well together, you should already have three aspects to your discussion of the writer's central point. Use these aspects in the same sequence when discussing the combination of visual text and written text.

Class assignment with assessment sheets – 1

Leaving Certificate paper I 2003 Text 2

A strange companion

This extract is adapted from The Golden Horde, Travels from the Himalaya to Karpathos, *published in 1997, in which sixty-five-year-old Sheila Paine describes her travels through some of the turbulent territories of the former Soviet Union. The extract begins at the point when Sheila returns to Saratov station to try once again to buy a ticket for a train journey.*

The scene at Saratov station was exactly as I had left it, as if none of the crowds had ever managed to get tickets or to go home or to

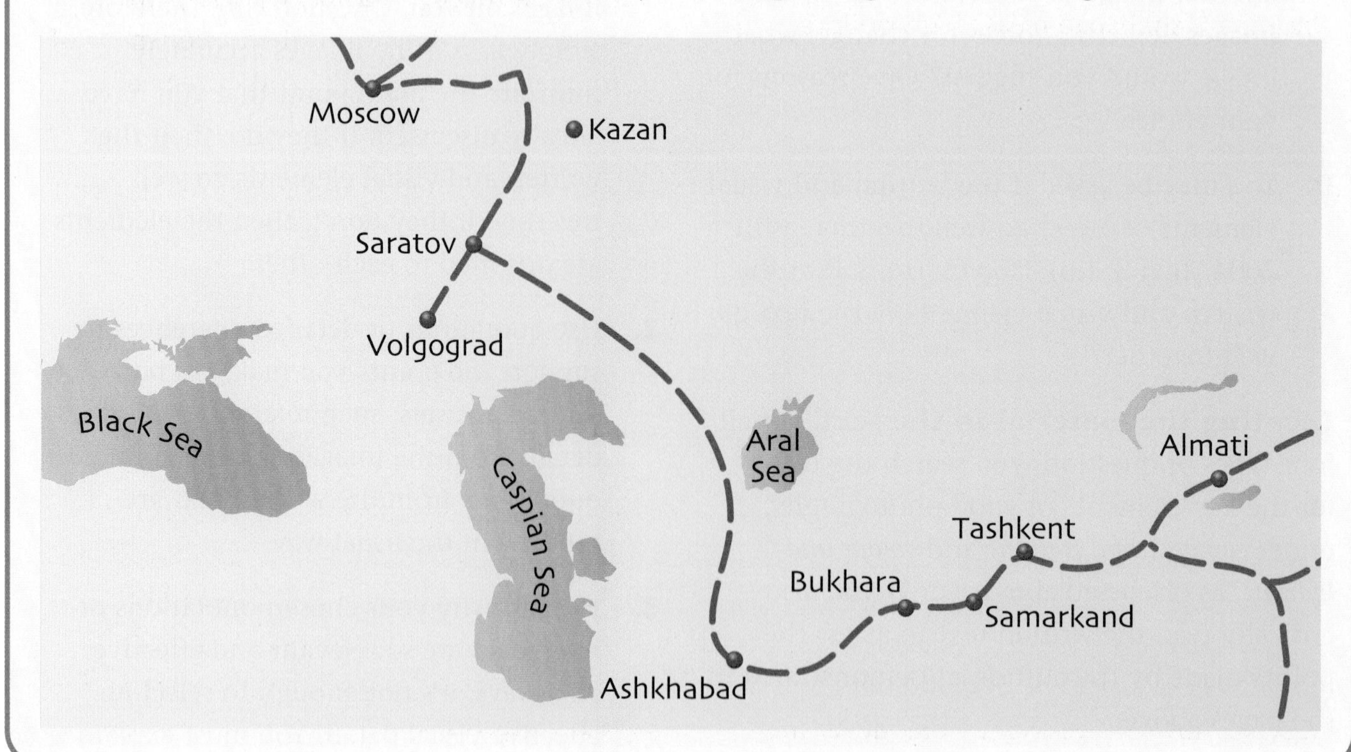

depart on trains. I joined the battle to buy a ticket once more until, totally exasperated, I was driven to shout out loud, 'God, where do they find these people?' Behind me a voice repeated, 'Yes, God, where are they finding these people?' I turned to see a slim, fine-featured girl with a long blonde ponytail, wearing heavy mountaineering boots, jeans and anorak, and carrying a massive orange rucksack. She held out her hand. 'I'm Alexandra,' she said.

I had a travelling companion.

Alexandra had taken a year off studying to travel. She had huge funds of energy but very little money. 'I need no money,' she said. 'I am of those travellers who live with the inhabitants.'

At the end of three further hours of queuing and pleading, the woman behind the grille was still saying *niet* – no. During my attempts to buy a ticket I tried to look rather lost and forlorn and held up my money deferentially, bleating 'Ashkhabad please.' Alexandra's approach was spectacularly different. She pummelled her rucksack, kicked the wall with her hefty boots, flung her passport to the ground, screamed 'I kill these people,' clenched her fists and punched the grille. However, neither of our techniques worked until Alexandra said, 'You have twenty dollars?' 'Yes,' I replied handing her a particularly crisp clean note. Some time later she returned grinning broadly and waving two tickets. 'We just didn't understand the system,' I said.

In all travelling it's usually best to go along with whatever the wind blows you and, as Alexandra had by total chance become part of my journey, I decided to stick with her and just see how things went. I had never met anybody quite so extraordinary and, although she might spell trouble later, she had succeeded in getting us on the train from Moscow to Ashkhabad. As we went to board the train I noticed that right at the end of the platform there was a scene of mayhem. A rusty coach with missing windows and our number on it had been tagged on to the train and was already full. Old women were being pushed through the windows head first, their boots and woolly stockings dangling above the platform. Alexandra went to work with her boots on the dense mass of people at the carriage door and we finally found our places in an open compartment with four bunks. Men lay draped on the luggage racks like leopards lounging on tree branches, some sat on the floor and others were piled on our bed. Now Alexandra used her rucksack to push them along and by the time the train pulled out the passengers had, by some hefty manipulation on her part, been reduced to those with places – the two of us, an old lady nursing toothache in a sparkly scarf, two polite young Turkmen – and an assortment of shifty men with no tickets and dozens of boxes of smuggled cigarettes.

We were to be on the train for three days and three nights.

The train trundled through golden open steppeland. At various stations people sold small silvery salted fish, cucumbers, tomatoes and beer. The old lady with the toothache shared her crushed hard-boiled eggs. Alexandra produced a huge bag of boiled millet, a dry loaf and a big silver knife. The men in the luggage racks leant down and helped themselves to everything. I rubbed vodka on the old lady's tooth and gave her aspirin.

The train chugged on. Men on horseback rode over the steppe herding their horses and sheep. The scene had changed from Russian to Mongol. At night it was bitterly cold as the wind howled through the glassless window. 'You should think to bring your sleeping bag,' said Alexandra.

By the second morning tempers were frayed. The old lady had produced more hard-boiled eggs, Alexandra her millet and bread. Then, suddenly all hell broke loose.

'I kill him. My knife. Where is my knife? I kill who steals it.'

Boots and arms lashed out, eyes stared down. Then, plop, in all the thrashing the knife fell from the grasp of a fat-lipped luggage-rack man on to the bed below.

The old lady got off the train in the night at one of the bleak Soviet towns along the banks of the Amu Darya river. A miserable place, she had said, and so far from her daughter in Saratov. The polite young Turkmen had helped her off while the fat-lipped thief on the rack above had grabbed her bed. He was now fast asleep.

'Some poor girl will be married off to him,' I said.

At the thought of this Alexandra leapt up, threw his baggage off our beds on to the floor and hid his shoes further along the coach.

Question A

(i) What impression do you get of the railway station at Saratov from your reading of the above extract? Support your answer by reference to the text. (15)

(ii) To what extent would you agree with Sheila's description of Alexandra as 'extraordinary'? Support your view by reference to the text. (15)

(iii) Would you like to have shared this train journey with Sheila and Alexandra? Give reasons for your answer. (20)

(i) What impression do you get of the railway station at Saratov from your reading of the above extract? Support your answer by reference to the text. (15)

P/C	You are expected to clearly describe the 'impression' or image or perception of Saratov station that Sheila Paine presents in her description; essentially a picture of a chaotic and corrupt place. Keeping in mind that a description of a location employs imagery, adjectives, atmosphere and colour, you are expected to illustrate and support your judgment with reference to at least two of the following points: (a) the station is overcrowded, permanently occupied by stranded hordes; (b) the station is chaotic, where the simple act of purchasing a ticket becomes a 'battle'; (c) the station is inefficient, since it prevents rather than facilitates travel; and (d) the station is staffed by corrupt officials, since tickets are unavailable without a bribe. Further, you are expected to organise your answer so that the clear expression of your assessment is coherently supported by references, quotations and analysis.	0=NG 1=NG 2=F 3=E 4=D 5=C 6=C 7=B 8=A 9=A1
	☐ Your answer is accurate and well organised.	
	☐ Your answer is accurate but too brief. More detail required.	
	☐ You fail to offer a clear understanding of what constitutes an impression of a place and of how that impression is conveyed by descriptive writing.	
	☐ Your answer is poorly organised.	/9
L/M	You are expected to express yourself precisely, employing words and phrases from your own vocabulary to demonstrate your understanding of the original text. Marks are lost if you merely repeat the wording of the text without interpretation. Consistently poor spelling and/or poor grammar result in the loss of 1 mark.	0=NG 1=F 2=E 3=D 4=C 5=B 6=A
	☐ Your written expression is accurate, controlled and varied.	
	☐ Your written expression is average and needs to be more precise.	
	☐ Your written expression is below average.	
	☐ Your spelling/grammar are poor.	/6
Total		/15

(ii) To what extent would you agree with Sheila's description of Alexandra as 'extraordinary'? Support your view by reference to the text. (15)

P/C	You are expected to offer some understanding of what the word 'extraordinary' implies, such as remarkable, exceptional, astonishing, marvellous, striking and so on. Keeping in mind that any description of character relies on dialogue, appearance and behaviour, you are expected to illustrate and support your assessment with reference to at least two of the following: (a) how Alexandra spoke; in a very flamboyant manner; (b) how Alexandra looked; in mountaineering boots, jeans and a ponytail; and (c) how Alexandra behaved; resourcefully and not particularly delicately. Further, you are expected to organise your answer so that the clear expression of your assessment is coherently supported by references, quotations and analysis.	0=NG 1=NG 2=F 3=E 4=D 5=C 6=C 7=B 8=A 9=A1
	☐ Your answer is accurate and well organised.	
	☐ Your answer is accurate but too brief. More detail required.	
	☐ You fail to offer a clear understanding of what constitutes an 'extraordinary' person and of how that character might be created by descriptive writing.	
	☐ Your answer is poorly organised.	/9
L/M	You are expected to express yourself precisely, employing words and phrases from your own vocabulary to demonstrate your understanding of the original text. Marks are lost if you merely repeat the wording of the text without interpretation. Consistently poor spelling and/or poor grammar result in the loss of 1 mark.	0=NG 1=F 2=E 3=D 4=C 5=B 6=A
	☐ Your written expression is accurate, controlled and varied.	
	☐ Your written expression is average and needs to be more precise.	
	☐ Your written expression is below average.	
	☐ Your spelling/grammar are poor.	/6
Total		/15

(iii) Would you like to have shared this train journey with Sheila and Alexandra? Give reasons for your answer. (20)

<table>
<tr><td>P/C</td><td>You are expected to appreciate that this is an invitation to develop material beyond the text by indicating your personal preferences and also to appreciate that there are two aspects to the query: whether or not you would have enjoyed the journey, and whether or not you would have enjoyed the company. In support of your view of the journey and keeping in mind that only the material in the text is relevant, you might mention the discomforts and difficulties on the one hand and the novelty and excitement on the other. In support of your attitude to the pair as travelling companions and keeping in mind that only the material in the text is relevant, you might consider Sheila too watchful and Alexandra too loud, or both interesting in their different ways. Further, you are expected to organise your answer so that the clear expression of your assessment is coherently supported by references, quotations and analysis.
<table>
<tr><td></td><td>Your answer is accurate and well organised.</td></tr>
<tr><td></td><td>Your answer is accurate but too brief. More detail required.</td></tr>
<tr><td></td><td>You fail to offer a clear understanding that you were asked to consider both the journey and the company.</td></tr>
<tr><td></td><td>You fail to confine yourself to a close reading of the text and instead you introduce irrelevant personal preferences.</td></tr>
<tr><td></td><td>Your answer is poorly organised.</td></tr>
</table></td><td>0=NG
1=NG
2=E
3=E
4=F
5=D
6=D
7=C
8=C
9=B
10=B
11=A
12=A

/12</td></tr>
<tr><td>L/M</td><td>You are expected to express yourself precisely, employing words and phrases from your own vocabulary to demonstrate your understanding of the original text. Marks are lost if you merely repeat the wording of the text without interpretation. Consistently poor spelling and/or poor grammar result in the loss of 1 mark.
<table>
<tr><td></td><td>Your written expression is accurate, controlled and varied.</td></tr>
<tr><td></td><td>Your written expression is average and needs to be more precise.</td></tr>
<tr><td></td><td>Your written expression is below average.</td></tr>
<tr><td></td><td>Your spelling/grammar are poor.</td></tr>
</table></td><td>0=NG
1=F
2=E
3=D
4=D
5=C
6=B
7=B
8=A

/8</td></tr>
<tr><td>Total</td><td></td><td>/20</td></tr>
</table>

Class assignment with assessment sheets – 2

Leaving Certificate paper I 2008 Text 1

This text is adapted from Jon Savage's book, Teenage, the Creation of Youth, 1875–1945, *in which he traces the history of the modern teenager.*

Modern teenagers are the ultimate psychic match for the times: living in the now, pleasure-seeking, product-hungry, embodying the new global society.

But where did teenagers come from? Teenage culture is not a modern phenomenon. Teenagers did not simply appear fully formed when the term entered everyday use in the 1940s. In fact the whole business machinery of modern youth culture – hit songs, heavily marketed products, commercial venues for dancing – was up and running, particularly in America before the 20th century even began.

The phrase 'juvenile delinquent' was coined in America around 1810 in response to teenage gangs who, with their own dress codes, rituals and street-corner poses, were filling newspapers and populating novels. The *Daily Graphic* described an 1890s London gang member as having 'a peculiar muffler twisted around the neck, a cap set rakishly forward, well over the eyes, and trousers very tight at the knee and loose at the foot.' In 1899 Clarence Rook's South London novel *The Hooligan Nights* featured a highly strung 17-year-old male protagonist with a darting gaze 'like the eyes of a bird perpetually prepared for conflict.' It is hard not to imagine Victorian adults keeping away from him on the top deck of a tram.

It was the American social psychologist G. Stanley Hall who coined the term 'adolescence' in 1898 and defined it as 'a period of ten years, from twelve or fourteen to twenty-one or twenty-five'. Characterising it as a period of 'storm and stress', he advised adults to treat adolescents with sympathy, appreciation and respect before subjecting them to the relentless responsibilities of adult industrial life. The term 'generation' up to this had been used to describe 'all men living more or less in the same time' but now it began to refer to 'the new generation', the idea of youth as a separate class, with its own institutions and values.

In Britain this took the form of small earnest groups such as the Woodcraft Folk who offered young people contact with nature and loyalty to the community. Their counterparts in Germany were the Wandervogel, adolescents who rebelled against authoritarian schooling before World War One by hiking, camping and singing folk songs. In France there were the Zazous who listened to jazz and swing, wore extravagant clothes and flirted like there was no tomorrow.

The decade of the Roaring Twenties introduced an international party scene of pleasure-seeking bright young people, similar to today's celebs, Paris Hilton and Lindsay Lohan, who saturate our own media. Bobby-soxers, the female swing fans with their sporty outfits and dance-ready shoes, screamed en masse for Frank Sinatra and laid the groundwork for gyrating rock'n'rollers, Elvis Presley fans and 'Beatlemania'.

In 1944 the magazine *Seventeen* was published, a fashion and pop magazine aimed at high-school girls. It was a landmark crystallization of teenage identity. Now teenagers were neither adolescents nor juvenile delinquents. They were a separate consumer grouping. '*Seventeen* is your magazine,' proclaimed the first issue. 'It is interested only in you and everything that concerns, excites, annoys, pleases or perplexes you.'

1945 was Year Zero, the start of a new era after the atrocities of World War Two and the unleashing of the ultimate terror weapon, the atomic bomb. The best placed group to flourish in a post-war era were the young. 'Their lives are lived principally in hope,' Aristotle had once written of the young, while for Stanley Hall, adolescence was nothing less than 'a new birth'.

The future would be *Teenage*.

Question A

(i) 'Teenage culture is not a modern phenomenon.' Give three pieces of evidence that the writer, Jon Savage, uses to support this statement. (15)

(ii) Comment on three features of the style of writing which contribute to making this an interesting and informative text. Refer to the text in support of your answer. (15)

(iii) Do you think the writer of this text is sympathetic to the modern teenager? Give reasons for your view with reference to the text. (20)

(i) 'Teenage culture is not a modern phenomenon.' Give three pieces of evidence that the writer, Jon Savage, uses to support this statement. (15)

<table>
<tr>
<td>P/C</td>
<td>You are expected to understand that only factual evidence could support such a claim. You are expected to notice the importance of the word 'culture' in the sentence and that therefore the evidence has to support the long-standing existence of teenage culture and not just of teenagers. In support of your answer, you might advance any three of the following as supporting evidence: (a) the existence of a distinctive youth culture, expressed through dress and behaviour, in the nineteenth century; (b) the existence of a distinctive youth culture in nineteenth-century fiction; (c) the recognition in the language of the late nineteenth century in America of the existence of a distinctive youth culture; (d) the existence of alternative youth cultures in early-twentieth-century Europe; (e) the existence of celebrity youth culture in the 1920s; (f) the expression of a distinctive youth culture through dedicated magazines in the 1940s; (g) the recognition of youth culture as different in post-war Europe. Further, you are expected to organise your answer so that the clear expression of your assessment is coherently supported by references, quotations and analysis.
<table>
<tr><td></td><td>Your answer is accurate and well organised.</td></tr>
<tr><td></td><td>Your answer is accurate but too brief. More detail required.</td></tr>
<tr><td></td><td>You fail to understand what constitutes factual evidence.</td></tr>
<tr><td></td><td>You fail to offer a clear understanding of the concept of a 'youth culture'.</td></tr>
<tr><td></td><td>Your answer is poorly organised.</td></tr>
</table>
</td>
<td>0=NG
1=NG
2=F
3=E
4=D
5=C
6=C
7=B
8=A
9=A1

/9</td>
</tr>
<tr>
<td>L/M</td>
<td>You are expected to express yourself precisely, employing words and phrases from your own vocabulary to demonstrate your understanding of the original text. Marks are lost if you merely repeated the wording of the text without interpretation. Consistently poor spelling and/or poor grammar result in the loss of 1 mark.
<table>
<tr><td></td><td>Your written expression is accurate, controlled and varied.</td></tr>
<tr><td></td><td>Your written expression is average and needs to be more precise.</td></tr>
<tr><td></td><td>Your written expression is below average.</td></tr>
<tr><td></td><td>Your spelling/grammar are poor.</td></tr>
</table>
</td>
<td>0=NG
1=F
2=E
3=D
4=C
5=B
6=A

/6</td>
</tr>
<tr>
<td>Total</td>
<td></td>
<td>/15</td>
</tr>
</table>

(ii) Comment on three features of the style of writing which contribute to making this an interesting and informative text. Refer to the text in support of your answer. (15)

<table>
<tr><td>P/C</td><td>The expressions 'style of writing' and 'interesting' are extremely vague, typical of this type of Leaving Certificate question, so you should really pin them down and clarify them as quickly as possible. It is essential, therefore, to state clearly, at the beginning of your answer, what precisely you expect from interesting, informative writing and what you find consistent with that in the author's style. To support your judgment, you might refer to and illustrate three of the following: (a) the relaxed, colloquial language, suited to the topic, such as 'up and running' and 'like there was no tomorrow'; (b) the precision and simplicity of the language, on the other hand, when providing factual material; (c) the effective use of quotations from various sources; (d) the effective use of colourful examples and illustrations; (e) the ability to synopsise and explain broad historical developments.
<table><tr><td></td><td>Your answer is accurate and well organised.</td></tr><tr><td></td><td>Your answer is accurate but too brief. More detail required.</td></tr><tr><td></td><td>You fail to offer a clear understanding of what constitutes interesting and effective informative writing.</td></tr><tr><td></td><td>Your answer is poorly organised.</td></tr></table></td><td>0=NG
1=NG
2=F
3=E
4=D
5=C
6=C
7=B
8=A
9=A1

/9</td></tr>
<tr><td>L/M</td><td>You are expected to express yourself precisely, employing words and phrases from your own vocabulary to demonstrate your understanding of the original text. Marks are lost if you merely repeat the wording of the text without interpretation. You are expected to demonstrate your knowledge and control of a critical vocabulary appropriate to discussing the style of a written text. Consistently poor spelling and/or poor grammar result in the loss of 1 mark.
<table><tr><td></td><td>Your written expression is accurate, controlled and varied.</td></tr><tr><td></td><td>Your written expression is average and needs to be more precise.</td></tr><tr><td></td><td>Your written expression is below average.</td></tr><tr><td></td><td>Your spelling/grammar are poor.</td></tr></table></td><td>0=NG
1=F
2=E
3=D
4=C
5=B
6=A

/6</td></tr>
<tr><td>Total</td><td></td><td>/15</td></tr>
</table>

(iii) Do you think the writer of this text is sympathetic to the modern teenager? Give reasons for your view with reference to the text. (20)

<table>
<tr><td>P/C</td><td>You are expected to offer some understanding of what the word 'sympathetic' means, such as in favour of, approving of, well disposed to, receptive to, and so on. You are expected to locate and use words and phrases that express or imply such sentiments and attitudes. In support of your answer, you might note some of the following: (a) the absence of any direct criticism of teenagers by the author combined with an ironic treatment of the criticism that is reported; (b) the consistent use of such approving terms, particularly adjectives, as 'earnest', 'rebelled against authoritarian schooling' and 'extravagant'; (c) the indulgent, approving tone throughout, as in 'bright young people'; (d) the use of teenage culture as a positive contrast to evils such as 'the atomic bomb'; (e) the presentation of adult life as rather grim, disapproving and constrained; (f) the use of glowing quotations from authorities approving of youth and their application to modern young people.
<table>
<tr><td></td><td>Your answer is accurate and well organised.</td></tr>
<tr><td></td><td>Your answer is accurate but too brief. More detail required.</td></tr>
<tr><td></td><td>You fail to offer a clear understanding of what 'sympathetic' means and of how it might be expressed in the choice of language and content.</td></tr>
<tr><td></td><td>Your answer is poorly organised.</td></tr>
</table></td><td>0=NG
1=NG
2=E
3=E
4=F
5=D
6=D
7=C
8=C
9=B
10=B
11=A
12=A

/12</td></tr>
<tr><td>L/M</td><td>You are expected to express yourself precisely, employing words and phrases from your own vocabulary to demonstrate your understanding of the original text. Marks are lost if you merely repeat the wording of the text without interpretation. Consistently poor spelling and/or poor grammar result in the loss of 1 mark.
<table>
<tr><td></td><td>Your written expression is accurate, controlled and varied.</td></tr>
<tr><td></td><td>Your written expression is average and needs to be more precise.</td></tr>
<tr><td></td><td>Your written expression is below average.</td></tr>
<tr><td></td><td>Your spelling/grammar are poor.</td></tr>
</table></td><td>0=NG
1=F
2=E
3=D
4=D
5=C
6=B
7=B
8=A

/8</td></tr>
<tr><td>Total</td><td></td><td>/20</td></tr>
</table>

Class assignment with assessment sheets – 3

Leaving Certificate paper I 2007 Text 3

Forces for change?

Question A

(i) Select *one* of the visual images in this collection for the front cover of a book entitled *Forces for Change in Our World*. Give reasons why you consider your chosen image to be the most effective and/or suitable. (15)

(ii) Does this set of images represent a balanced view of our changing world? Support your view by reference to the images. (15)

(iii) If asked to select another image to expand this group of images depicting forces for change, what image would you suggest? Give reasons for your choice. (20)

1. The Ballot Box

2. War

6. Protest

3. Natural Disaster

5. Science and Technololgy

4. The Smoking Ban

(i) Select *one* of the visual images in this collection for the front cover of a book entitled *Forces for Change in Our World*. Give reasons why you consider your chosen image to be the most effective and/or suitable. (15)

<table>
<tr>
<td>P/C</td>
<td>You are expected to justify your selection in terms of the content and/or the visual impact of your chosen image, but preferably a combination of both. In terms of content, all images are presented as potential forces for change, so you are expected to explain why your chosen image is more relevant than any of the others, what type of change it promises to bring about and why that type of change is more significant than any other. For example, image 6 presents people attempting to shape their own lives and image 3 presents the changes wrought by nature, two universal and powerful forces. In terms of style, you are expected to explore the impact of your chosen image with reference to at least one, but preferably all three, of the following: composition, framing, lighting. For instance, the composition of image 2 creates a sense of tension, the framing of image 4 forces us to focus on the cigarette and the vibrant colours of image 6 create a certain energy and hope. Further, you are expected to organise your answer so that the clear expression of your assessment is coherently supported by detailed references and analysis.
<table>
<tr><td></td><td>Your answer is accurate and well organised.</td></tr>
<tr><td></td><td>Your answer is accurate but too brief. More detail required.</td></tr>
<tr><td></td><td>You fail to offer a clear understanding of what might constitute a powerful image for the cover of a book on a specific subject.</td></tr>
<tr><td></td><td>Your answer is poorly organised.</td></tr>
</table>
</td>
<td>0=NG
1=NG
2=F
3=E
4=D
5=C
6=C
7=B
8=A
9=A1

/9</td>
</tr>
<tr>
<td>L/M</td>
<td>You are expected to express yourself precisely, employing words and phrases from your own vocabulary to demonstrate your understanding of the original text. Marks are lost if you merely describe the content of an image without interpretation. You are expected to demonstrate your knowledge and control of a critical vocabulary appropriate to discussing a visual text. Consistently poor spelling and/or poor grammar result in the loss of 1 mark.
<table>
<tr><td></td><td>Your written expression is accurate, controlled and varied.</td></tr>
<tr><td></td><td>Your written expression is average and needs to be more precise.</td></tr>
<tr><td></td><td>Your written expression is below average.</td></tr>
<tr><td></td><td>Your spelling/grammar are poor.</td></tr>
</table>
</td>
<td>0=NG
1=F
2=E
3=D
4=C
5=B
6=A

/6</td>
</tr>
<tr>
<td>Total</td>
<td></td>
<td>/15</td>
</tr>
</table>

(ii) Does this set of images represent a balanced view of our changing world? Support your view by reference to the images. (15)

<table>
<tr>
<td>P/C</td>
<td>You are expected to understand that the key phrase in the question is 'a balanced view' and that you are asked to assess the set of images only in relation to this. It follows that some understanding of what 'a balanced view' actually means is required, such as an equal representation of positive and negative features or a treatment of change in a wide enough range of areas to offer a comprehensive treatment, or both. One way or the other, you should discuss more than one image and explore the arrangement of the images and how they relate to each other. Further, you are expected to organise your answer so that the clear expression of your assessment is coherently supported by detailed references and analysis.
<table>
<tr><td></td><td>Your answer is accurate and well organised.</td></tr>
<tr><td></td><td>Your answer is accurate but too brief. More detail required.</td></tr>
<tr><td></td><td>You fail to offer a clear understanding of what constitutes 'a balanced view' and how such a balance might be presented by the selection and arrangement of a number of images.</td></tr>
<tr><td></td><td>Your answer is poorly organised.</td></tr>
</table>
</td>
<td>0=NG
1=NG
2=F
3=E
4=D
5=C
6=C
7=B
8=A
9=A1

/9</td>
</tr>
<tr>
<td>L/M</td>
<td>You are expected to express yourself precisely, employing words and phrases from your own vocabulary to demonstrate your understanding of the original text. Marks are lost if you merely describe the content of an image or a number of images without interpretation. You are expected to demonstrate your knowledge and control of a critical vocabulary appropriate to discussing a visual text. Consistently poor spelling and/or poor grammar result in the loss of 1 mark.
<table>
<tr><td></td><td>Your written expression is accurate, controlled and varied.</td></tr>
<tr><td></td><td>Your written expression is average and needs to be more precise.</td></tr>
<tr><td></td><td>Your written expression is below average.</td></tr>
<tr><td></td><td>Your spelling/grammar are poor.</td></tr>
</table>
</td>
<td>0=NG
1=F
2=E
3=D
4=C
5=B
6=A

/6</td>
</tr>
<tr>
<td>Total</td>
<td></td>
<td>/15</td>
</tr>
</table>

(iii) If asked to select another image to expand this group of images depicting forces for change, what image would you suggest? Give reasons for your choice. (20)

<table>
<tr>
<td>P/C</td>
<td>This is a somewhat dangerous question, since it seems to offer you a great deal of freedom, but actually insists that you begin with a precise understanding of the original text. The key phrase in the question is 'to expand this group of images'. This means that you are expected to understand what impression the collection is trying to project (your answer to (ii) above) and you are expected to precisely describe another image that fits in well with this impression (using the techniques for exploring images already employed in your answer to (i) above). For instance, if you decide that the set of images does not offer a balanced view, then you should suggest an image that would restore the balance; but if you insist that the set was balanced, then you should suggest an image that would maintain that balance. In describing your additional individual image, you are expected to present it with reference to its content and at least one, but preferably all three, of the following technical aspects: composition, framing, lighting. Further, you are expected to organise your answer so that the clear expression of your assessment is coherently supported by detailed references and analysis.
<table>
<tr><td></td><td>Your answer is accurate and well organised.</td></tr>
<tr><td></td><td>Your answer is accurate but too brief. More detail required.</td></tr>
<tr><td></td><td>You fail to offer a clear understanding of what the 'group' of images is trying to achieve and of how an additional image would 'expand' that group by adding to but not changing its impact.</td></tr>
<tr><td></td><td>Your answer is poorly organised.</td></tr>
</table>
</td>
<td>0=NG
1=NG
2=E
3=E
4=F
5=D
6=D
7=C
8=C
9=B
10=B
11=A
12=A

/12</td>
</tr>
<tr>
<td>L/M</td>
<td>You are expected to express yourself precisely, employing words and phrases from your own vocabulary to demonstrate your understanding of the original text. Marks are lost if you merely repeat the wording of the text without interpretation. You are expected to demonstrate your knowledge and control of a critical vocabulary appropriate to discussing a visual text. Consistently poor spelling and/or poor grammar result in the loss of 1 mark.
<table>
<tr><td></td><td>Your written expression is accurate, controlled and varied.</td></tr>
<tr><td></td><td>Your written expression is average and needs to be more precise.</td></tr>
<tr><td></td><td>Your written expression is below average.</td></tr>
<tr><td></td><td>Your spelling/grammar are poor.</td></tr>
</table>
</td>
<td>0=NG
1=F
2=E
3=D
4=D
5=C
6=B
7=B
8=A

/8</td>
</tr>
<tr>
<td>Total</td>
<td></td>
<td>/20</td>
</tr>
</table>

Chapter Five: Answering Question B

Introduction

For 50 marks, Question B asks you to pretend that you are someone other than who you really are, stuck in a situation in which you're unlikely to ever really find yourself, and then asks you to use language appropriate to that character and that situation. It's an exercise in style and the key issue is credibility. Does your finished product look, sound and feel like what it is supposed to look, sound and feel like? If it does, you'll score highly; if it doesn't, you won't.

Each Question B specifies three things: (i) the content or subject-matter you must use; (ii) the format you must present it in; and (iii) the style of writing you must employ. In 2008, Text 1, Question B – 'Write a letter to Jon Savage responding to this extract from his book and giving your own views on today's teenage culture' – the topic is teenage culture, the format is a letter and the style is argumentative. In 2008, Text 2, Question B – 'two diary entries: one written by Alexander, recalling his encounter with Eva in Tompkins Square Park and the second by Zach, giving his thoughts on hearing that Eva has purchased the violin' – the subject-matter is the two specified incidents, the format is diary entries and the style is narrative. In 2008, Text 3, Question B – 'Students in your school have been invited to contribute articles to the school website on issues relevant to young people. This week's issue is "We are what we wear". Write an article for the website expressing your views on the topic' – the topic is 'We are what we wear', the format is an article and the style is argumentative. In 2005, Text 3, Question B – 'Imagine that as a reporter for a local newspaper you plan to interview a celebrity of your choice. Write a proposal/memo for the editor of your newspaper in which you explain why you want to interview this celebrity and giving an outline of the areas you hope to explore in the course of the interview' – the subject-matter is the outline and content of the interview, the format is a memo and the style is informative.

It's impossible to predict the topic, but the range of formats is limited and, of course, there are only three styles – informative, argumentative and narrative.

Informative Question B

Description. When the primary purpose of the task you are given is to supply useful or helpful information to others, then the task is an exercise in the language of information. Whether you adopt a formal or informal approach to providing the information depends on the circumstances. *Formal* relies on fact, evidence, statistics and a largely neutral writing style; *informal* will employ anecdote, personal experience and a more relaxed style. For instance, 2004, Text 2, Question B – 'Imagine that Mr Pappleworth is asked, on the basis of Paul's first day at work, to write a report giving his impressions of Paul Morel as an employee. Write the text of his report' – requires a formal style, whereas 2004, Text 1, Question B – 'You have been asked to give a short talk to a group of students who are about to start first year in your school. Write out the text of the talk you would give' – would benefit from a more relaxed approach.

The formats. A talk offering advice (2001), a letter listing contents (2003), a talk offering information and advice (2004), a report on a new employee (2004), a memo outlining information (2005), a letter providing information (2006), an informative election leaflet (2007).

The key elements. A comprehensive list of the key elements of an effective informative text was provided in Part One, Chapter One, pages 9 and 12–13. They don't change. The same list is used for answering both Question A and Question B. The only difference is that your own role has been reversed. In answering Question A you are a critic; in answering Question B you are a writer. The features that you looked for in another's work you now must provide in your own. Before continuing with the samples in this chapter, re-read the sections on the key elements of an effective informative text, paying particular attention to the structure of such a text, which should consist of:

- **an introduction,** providing a context for and/or background to the material that is to follow;
- **a development,** organising the material into categories and/or under themed headings;
- **a conclusion,** offering an assessment and/or recommendation on the basis of the material supplied.

When writing, the initial emphasis should be on structure. You must make a plan before beginning. When you undertake an unfamiliar journey, you consult a map. When you create something original, you provide your own map. Otherwise, you have no idea where you're going. You'll get lost. And if you are lost, all your knowledge and all your talents – the content and style of your text – will be devalued. In each of the following samples, therefore, my plan precedes my answer.

Sample 1 2007 Text 1 Question B

Imagine you are running for the position of Student Council President in your school. Compose an informative election leaflet encouraging students to vote for you. It should outline your own leadership qualities and the changes you would like to introduce into your school.

Plan

Structure: An *introduction,* providing a context or background; in this case a general profile of the candidate. A *development,* organising the material into categories or under headings; in this case, as instructed, *leadership qualities* and *changes.* A *conclusion,* offering an assessment or recommendation; in this case a simple *Vote for Me* request.

Content: As specified by the question, *leadership qualities* and *changes in the school.*

Style: Initially, factual, with an emphasis on clarity. But there's also the need to convince, to sell oneself as a candidate, so I'll incorporate, where appropriate and without neglecting the need to be informative, some of the rhetorical techniques used in argumentative and persuasive texts.

Sample answer

John Lancaster

About the Candidate

I am a fifth-year student at Ford Community School.

I am an elected member of the current Student Council. Since first standing for election five years ago I have been a continuous member of the Council and I have represented my form year in successive elections. I have never failed to top the poll for my year and in the last campaign I polled more than twice the number of votes cast for my nearest rival.

I am also a member of the School Library Committee, the Sports Council and the Literary & Historical Society.

Although not a member of any political party, I have been active in many local campaigns associated with the school, most notably the recent Fund Raising Day for the Children's Hospital.

A Leader on the Field

- In our school's most successful ever sporting campaign, I captained the junior rugby team to victory in the Leinster Junior Cup two seasons ago. As newly-appointed captain of our senior squad, I hope to contribute to another outstanding achievement in the Senior Cup this year.
- I believe that every student should give back to the school as much as they take from it by dedicating their particular talents to the benefit of others. For the past three years I have been wholly involved in the coaching and organisation of First Form teams and nothing has given me greater pleasure in that area than coaching the First Form C Soccer team to victory in their Inter-Schools Tournament last May.

A Leader in the Committee Room

- Your voices *must* be heard by the school authorities and *must* be attended to. A leader is powerless unless he is also a representative. For the past year, I have been your voice on the school's Governing Body. To ensure that I accurately reflect your views, I have repeatedly requested written submissions from concerned students, a strategy that has been increasingly successful in making a decisive impact.

- A leader must also be a focal point. Too often in Fifth and Sixth Form assemblies and in class meetings the discussions disintegrate into slanging matches and confused shouting matches. Over the past year I have consistently proposed that, although all voices are equal, only one can be heard at a time. A leader is also, on occasions, only a chairman. I am happy to have filled that role.

Changes on the Field

- Everyone accepts that the current cricket pavilion is too old, too dilapidated, totally inadequate and bordering on a disgrace. No one does anything but moan about it, however. I will change that. A committee must be formed to undertake the construction of a new pavilion, a fund-raising co-ordinator must be appointed, plans must be submitted and planning approval sought . . . all before the beginning of the next academic year.

- Currently, the major sports are extremely well catered for in the school, and everything else is officially neglected. In fairness to all, this must change. All students must have the opportunity to participate in a wider range of sports and each student should be entitled to structured coaching to prepare for competition. This will be a priority for me over the next year.

Changes in the Committee Room

- At the moment, meetings of the school's Governing Body accept 'contributions, observations and recommendations' from the two students' representatives. This reduces us to the role of observers, without any powers. I will insist that in future the agenda for these meetings should contain a sub-section entitled STUDENT ISSUES, which will then be formally debated by all and voted on.

- Since we ourselves must behave as we expect others to, I will also insist that all future student class meetings and Form assemblies should be conducted according to a prepared agenda and chaired by an elected student.

MANIFESTO

I cannot improve everything that displeases us about our wonderful school in a single year as President, but I will change those things that I promise to change.

VOTE NO 1

JOHN LANCASTER

FOR STUDENT COUNCIL PRESIDENT

and support TINA O'LEARY for

INFORMATION OFFICER

Analysis

Structure: I have followed the intended structure, introducing myself, organising the material on leadership qualities and changes under themed headings and sub-dividing with bullet points, and concluding with a manifesto, which is an assessment of everything that has gone before, and a recommendation.

Content: Note that the question demanded equal treatment of two aspects – leadership qualities and changes – and that I devoted equal amounts of space to these.

Style: The language is neutral in the opening section. Facts are recorded. Once I need to become persuasive, however, the style becomes more colourful. Note in particular how the function of the *adjectives* changes. In the introduction, the adjectives are neutral and factually descriptive – 'a *continuous* member' and '*successive* elections' – but in the development they, and the adjectival clauses – '*most successful ever* sporting campaign' and '*outstanding* achievement' – become livelier, more expressive and suggestive. Note also the role of *adverbs* in persuasive writing. The word 'wholly' is not strictly necessary in the phrase 'For the past three years I have been wholly involved in the coaching', but you will agree that it suggests far greater commitment and dedication than the basic 'I have been involved'. If you want to further understand the power of adverbs and adjectives, take 'increasingly' and 'decisive' out of the following sentence: 'a strategy that has been increasingly successful in making a decisive impact', and consider the vastly reduced effect of 'a strategy that has been successful in making an impact'.

'Your voices *must* be heard by the school authorities and *must* be attended to' uses *emphasis* and *repetition* to convince. It is also an example of the *assertive, self-confident tone* throughout. You cannot hope to persuade if you display uncertainty. Since all the expressions mean more or less the same thing, the phrase 'the current cricket pavilion is too old, too dilapidated, totally inadequate and bordering on a disgrace', uses *repetition through variation* effectively. Again, you can appreciate just how powerful it is by simply stopping at 'the current cricket pavilion is too old', which makes the same point, but nowhere near as strongly.

Finally, unrelieved negativity is very unappealing in a text and criticism should always be balanced by praise or optimism. In the phrase 'I cannot improve everything that displeases us about our wonderful school', the adjective 'wonderful' allows the writer to avoid both the unattractive self-satisfaction and the carping inherent in 'I cannot improve everything that displeases us about our school'.

Sample 2 2006 Text 2 Question B

Write a letter to a famous writer or celebrity or sports personality of your choice offering your services as a ghost writer for a future book. In your letter you should outline the reasons why you believe you would make a successful ghost writer for your chosen author.

Plan

Structure: An *introduction*, providing a context or background; in this case two paragraphs explaining what I want and who I am. A *development*, organising the material into categories or under headings; in this case two paragraphs outlining the process involved in creating a ghost-written autobiography and the client's part in it. A *conclusion*, offering an assessment or recommendation; in this case a simple re-assurance that the project will be enjoyable and successful.

Content: As specified by the question, *services as a ghost writer* and *reasons* for the project's success. However, to put a little colour into the piece I'm going to look for someone in the news, someone involved in a little controversy, someone difficult or notorious.

Style: You will have noticed by now that there seems to be an element of persuasion in most informative tasks that are set in the Leaving Certificate examination. There has to be an emphasis on clarity here, but also a need to convince, to sell oneself as a ghost writer, so I'll incorporate, where appropriate and without neglecting the need to be informative, some of the rhetorical techniques used in argumentative and persuasive texts. Because this letter is addressed to an individual and not to a group, I intend opening on a personal, flattering note.

Sample answer

'Hades'
Faithleg
Co. Waterford

Cristiano Ronaldo dos Santos Aveiro
c/o Manchester United FC
Manchester

6 June 2009

Señor Aveiro,

Following your double triumph in being selected as both the Senior and the Young Footballer of the Year in England, and in the wake of José Mourinho's ungracious comments about your 'difficult childhood, no education',

could I suggest that now is the perfect time to consider publishing your own account of your life thus far; your autobiography. Not only have your dazzling football skills brought the attention of the world to you, but the world awaits your response to Señor Mourinho's unkind remarks. I know that your manager, Sir Alex Ferguson, has stoutly defended you in public, but what could be more interesting than your own story of your childhood and teenage years?

I am a ghost writer. I write books on behalf of my clients, whose names appear on the covers and whose life stories appear within these covers. Contractual restrictions forbid me to reveal the names of previous clients, but could I assure you that my area of experience is the English Premiership and that you are already professionally acquainted with all my previous clients. Many of these will confirm this to you, privately and in the strictest confidence, if you require testimonials.

Allow me to explain the process involved in creating your autobiography and to clarify your own part in it, assuring you that only the material you *want* to share with the public will appear in the finished work.

For a large project such as this, I always conduct a series of interviews with the subject. These are recorded and later transcribed. Obviously, the more relaxed the interviewing is and the less it resembles an interrogation or an obligation, then the more varied and interesting and colourful the material that will emerge. Nobody wants to confide in an unsympathetic listener. This has always been my particular strength in my profession. As others will confirm, again privately and in the strictest confidence, the interviews are really informal chats, during which we get to know each other. Usually, a few hours a week for several weeks is sufficient. If I need further material, we can arrange to meet again at your convenience.

After that, up to the approval of the first draft of the completed manuscript, the work is entirely mine, although you always retain the final say at each stage and I may occasionally need to consult you to confirm a detail or two. My previous work, under the names of others, of course, has been praised as 'full of insights', 'a gripping read', and 'providing the sort of intimacy every fan craves to experience'.

But, as I've said, it is neither my skills as a researcher nor my skills as a writer that will make this project even better than my previous work, but rather the colour and courage of your own life story.

I look forward to hearing from you, Sir.

Yours sincerely

Jason Coodabin

Analysis

Structure: Within the basic format of a personal letter – my address, recipient's address, date, salutation, signature – I followed my intended structure, offering contextual information, organising the material into categories that make it easier for the audience to understand, and ending with a persuasive recommendation.

Content: Note that the question demanded equal treatment of two aspects – *offering your services as a ghost writer for a future book* and outlining *the reasons why you believe you would make a successful ghost writer for your chosen author* – and that I devoted equal amounts of space to these.

Style: Initially, the language is flattering, simply because I want something from this person. Note how the expressive *nouns* – 'double *triumph*' – the colourful *adjectives* – '*dazzling* football skills' – and the forceful *adverbs* – '*stoutly* defended you' – all feed into this. In the second paragraph, because I need to explain rather than persuade, clarity becomes more important. The *adjectives* – '*contractual* restrictions' – the adverbs – '*professionally* acquainted', '*privately* . . . confirm' – and the *nouns* – '*books*', '*names*', '*covers*' – become neutral, merely factual. 'This has always been my particular strength in my profession' is an example of the *assertive, self-confident tone* that is maintained throughout and that is essential in persuasive writing.

Homework and tasks

Under the headings used for analysis above – structure, content and style – assess the following text as an informative Question B.

Web safety

Of all the websites, one that has attracted attention recently is the social network myspace.com. Most of this attention has come from the media and illustrates every reason why the website should be shut down. The threat of predators is indeed a harsh reality, but shutting down the site is not the answer. If myspace were shut down, another better site would quickly take its place. Therefore, the approach is to teach teens how to use the site, and others like it, safely. Unless teens are educated about the adults who may be predators and how to avoid them, the problem will persist.

The key to staying safe on the internet is to make sure that your profile is secure. The simplest way to do this is by changing the privacy setting on your profile to 'private'. This protects your information so that only the people on your friend-list can view it. Although this is effective, it is not foolproof. Predators can find ways to view your profile if they really want to, whether through hacking in or manipulating their way onto your friend-list. Because of this, you should never post too much personal information. Some people actually post their home and school addresses, date of birth, and other personal info, often letting predators know exactly where they will be and when. The most info that is safe is your first name and state. Anything more is basically inviting a predator into your life.

Another big issue is photos. I suggest completely skipping photos, but if you are going to include some, make them innocent and fun, not provocative. Also, never post a photo of a friend online without asking permission.

Most importantly, never, under any circumstances, agree to a real-life meeting with anyone you meet online. No matter how well you think you know this person, there are no guarantees that they have told the truth. A good example is John Contos, who in his myspace.com profile said he was 16. Two 16-year-old girls and a 14-year-old believed him and agreed to meet him. He was actually 27! There is also evidence that he exploited a number of girls before them.

These situations do happen and you need to be aware. You should feel free to chat with people you meet on the site, but just remember that not everyone is who they say they are. Hopefully, the next time you edit your profile, you'll be more informed about the dangers of internet predators and take the steps to defend yourself.

Argumentative Question B

Description. When the primary purpose of the task you are given is to express your opinion on a particular topic, or to give your point of view on some issue, then the task is an exercise in writing an opinion piece, or, as it is known in Leaving Certificate terms, an argumentative text. For instance, 2004, Text 3, Question B – 'Write a letter to one of the people from the collection of visual images in the text, indicating what appeals and/or does not appeal to you about the work which that person does' – clearly demands the communication of your opinion. Apart from requiring minor adjustments in presentation, it doesn't really matter in what format you are asked to work it: letter, radio talk, magazine article, public address. As always, the choice between formal and informal approaches is a matter of individual taste. However, a formal approach, if not skilfully managed, can too easily lead to pomposity, and a relaxed, personal, though passionate, style is usually the preferred option.

The formats. An article expressing admiration or condemnation (2001), a letter communicating your judgment of a photograph (2002), a radio talk supporting a human right (2002), a letter expressing your opinions on a particular career (2004), a letter communicating your judgment of a photograph (2005), a report offering your views on exploitation in advertising (2006), a radio talk on social change (2007), a letter offering your views on the smoking ban (2007), a letter offering your views on teenage culture (2008), an article on clothes as an expression of personality (2008).

The key elements. A comprehensive list of the key elements of an effective argumentative text was provided in Part One, Chapter Two, pages 24 and 27–28. They don't change. The same list is used for answering both Question A and Question B. The only difference is that your own role has been reversed. In answering Question A you are a critic; in answering Question B you are a writer. The features that you looked for in another's work you now must provide in your own. Before continuing with the samples in this chapter, re-read the sections on the key elements of an effective argumentative text, paying particular attention to the structure of such a text, which should consist of:

- **an introduction,** describing an anecdote, social rather than personal, to introduce the point you wish to make;
- **a development,** applying that point to two or three areas of social life;
- **a conclusion,** returning to recycle or complete the opening anecdote and to re-state your point.

When writing, the initial emphasis should be on structure. You must make a plan before beginning. When you undertake an unfamiliar journey, you consult a map. When you create something original, you provide your own map. Otherwise, you have no idea where you're going. You'll get lost. And if you are lost, all your knowledge and all your talents – the content and style of your text – will be devalued. In each of the following samples, therefore, my plan precedes my answer.

Sample 1 2007 Text 2 Question B

Imagine your local radio station is producing a series of programmes entitled 'Changing Times', in which teenagers are asked to give their views on the changes they welcome in the world around them. You have been invited to contribute. Write out the text of the presentation you would make.

Plan

Structure: An *introduction*, describing an anecdote, social rather than personal, to introduce the point I wish to make, in this case a story about old Ireland, which was mono-cultural, leading to the point that the new Ireland, which is multi-cultural, is better.
A *development*, applying that point to two or three areas of social life, in this case a demonstration that financially and culturally we have benefited from the change.
A *conclusion*, returning to recycle or complete the opening anecdote and to re-state my point, in this case a reference back to the old Ireland described in the opening and a re-affirmation of the view that the new Ireland is an improvement.

Content: As specified by the question, *the changes* you *welcome in the world around* you. As is almost always the case, there are two aspects, then. I must describe the changes and I must argue for why I welcome them.

Style: The combination of styles is indicated in the previous sentence: the best of descriptive techniques in presenting the anecdotes and illustrations, the best of rhetorical techniques in advancing the opinions.

Sample answer

My father often tells the story – a little *too* often, to be perfectly honest – of the time his closest friend in university caused a major traffic pile-up merely by strolling down Grafton Street in Dublin. The reference to traffic on Grafton Street, which has long been pedestrianised, will date the story, of course, to a period when Ireland was a small, insular and remote island. My father's friend didn't have two heads or a rare tropical plant growing out of his left shoulder; he distracted car drivers and caused chaos simply because he was a black man, a political refugee from the apartheid regime in South Africa, and therefore a rarer sighting in Ireland than a wild cheetah.

Today, of course, an individual black man on Grafton Street would not be noticed among all

the others, from Nigeria, from Chad, from Jamaica, from London; nor would a foreigner of any nationality attract the slightest interest. The streets of our capital city, and most other parts of our country, are teeming with Poles and Polynesians, French and Finns, Spaniards and Swedes. Of all the changes that have occurred in our society in recent times, this huge influx of peoples from other cultures is the most colourful, the most beneficial and the most welcome.

It is not only that most foreigners are migrant workers, or that they bring with them the skills and the energies that have helped to re-vitalise our economy. Looking around now, it is almost impossible to believe that there was once a time when our building sites weren't crowded with Polish craftsmen and craftswomen, when our hospitals weren't staffed by experts from India and the Philippines. But the benefits to the labour market are only the most direct and the most visible.

Much more subtle, more complex, and far more incalculable, are the rich effects on our own culture in its interaction with the cultures of others. New music is all around us. Walk down Grafton Street today and you might hear a mariachi band, a Lithuanian folk song and an African ensemble at different junctions. New restaurants appear in our cities and new dishes on their tables. New ideas are in the air. In the bars off Grafton Street, you are as likely to hear animated discussions about Togo's chances of reaching the next soccer World Cup as you are to catch a couple of jackeens complaining about an Italian being appointed as the manager of Ireland.

The Ireland of my father's time, as he often described it himself, was uniformly grey. Contemporary Ireland is a blaze of colour. Even the most miserable among us would have to be cheered by such an improvement.

Analysis

Structure: The opening anecdote – described in outline rather than in detail, since it does not exist for its own sake, but only to serve the argument – leads to the expression of my central point in the last sentence of the second paragraph, 'this huge influx of peoples from other cultures is the most colourful, the most beneficial and the most welcome'. That point is then applied to two areas of social life, the economic and the cultural. Finally, the opening anecdote is recycled – old Ireland was a 'grey' place – and the central point is repeated, though the expression of it is varied, 'cheered' being a synonym of 'welcome' and 'improvement' being a synonym of 'changes'.

Content: There is one point, and only one point, that 'this huge influx of peoples from other cultures is the most colourful, the most beneficial and the most welcome' of the changes that have occurred. Everything else supports and illustrates this. There are multiple examples – a single occurrence is not enough to demonstrate a trend – but please note that most are only referred to and not developed in detail. In the short Question B, there is no role for elaborate description.

Style: The opening strikes a *personal note* – 'My father often tells the story' – which is always very attractive. Note, however, that the story itself is not domestic, which would be of limited relevance to 'changes in the world', but social, illuminating the shared, public world. Nevertheless, the style is descriptive rather than rhetorical, using colourful *imagery* such as 'a rare tropical plant growing out of his left shoulder', and 'rarer . . . than a wild cheetah', clusters of *adjectives* – 'small, insular and remote' – and deliberate *exaggeration* for effect – 'a major traffic pile-up'. But in an argument, you tell a story only to make a point. The second paragraph is therefore interpretative rather than descriptive, as it reflects on the anecdote and reveals the reason for using it. The two paragraphs are linked by the standard device of using the opening sentence in the new paragraph to *refer back before moving forward*. This basic technique is used throughout. For instance, in the opening sentence of the fourth paragraph, 'Much more subtle, more complex, and far more incalculable' all refer back, by way of comparisons again, to the material that preceded it, while 'are the rich effects on our own culture' introduces the topic for the current paragraph. *Examples and illustrations* are plentiful throughout. Note in particular the sections 'Poles and Polynesians, French and Finns, Spaniards and Swedes' and 'mariachi band, a Lithuanian folk song and an African ensemble'. The use of extensive illustrations always adds richness and variety to an argument. 'New restaurants appear in our cities and new dishes on their tables. New ideas are in the air' uses *repetition* for the sake of *emphasis* and is also a further example of the effective use of multiple illustrations. And since I have never heard anyone discussing Togo's chances of reaching the FIFA World Cup, and never expect to hear anyone doing so, that's a perfect example of the type of *ironic exaggeration* that is expected in argument.

Sample 2 2005 Text 2 Question B

Write a letter to a photographic magazine in which you propose one of the four images for the award 'Best War Photograph of the Year'.

Plan

Structure: The use of an anecdote to introduce a central point is not appropriate here, since the story is already presented to me, in the form of the photograph itself. Nevertheless, the basic shape of my response remains the same: an introduction that clearly states my point, in this case the reasons for my choice; a development that expands on and illustrates those reasons; a conclusion that re-states my point.

Content: A comprehensive discussion of any photograph should include treatment of both its subject-matter and its technical merits, such as composition, framing and use of colour and lighting, as illustrated in Part Two, Chapter Four, 'Reading an image or a set of images'.

Style: This is not a debate, but the expression of a critical judgment. The more colourful rhetorical devices – exaggeration, sarcasm, rhetorical questions – will be less useful than passion, conviction and enthusiasm.

Sample answer

My nomination for 'Best War Photograph of the Year' is Image No. 2, 'El Salvador 1986, An Afternoon Dance'. Unlike many war photographs, it doesn't glamorise, romanticise or over-dramatise violence; and what it does instead is to suggest many of the precious things that are threatened by war – pleasure, relaxation, relationships, tenderness, youth.

There is no glamour in this photograph. In fact, your eyes can't help being drawn away from the three humans to those prominent patches of peeled paint and plaster on the walls. Are those pockmarks bullet holes or just natural decay? So much is suggested by the photographer's selection of the background. One thing is certain, however. This is a modest room. These are modest, ordinary people. The woman is a little too heavy, the man a little too short, the boy a little too gangly. Their clothes are basic.

But what I like best about the photograph is that everything that's worth fighting for is also contained within its frame. None of the three humans is looking directly at the camera, and yet all of them are also slightly awkward. The man has a self-conscious smile, the woman is rather stiff, and the boy is looking anxiously outside the frame. Whether this tension is caused by the man's gun, the photographer's unseen presence, the possibility of an ambush or the fact that the boy may be cramping the dancers' style is something we cannot tell from the image. But it doesn't matter. The whole image captures a moment of awkward, mysterious tenderness that we know won't last. Except, of course, that it does survive – in the photograph itself.

A great photograph should capture a truth that the whole world can identify with. This one does just that. Which is why I nominate it as my War Photograph of the Year.

Analysis

Structure: A simple but very precise opening paragraph, which identifies my choice and offers my reasons. Each of these reasons then becomes the subject of a separate paragraph. I explain what I mean by claiming that there is no glamour in the image and I use details from the photograph to support and illustrate this. Then I explain what I mean by suggesting that the image captures the beauty and fragility of life, again using details in support. The final paragraph re-states my original point, but varies the expression of it.

Content: Both the subject-matter (the human figures and the setting) and the technique (particularly composition and framing) are given equal value. The Chief Examiner's Report in 2005 recorded that: 'Candidates often wrote convincingly on their chosen image. Many used persuasive language indicating their consciousness of audience/reader in the task. Less successful candidates tended to drift from the photograph into a generalised discussion of war. Some excellent answers dealt with the technical merits of their chosen image.'

Style: The use of *expressive adjectives* is essential when conveying personal enthusiasm during a critical analysis. The best examples here are '*precious* things' and '*awkward, mysterious* tenderness'. The language is highly *personal* throughout: '*My* nomination', 'what *I* like best', 'tenderness that *we* know won't last', '*I* nominate'. Judgments are always delivered with *conviction*, since uncertainty betrays lack of fervour as well as loss of confidence: 'there is no glamour', 'one thing is certain', 'it doesn't matter'. *Repetition* for *emphasis and clarification* – 'This is a modest room. These are modest, ordinary people' – is used lightly throughout. The *rhetorical question* – 'Are those pockmarks bullet holes or just natural decay?' – is employed to express wonder rather than aggression.

Homework and tasks

Under the headings used for analysis above – structure, content and style – assess the following text as an argumentative Question B.

Celebrity obsession

Our society is obsessed with celebrities. If you step back and look at the whole picture, it's really pretty ridiculous.

On the first day of school, instead of catching up with her clique, one girl was decorating her locker. A close friend broke free of the others to check it out and stopped in her tracks, stunned.

'Omigawd! I love him!' she yelled.

The locker was plastered with pictures of that hot kid from *She's the Man* and *Step Up*. What's his name? Neither girl was sure, but they'd know his body anywhere. That's what counts . . . right?

Two weeks into school, Locker Decorating Girl is assigned a current events project on the Middle East.

'I don't have time,' she complains. 'It's not like anyone cares.'

This is coming from a girl who has time to find pictures of what's-his-face to cover her locker. But she knows what's important: the release date for *Pirates of the Caribbean 3*; Zac Efron has gone brunette; and Brad Pitt and Angelina Jolie still aren't married. That's what counts . . . right?

It's been suggested that teens who obsess over celebrities often have poor relationships with family and peers. But why do everyday teenagers follow every move of favourite celebrities? Perhaps because an average person's life can't satisfy their love for drama, they turn to the country's icons, whose lives are faster and more interesting. Celebrities are portrayed as beautiful and indulge in anything they want. Their faces appear everywhere and we idolise them, we want to be like them.

By following their doings, society lives through them. Preoccupied with a favourite celebrity's mishaps, personal troubles are escaped. It is logical that teens with emotional and social problems worship celebrities. They might think that a celebrity would understand their problems better than friends or family. They create illusions and fantasies that convince them they have personal connections with their idols.

So what began as watching a few movies starring some no-name actor sprouts into a full-blown emotional problem that could impact a life forever. But that would never happen to you . . . right?

Narrative Question B

Description. When the primary purpose of the task is to describe an event or a sequence of events, then you are asked to demonstrate your narrative skills. For example, 2003, Text 3, Question B, 'Write three or four diary entries that record the details of a disastrous holiday (real or imaginary) that you experienced.' As noted in Part One, Chapter Three, 'The key elements of an effective descriptive or narrative text', however, 'Without credible, engaging characters, the description of events becomes merely anecdotal, that is, only a sketch, a yarn, lacking any depth or importance.' In recent years, the examination questions have recognised the central importance of character, so much so that the incidents are often given, leaving only the creation of a credible voice. In 2008, Text 2, Question B, for instance, the task was to capture and sustain two voices, using the events already described in the text itself: 'Write two diary entries: one written by Alexander, recalling his encounter with Eva in

Tompkins Square Park and the second by Zach, giving his thoughts on hearing that Eva has purchased the violin.'

The formats. A radio talk narrating a favourite comic moment (2001), a radio talk describing an interesting holiday (2003), three or four diary entries recording a disastrous holiday (2003), three diary entries of a late-nineteenth-century servant (2005), a diary entry of a boy in emotional turmoil (2006), two diary entries by different characters (2008).

The key elements. A comprehensive list of the key elements of an effective narrative text was provided in Part One, Chapter Three, pages 43 and 46–47. They don't change. The same list is used for answering both Question A and Question B. The only difference is that your own role has been reversed. In answering Question A, you are a critic; in answering Question B you are a writer. The features that you looked for in another's work you now must provide in your own. Before continuing with the samples in this chapter, re-read the sections on the key elements of an effective narrative text, paying particular attention to the creation of character and to the shaping of events, which should consist of:

- **an introduction**, describing a situation full of potential conflict or danger;
- **a development**, bringing this situation to the point of crisis;
- **a conclusion**, resolving this crisis, but leaving the future merely suggested rather than defined.

When writing any other text, the initial emphasis should be on structure, but by definition, creative work is subversive, original and unconfined. The structure outlined above is the basic shape of all stories, really, but it is of very limited use if you are unable to bring characters alive on the page. When writing a narrative, therefore, you should concentrate primarily on creating a credible voice and allow everything else – the shaping of the incidents and the theme – to emerge organically from this. Nevertheless, you should make a plan before beginning. I recommend beginning with one or two words that capture the character's voice: 'in turmoil', for instance, or 'in love' or 'frustrated'. This will help you keep your character consistent throughout the account. If appropriate, you can then organise the events in your narrative according to the structure outlined above.

Sample 1 2006 Text 1 Question B

'Hours later . . . the boy's soul raged . . .' Imagine that, in an attempt to control his feelings, the boy writes into his diary an account of the incident and his reactions to it. Write out his diary entry.

Plan

Voice: I note that the register is determined by the phrase 'in an effort to control his feelings'. I'm going to have to make the boy's *feelings* fairly obvious and I have to show him struggling with these; in other words, a little confused. I'm going to try and capture the boy's voice, so that, hopefully, the diary entry will feel like that of an upset, but intelligent, well-educated thirteen- or fourteen-year old.

Structure: Far less important than capturing the boy's voice, which is confused rather than organised, after all. Nevertheless, I'll attempt to use the events to build towards a crisis inside the boy and to suggest a continuation of his turmoil in the future.

Content: The content here is defined by 'an account of the incident and his reactions to it'. My material must cover these areas.

Style: The features of creative writing covered in Part One, Chapter Three, 'The key elements of an effective descriptive or narrative text', with particular emphasis on the techniques for bringing characters alive on the page.

Sample answer

Saturday, 02 October

He finally did it. All week he's been saying the same thing, morning and night, breakfast and supper. 'We'll go out some day soon and cut down that aul' tree Lady Sarah wants rid of.' But every time he said it he had this smirk on his gob, just like Mr Maher says of Tubs. Take that smirk off your gob, Tubbin! It was like he had a private joke no one else could get. Well, now I know. Big joke! I hate it when he's smirking like that. Like the time he said to the Dennehys that Mum had a cut on her nose 'cause she'd let the razor slip and everyone laughed and Mum cried again and I still don't know why. I hate it when he's like that.

Mum says getting angry only makes him laugh even more and I have to remember that. When he woke me up I didn't want to go. The better form he's in the worse for everyone else and he was as bad as when he's drunk, shouting and laughing out loud. I didn't know why he needed me anyway. 'You're only cutting down an ash. You're always saying I'm in the way anyway.' Soon as you cross him of course it's up with the hand, threatening you. Whenever he has no answer he hits you and wins the argument when you're unconscious. That's another thing I hate him for. Mum says to let him win but I think he wants the fight anyway 'cause I know she gets it whether she agrees with him or not.

I like Lady Sarah's grounds but not with him. Soon as you want to play or anything he's mocking you. 'Would you stop your fooling like an amadán, you, and get on with the job!' First I found out the reason for the smirk 'cause he started hacking away at a great big beech tree right on the driveway and when I said he'd made a mistake and it wasn't an ash he jabbed me in the ribs and put on a stupid voice. 'Aren't you the expert all of a sudden? Would you go away out of that, you half-wit. Sure, you wouldn't know your ash from your elbow.' He thought that was hilarious and roared laughing like a madman all the time he was hacking down the beech but my stomach was in a knot and I felt like getting sick 'cause Lady Sarah would have him for it and she'd get him sacked off the force and we'd lose the station house and all and have nowhere to stay and Mum would get ill and die on us.

Next I found out why he wanted me there 'cause when Lady Sarah did turn up and started crying like he'd murdered one of her children – that's how she said it – he started to blame me saying I was responsible. That's when I hated him most of all. Mum says not to go tell Lady

Sarah that I told him it wasn't an ash, that Lady Sarah already knows that, but even though I know she knows I'd like to tell her anyway. I don't know what to do. Mum is crying again now. I can hear her. Lady Sarah is crying. He makes everybody cry. I'm not going to cry. But I don't know what to do. I want to do whatever stops Mum and Lady Sarah from crying, but I don't really know what it is yet.

Analysis

Voice: I specified for myself that I had to concentrate on the boy's feelings and that he was confused. Firstly, note how the description of every event is followed by the boy's emotional response to it, using appropriate phrasing and vocabulary: 'I hate it when he's smirking like that', 'That's another thing I hate him for', 'I like Lady Sarah's grounds, but not with him', 'my stomach was in a knot and I felt like getting sick', 'That's when I hated him most of all.' You can see that the voice is dominated by a single word: hatred. As demanded by the question, of course, he is struggling to control that hatred: 'Mum says getting angry only makes him laugh even more and I have to remember that.' and 'Mum says not to go tell Lady Sarah that I told him it wasn't an ash, that Lady Sarah already knows that, but even though I know she knows I'd like to tell her anyway.'

Secondly, note how expressions of confusion are threaded through the text, from 'It was like he had a private joke no one else could get' through 'I still don't know why' and 'I think', onto the crisis at the end, 'I'm not going to cry. But I don't know what to do. I want to do whatever stops Mum and Lady Sarah from crying, but I don't really know what it is yet.' This demonstrates the real virtue of planning a narrative text. The character's voice remains consistent. A consistent character is a credible character. And a credible character will get you full marks in the narrative Question B.

Structure: Quite clearly, the structure of my text consists simply of using the incidents to build up the 'rage' and confusion inside the boy to the point of crisis. All stories should have forward momentum, a gathering of pace, and that's how I achieve that effect here.

Content: As instructed, full use is made of the incidents described in the text, but without parroting the original phrasing. When recycling material, it is important to do so through the distinctive voice of the character, using their particular perspective and particular vocabulary.

Style: Part One, Chapter Three observed, 'Almost all stories concern themselves with human characters. It is essential, therefore, that you learn how to bring such characters alive on the page. There are four aspects that you should pay close attention to: *appearance, behaviour, dialogue* and *reflections* . . . how a character looks, what a character does, what a character says and what a character thinks or feels.' Here, as explored in the section on *voice* above, I use thoughts and feelings to capture the boy's character. The father's personality, on the other hand, is depicted through *appearance* – 'he had this smirk on his gob' – *behaviour* – 'Soon as you cross him of course it's up with the hand, threatening you' – and *dialogue* – 'Sure, you wouldn't know your ash from your elbow'. All three, you will note, contribute to the portrait of a bully. Consistency again.

Sample 2 2005 Text 1 Question B

'On Saturday afternoons Margaret Ann would go to the market to buy the meat for Sunday.' Write *three diary entries* that Margaret Ann might have written over a series of Saturday evenings. Your writing should relate to her experience as described in the passage.

Plan

Voice: At the time of the events that are covered in the text, towards the end of the nineteenth century, Margaret Ann was a young woman working as a domestic servant in Carlisle in the north of England. My chances of authentically capturing this character's voice are slim enough, really, but I must make an imaginative effort and I must enjoy the challenge. I have decided to opt for a vaguely old-fashioned phrasing, syntax and vocabulary. I note from the text that Margaret Ann is calm and reserved and self-effacing. These are the qualities I will use to define her voice for the diary entries.

Structure: Less important than capturing the character's voice, but the request for 'three diary entries' perfectly suits the standard three-part narrative structure of conflict-crisis-resolution. I'm going to invent a little conflict within Margaret Ann in the form of competition from another woman for the attentions of Thomas Hind.

Content: The content here is defined by 'Your writing should relate to her experience as described in the passage.'

Style: The features of creative writing covered in Part One, Chapter Three, 'The key elements of an effective descriptive or narrative text', with particular emphasis on the techniques for bringing characters alive on the page.

Sample answer

Saturday, April 17th, 1897

When I met them on Shadowgate, his sisters politely enquired, but at the market he chose not to. He could not have failed to observe the crudely applied bandage, since I clumsily proffered him the coins with my left hand, instead of my right, as I usually do. Cutting my finger last night, while I was dreamily slicing the last of this week's ham, my thought was all for the conversation it would ease and not at all for the pain.

'Three pound of sausage, Mr Hind, please.'

'Your hand, Miss Stephenson! Have you been injured?'

'Oh, it is nothing but a scratch, I assure you.'

'Come, you must allow me to . . .'

I am undoubtedly foolish in my thoughts when idle, for the stall was busy as usual, and not the secluded spot I had imagined. Mrs Macey was again accompanied by her pretty and vivacious daughter, who drew a blush from Mr Hind when she complimented his neat appearance, much to the amusement of the other customers.

Saturday, April 24th, 1897

Except for presumption, vanity is the most uncomfortable of my many failings. The new bonnet bought for church was not obliged to wait until the Sabbath for an outing, but instead set out to attract attention a day earlier this afternoon. I did not go by Shadowgate, fearing to meet his sisters as usual, for any other woman would so easily have understood the scheming behind my poor ruse and might have thought the less of me.

'A man is not so charmed by bright colours as a lady, Miss Stephenson.'

'Oh, I had no thought of charming . . .'

'Of charming who, dear?'

My detour was my chastisement, however. On Victoria Peace, I was overtaken by Mrs Macey and her pretty daughter, and was obliged to accompany them all the way to the market. Beside the splendour of Miss Macey's outfit, my poor bonnet seemed dull and lifeless. As I must have myself. Mr Hind kept his eyes averted, attending to his duties, as he served us all, though whether from shyness in the presence of beauty or embarrassment at my own poor appearance I know not.

Saturday, 1st May, 1897

Ill today. The mistress ordered me to stay in bed, so wretched did I look, but I insisted that I was strong enough to manage my chores. Otherwise, young Cathy would have been sent to market to buy the meat and other necessities. My brain must have been slightly feverish, for I imagined a disaster arising from this.

'Did he ask why I had not come as usual, Cathy?'

'No, Margaret, indeed not, he asked me about my own age and whether so pretty a thing as I had a young man of her own . . .'

Had I seen him, it would have been ample recompense for the aching in my limbs while scrubbing the stairs and washing the dishes after breakfast this morning. But he was not there today. Nor were his sisters on Shadowgate as usual. It is rumoured that their mother is gravely ill and there was a sense of gloom among those queuing at his stall today, except for Miss Macey, who so encouraged one of Mr Hind's assistants that he left a bright smear of blood on the shoulder of her dress where his hand had playfully touched her. For once, I do not think the other customers were pleased by her demeanour. I will ask his sisters at church tomorrow for news of their mother.

Analysis

Voice: I specified two things for myself, that I should use old-fashioned phrasing and vocabulary in an effort to suit the historical period, and that Margaret Ann's voice should be characterised by calmness and self-effacement. I have little idea whether such expressions as 'The new bonnet bought for church was not obliged to wait until the Sabbath for an outing' are at all authentic, but I'm demonstrating that I know what is required and that I'm making an enthusiastic effort to provide it. According to the Chief Examiner's report for 2005, such engagement with the task is always highly rewarded. The only error I could have made was to write in a contemporary idiom. Here, the words 'bonnet' and 'Sabbath' are no longer in common usage and the construction 'was not obliged to wait until' sounds terribly dated. As for Margaret Ann's voice, it consistently strikes, as I intended, a note of self-effacement: 'I am undoubtedly foolish in my thoughts when idle' from the first entry; 'my poor bonnet seemed dull and lifeless' from the second; and 'I imagined a disaster arising from this' from the last.

This is a diary, however, and since a person always confides more to a diary than to others, I have taken the opportunity to gently reveal Margaret Ann's private dreams and hopes and anxieties. Note how both the self-effacement and the mild fantasies are threaded through the text, appearing in each separate diary entry. This demonstrates the real virtue of planning a narrative text. The character's voice remains consistent. A consistent character is a credible character. And a credible character will get you full marks in the narrative Question B.

Structure: Three diary entries allows me scope for a little drama. In the first, I set up a conflict within Margaret Ann as she observes an attractive rival, Mrs Macey's 'pretty and vivacious daughter', who makes a play for Margaret's love-interest, Thomas Hind. In the second, Margaret Ann responds to this challenge by dressing up in her Sunday best, but runs into a minor crisis when even her best seems 'dull and lifeless' compared to the beauty of Mrs Macey's daughter. Surely, Thomas will have his head turned away from Margaret? In the final entry, the crisis is resolved. Mrs Macey's daughter makes a fool of herself by coquettishly making a play for one of the butcher's assistants and leaves the field clear for the more composed Margaret Ann to impress by comparison.

Content: As instructed, full use is made of the incidents described in the text, but without parroting the original phrasing. When recycling material, it is important to do so through the distinctive voice of the character, using their particular perspective and particular vocabulary.

Style: Part One, Chapter Three observed, 'Almost all stories concern themselves with human characters. It is essential, therefore, that you learn how to bring such characters alive on the page. There are four aspects that you should pay close attention to: *appearance, behaviour, dialogue* and *reflections* . . . how a character looks, what a character does, what a character says and what a character thinks or feels.' Here, as explored in the section on voice above, I use reflections and imagined dialogue to capture Margaret Ann's character. The other characters are depicted through appearance – Mrs Macey's daughter is 'pretty and vivacious' and 'so encouraged one of Mr Hind's assistants that he left a bright smear of blood on the shoulder of her dress where his hand had playfully touched her' – and behaviour – the girl 'drew a blush from Mr Hind when she complimented his neat appearance' and 'Mr Hind kept his eyes averted, attending to his duties, as he served us all.'

Homework and tasks

In relation to the following prison diaries, put a single term on the voice of each character and select the words and phrases that most vividly express that character.

Paula Curtis, 24

Serving eight months for money laundering and having fake documents, HMP Holloway, London

I was pregnant when I came here in September and was put in C4, a unit for pregnant women. After my daughter Simi was born, I went to D4, the mother-and-baby unit. There are 10 of us on here, with babies ranging from newborn to eight months. Then you have to move to another prison, which takes mothers and babies up to 18 months. My day started at 6 – that's the time my baby wakes up. The officers come around at seven and say good morning; you have to be ready by 7.30 and then you have breakfast. After that, my baby goes to a crèche and I have classes from nine. We can study for qualifications. My favourite class is art: I'm learning how to make a baby blanket by sewing together different patches. I'm also learning how to cook for my baby. She's my first, I want to get it right. We break off for lunch at 12, then from two you can go back to education or stay on the unit with your baby or go to the gym. The crèche is nice, with toys. We have dinner about five and there are five or six choices, including vegetarian. It's not bad. At eight we go to our rooms. I have a toilet, a single bed and my baby's crib in my room, as well as a telly and a cupboard. People can send you bed covers, so you're not using prison stuff. I've got another 11 weeks to go.

Bekir 'Dukie' Arif, 53

In the 10th year of a 24-year sentence for drug distribution, Whitemoor maximum security prison, near Peterborough

Another interrupted night's sleep; the night screw, who must wear size-18 boots, given the noise he makes, shone his torch in my face

every hour. Unlocked at five to eight and I made an application for money to go on my Pin numbers, so I can make phone calls. Called to labour at 8.55, checked off the wing with a rubdown and metal detector. The work – breaking up used CDs – is about as mind-numbing as it gets. Finished work at 11.10am, checked back on wing, then exercised in a small yard – totally inadequate. Gave my lunch away, as usual, then back to work in the afternoon. Locked up until just gone five, then association till 7.10 before lock-up for the night. My big concern right now is that my daughter visited me regularly until she was 16. Then she was deemed an adult and had to be security cleared. Up to now, this has taken 19 months, which was when I last saw her. This is my own daughter, remember.

Prisoner Y, 40

Serving life under the two-strikes law for rape, kidnap and eight robberies, Wakefield high-security prison, North Yorkshire

I woke up at 7.30, had a wash, tidied myself up and pottered about in my cell. Unlock is around eight. I don't bother with breakfast, I just get a carton of milk. Prison food is horrible. I cook my own stuff with four inmates – we all put in money and share a 'food boat'. Around 8.30 I go to work as a cleaner. I've done cleaning jobs in a lot of jails so I'd say I was pretty good. You do not get security-cleared to clean on the wings with minimal staffing if you're an idiot. I get paid £18 a week, and spend £12 of this on food – mostly tinned stuff and fresh veg. I've met prisoners who are brilliant cooks. You learn off the Asian guys how to do the curries and an Albanian taught me how to do pizza. I've been in prison most of my life. Most of my offences are drugs-related, and for a long time I had issues with addressing my behaviour. This place has been good for me. Before, prison was just an occupational hazard. When I left jail after a stint, I'd say, 'You'll never see me again,' but I'd be back in six months. Now I've done courses, had risk-reducing therapy and am about to do a course for sex offenders so that I have a chance when I get out. At seven we are locked up for the night. I write letters, watch TV, read and go to bed at 11–12. For me, it's easy to be occupied. If you can't read or write, and you're not into TV or music, you're in trouble. You'll get depressed and wound up.

The prison service has changed massively over the years. Gone are the days when you sat locked up for 23 hours a day. Even the abuse has gone over the past five years. The government or whoever has realised that the only way to stop people coming back is to concentrate on offending behaviour. There's a lot of psychology in the prison now.

I wouldn't say I was having a good time, but you've got to make the most of it. My next parole opportunity is later this year, but realistically it's going to be another three or four years before I get out. I'll have done 11 years then – double my tarrif. As well as the drugs, a huge issue for me was anger. But it's not a problem these days. Part of it is down to the courses, and part of it is just growing up. I'm more mature now.

Class assignments with assessment sheets

Instructions

- You should take 40 minutes to complete each assignment.
- You may find it beneficial to consult notes or ask for advice.
- The general theme is **Public communication**.
- There are four photographs.
- There are three assignments.

Question B

Assignment 1, Informative: Write a short report for your school magazine in which you give tips on body language that will create a positive impression while you are speaking in public.

Assignment 2, Argumentative: You have been asked to give a short talk on radio on the topic of **Street protests**. Write the script of the talk you would give.

Assignment 3, Narrative: Choose one of the people pictured below and write three diary entries that your chosen person might write during a protest campaign.

Assessment sheet – Assignment 1

Write a short report for your school magazine in which you give tips on body language that will create a positive impression while you are speaking in public.

<table>
<tr>
<td>P</td>
<td>In this exercise in informative writing, you are expected to supply a good deal of material that will clearly demonstrate to your audience of students the advantages of effectively using the body in public debate or communication. These materials should cover a fairly wide area, so that you present a fairly comprehensive profile of body language.
<table>
<tr><td></td><td>The material you provide is varied, interesting and relevant.</td></tr>
<tr><td></td><td>Some, but not sufficient relevant material provided.</td></tr>
<tr><td></td><td>Poverty of material, indicating a lack of knowledge.</td></tr>
</table>
</td>
<td>0–5=F/E
6–8=D
9–10=C
11–12=B
13–15=A

/15</td>
</tr>
<tr>
<td>C</td>
<td>You are expected to organise your response coherently, so that you clearly outline the various benefits of persuasive body language and clearly illustrate each in turn. You may structure the piece using a brief introduction, themed headings and a conclusion OR you may list the attractions in your introduction and then deal separately with each OR you may deal with separate situations in which public communication occurs, such as a formal debate, an informal group meeting, a family dinner, a wedding, and so on. One way or the other, you must organise the material so that you offer a sustained introduction to body language.
<table>
<tr><td></td><td>Your organisation of the material is effective.</td></tr>
<tr><td></td><td>Your organisation of the material is uneven.</td></tr>
<tr><td></td><td>Your organisation of the material is poor.</td></tr>
</table>
</td>
<td>0–5=F/E
6–8=D
9–10=C
11–12=B
13–15=A

/15</td>
</tr>
<tr>
<td>L</td>
<td>You are expected to employ informative techniques, such as clarity of language, amusing or enlightening illustrations, user-friendly presentation. You are expected to be aware of your target audience at all times, so that you are using language to inform an audience. You are expected to select a single register – humorous, serious, relaxed – and to maintain it consistently throughout. You are expected to reproduce the basic format of a magazine article.
<table>
<tr><td></td><td>Appropriate use of language.</td></tr>
<tr><td></td><td>Poor informative technique.</td></tr>
<tr><td></td><td>Inconsistency of register.</td></tr>
</table>
</td>
<td>0–5=F/E
6–8=D
9–10=C
11–12=B
13–15=A

/15</td>
</tr>
</table>

M		No problems with spelling and grammar. Problems with spelling. Problems with grammar.	4–5=D 6–7=C 8=B 9–10=A /10
Total			/50

Assessment sheet – Assignment 2

You have been asked to give a short talk on radio on the topic of street protests. Write the script of the talk you would give.

P	You are expected to adopt some attitude in relation to street protests, so this is an exercise in argument; in offering an opinion. You are expected to use material that (a) relates to contemporary or recent street protests, and (b) offers your own response to these. Merely agreeing or disagreeing in an abstract way with street protests is not sufficient. You must introduce illustrations and examples to substantiate your points. [ ] You show a good understanding of the topic and offer a relevant account. [ ] You show a poor understanding of the topic. [ ] You offer very little in way of examples and illustrations.	0–5=F/E 6–8=D 9–10=C 11–12=B 13–15=A /15
C	You are expected to organise your response coherently, so that you clearly state your own views and clearly support each of your views with appropriate illustrations or evidence or personal experience. You may structure the piece by raising the 'burning issue' in relation to street protests at the beginning and then offering examples to illustrate OR by considering some recent event, news item or personal experience and developing your response and your conclusion from this. Either way, you must organise the material so that you present a clear and coherent view on the topic. [ ] Your organisation of the material is effective. [ ] Your organisation of the material is uneven. [ ] Your organisation of the material is poor.	0–5=F/E 6–8=D 9–10=C 11–12=B 13–15=A /15

<table>
<tr><td>L</td><td>You are expected to employ argumentative techniques, such as rhetorical questions, emphasis, repetition, exaggeration, colour, and the rest. You are expected to be aware of your target audience at all times, so that you are using language to make an impression, to convince. You are expected to select a single register – humorous, serious, aggressive – and to maintain it consistently throughout. You are expected to reproduce the basic format of a radio talk.
<table>
<tr><td></td><td>Appropriate use of language.</td></tr>
<tr><td></td><td>Poor argumentative technique.</td></tr>
<tr><td></td><td>Inconsistency of register.</td></tr>
</table></td><td>0–5=F/E
6–8=D
9–10=C
11–12=B
13–15=A
/15</td></tr>
<tr><td>M</td><td><table>
<tr><td></td><td>No problems with spelling and grammar.</td></tr>
<tr><td></td><td>Problems with spelling.</td></tr>
<tr><td></td><td>Problems with grammar.</td></tr>
</table></td><td>4–5=D
6–7=C
8=B
9–10=A
/10</td></tr>
<tr><td>Total</td><td></td><td>/50</td></tr>
</table>

Assessment sheet – Assignment 3

Choose one of the people pictured below and write three diary entries that your chosen person might write during a protest campaign.

<table>
<tr><td>P</td><td>In this exercise in narrative writing, you are expected to invent material consistent with a protest campaign in the life of your chosen character. The protest campaign must be consistent with the character chosen, relating to student life, Greenpeace agitation, animal rights or homophobia (morbid anxiety about homosexuality). To add colour and interest, and to avoid making the material boring, you may invent a crisis or challenge that the character encounters during the course of the protest.
<table>
<tr><td></td><td>You show a good understanding of the requirement to provide material consistent with a protest campaign.</td></tr>
<tr><td></td><td>You show a poor understanding of the question.</td></tr>
<tr><td></td><td>You offer very little material consistent with the character.</td></tr>
</table></td><td>0–5=F/E
6–8=D
9–10=C
11–12=B
13–15=A
/15</td></tr>
</table>

<table>
<tr><td rowspan="4">C</td><td colspan="2">You are expected to organise the diary entries coherently, either by taking us through a typical protest – structuring it around time – or by taking us through a crisis or challenge for the character – structuring it around incident: problem, crisis and resolution. Either way, you must show that you have intentionally shaped the material.</td><td rowspan="4">0–5=F/E
6–8=D
9–10=C
11–12=B
13–15=A

/15</td></tr>
<tr><td></td><td>Your organisation of the material is effective.</td></tr>
<tr><td></td><td>Your organisation of the material is uneven.</td></tr>
<tr><td></td><td>Your organisation of the material is poor.</td></tr>
<tr><td rowspan="4">L</td><td colspan="2">You are expected to employ narrative techniques, such as description, dialogue, action, the creation of mood, the evocation of feeling. You are expected to be aware that a diary is written for oneself, and therefore confessional, and also that the style and standard of the writing must suit the personality of the diarist. You are expected to reproduce the basic format of a diary.</td><td rowspan="4">0–5=F/E
6–8=D
9–10=C
11–12=B
13–15=A

/15</td></tr>
<tr><td></td><td>Appropriate use of language.</td></tr>
<tr><td></td><td>Poor narrative technique.</td></tr>
<tr><td></td><td>Inconsistency of register.</td></tr>
<tr><td rowspan="3">M</td><td></td><td>No problems with spelling and grammar.</td><td rowspan="3">4–5=D
6–7=C
8=B
9–10=A
/10</td></tr>
<tr><td></td><td>Problems with spelling.</td></tr>
<tr><td></td><td>Problems with grammar.</td></tr>
<tr><td>Total</td><td colspan="2"></td><td>/50</td></tr>
</table>

Chapter Six:

Writing the Composition: The Short Story

Introduction

For 100 marks, you are asked to write a short story using a quotation from one of the texts on the examination paper as your title, a short story prompted by one or more of the images from the visual text on the examination paper or a short story featuring a character or a location suggested by one of the texts on the examination paper.

In 2008, the choice was between 'Write a short story in which the central character is a rebellious teenager (male or female)' and 'Write a short story in which setting/location is a significant feature. (Your story may be prompted by one or more of the locations depicted in Text 3 or by any other setting of your choice.)'

In 2007, the choice was between '"I tune in to conversations around me." (Text 2) Write a short story suggested by the above sentence' and 'Write a short story prompted by one or more of the images in Text 3.'

The Chief Examiner's Report on the compositions attempted by candidates in 2005 observed that 'As in previous years, the short story option continues to be the most popular' and advised, 'Candidates who wish to write compositions in the form of short stories would benefit from a short study of the genre by reading and analysing a number of examples. Too often a candidate writes a short story that is limited in scope to that of a simple anecdote which is lacking in narrative shape or any awareness of the reader's presence.'

Further, the instructions given to examiners correcting your Leaving Certificate short stories ask them to 'reward awareness of narrative shape' and they stress that 'an implicit link with the textual prompt given in the title is sufficient' or that 'a tenuous connection with the chosen image/s will suffice'. What all this means is that you are free to create whatever material you like, but that you must know how to shape this material into an effective short story.

How do you *shape* a short story? Well, let's read one and find out.

Ironclad rules

by Etgar Keret

Usually, we don't kiss around other people. Cecile, with her plunging necklines and lurid shoes is actually very shy. And I'm one of those guys who's always aware of every movement around him, who never manages to forget where he is. But it's a fact that on that morning, I did manage to forget, and we suddenly found ourselves, Cecile and me, hugging and kissing at a table in a coffee house like a pair of high school kids trying to steal themselves a little intimacy in a public place.

When Cecile went to the bathroom, I finished my coffee in one gulp. I used the rest of the time to straighten out my clothes and my thoughts. 'You're a lucky guy,' I heard a voice with a thick Texas accent say from very close by. I turned my head. At the next table was an older guy wearing a baseball cap. The whole time we were kissing, he was sitting practically on top of us, and we'd been rubbing and moaning into his bacon and eggs without even noticing. It was very embarrassing, but there was no way of apologizing without making it worse. So I gave him a sheepish smile and nodded.

'No, really,' the old guy went on, 'it's rare to hold on to that after you're married. A lot of people get hitched and it just disappears.' 'Like you said,' I kept on smiling, 'I'm a lucky guy.' 'Me too,' the old guy laughed and raised his hand in the air, to show me his wedding band. 'Me too. Forty-two years we're together, and it isn't even starting to get boring. You know, in my work, I have to fly a lot, and every time I leave her, let me tell you, I just feel like crying.' 'Forty-two years,' I gave a long, polite whistle, 'she must really be something.' 'Yes,' the old guy nodded. I could see that he was trying to make up his mind whether to pull out a picture or not, and I was relieved when he gave up on the idea. It was getting more embarrassing by the minute, even though he clearly had good intentions. 'I have three rules,' the old guy smiled, 'three ironclad rules that help me keep it alive. You want to hear them?' 'Sure,' I said, gesturing at the waitress for more coffee. 'One,' the old guy waved a finger in the air, 'every day I try to find one new thing I love about her, even the smallest thing, you know, the way she answers the phone, how her voice rises when she's pretending she doesn't know what I'm talking about, things like that.' 'Every day?' I said.

'That must really be hard.' 'Not that hard,' the old guy laughed, 'not after you get the hang of it. The second rule – every time I see the children, and now the grandchildren too, I say to myself that half of my love for them is actually for her. Because half of them is her. And the last rule –' he continued as Cecile sat down next to me, 'when I come back from a trip, I always bring my wife a present. Even if I only go for a day.' I nodded again and promised to remember that. Cecile looked at us a little confused; after all, I wasn't exactly the kind of person who starts conversations with people in public places, and the old guy, who'd probably realized that, got up to leave. He touched his hat and said to me, 'Keep it up.' And then he gave Cecile a small bow and left. "'My wife"?' Cecile grinned and made a face. "'Keep it up"?' 'It was nothing,' I stroked her hand, 'he saw my wedding band.' 'Ah,' Cecile kissed me on the cheek. 'He looked a little weird.'

On the flight back home, I sat alone, three seats all to myself, but as usual I couldn't fall asleep. I was thinking about the deal with the Swiss company, which I didn't actually think would get off the ground, and about that PlayStation I bought for Roy with the cordless joystick and everything. And when I thought about Roy, I kept trying to remember that half of my love for him is actually for Mira, and then I tried to think about one small thing I love about her – her expression, trying to stay cool, when she catches me in a lie. I even bought her a present from the duty-free cart in the plane, a new French perfume, which the smiling young flight attendant had said everyone was buying now and even she herself was using it. 'Tell me,' the flight attendant said, extending the back of her bronzed hand towards me, 'isn't that a fantastic scent?' Her hand really did smell great.

A critical reading

'Usually, we don't kiss around other people. . . . But it's a fact that on that morning . . . we suddenly found ourselves . . . hugging and kissing at a table in a coffee house'. As observed in Part One, Chapter Three, 'the opening few sentences of a narrative have a great deal of work to do. Ideally, they should simultaneously introduce character, situation and theme, while at the same time stimulating the reader's interest in what is about to happen. The situation described must be full of promise, full of potential tension or conflict or danger.' You will notice two important things about the opening of this story: (i) it immediately engages our interest in the characters; and (ii) it immediately plunges the reader into the heart of the incident that the story is shaped around.

Properly understood, the short story is an exploration of the inner life of a character caught in a situation that defines their personality. Different writers have different techniques for dropping you, at the opening of a story, into both the characters' lives and the central incident. Here, Keret offers a very brief profile of the two characters and then immediately introduces a situation in which they're behaving oddly. He opens in the middle of an incident, in the middle of a relationship, in the middle of two lives. A couple momentarily forget themselves and are all over each other in a café. How did they get there? What were they doing beforehand? What do they work at? Why are they so suddenly unrestrained? These are important questions. But they are only questions, and only important because they are not answered by the opening. The function of a good opening is to arouse the reader's interest, not to satisfy it. Here, we already have a hundred queries about this couple. In other words, we're hooked.

'Cecile, with her plunging necklines . . . is actually very shy.' Again, as observed in Part One, Chapter Three, 'Almost all stories concern themselves with human characters. It is essential, therefore, that you learn how to bring such characters alive on the page. There are four aspects that you should pay close attention to: *appearance, behaviour, dialogue* and *reflections* . . . how a character looks, what a character does, what a character says and what a character thinks or feels. Appearance covers all visible features, including body language, facial expressions, gestures, clothes and physique.' Here, notice how the character of Cecile is swiftly but precisely created. There are no lengthy physical descriptions, no attempt to capture a 'photograph' of her. Instead, we are offered two pieces of information, which happen to contradict each other. She dresses rather provocatively, but she's actually quite reserved, even modest. This reveals the essence, rather than just the surface, of the character.

'I'm one of those guys who's always aware of every movement around him.' There is no physical description of the male narrator, partly because narrators rarely need to remind themselves what they look like, but mostly because such descriptions are not at all necessary. Here, nothing at all is provided except the essential portrait of the narrator as cautious, watchful, alert, perhaps verging on neurotic, and certainly very tense.

'"You're a lucky guy," I heard a voice with a thick Texas accent say from very close by . . . an older guy wearing a baseball cap . . . raised his hand in the air, to show me his wedding band . . . trying to make up his mind whether to pull out a picture or not'. Notice how the third character in the story is created primarily through a voice. Again, there is no physical description of this man, but you can 'see' him through what he says and how he sounds – a big, kindly, friendly, innocent American, as big and straightforward as the state he comes from, which is Texas. Follow the development of this portrait through the dialogue as the story advances. Once more, the key to bringing the character alive on the page is to rely on dialogue, gesture and significant detail. The baseball cap is particularly revealing, a different world from Cecile's plunging neckline, and the wedding band and family snapshots both contribute to the profile of a solid, dependable, conventional type. The really important thing is the consistency of the detail, all feeding into the same impression. As mentioned so often before, a consistent character is a credible character.

'"Like you said," I kept on smiling, "I'm a lucky guy."' As a further study in the use of dialogue and how it can be skilfully used to create both character and situation, contrast the rather unwelcoming tension in the narrator's short responses with the beefy, expansive sentences of the Texan. Quite clearly, the narrator does not want to get involved in this conversation, but is probably too wary to risk being rude.

'On the flight back home, I sat alone, three seats all to myself'. The time-frame of this story is remarkably short. The action takes place over a few hours, at most. The couple are parting in the café – hence their hunger for one another – and the narrator has to take his flight immediately afterwards. Concentrating on a single situation, within a limited time span, gives an intensity to a story that is not possible to achieve if the events are spread over years. Nevertheless, this very short period of time offers an insight into an entire life. Those few hours *define* these characters. This is how they will be forever.

'I was thinking about the deal with the Swiss company . . . and about that PlayStation I bought for Roy'. Only now, very late in the story, are some details being provided to answer the questions that were raised by the opening. Who are these people? Why are they behaving like this? The incident in the café is over, the story has settled, and there is time for a little background. This background is not provided merely for its own sake, however; it is essential to an understanding of the central character and therefore an integral part of the story.

'And when I thought about Roy, I kept trying to remember that half of my love for him is actually for Mira, and then I tried to think about one small thing I love about her'. Finally, we learn that the narrator is not married to Cecile, as the big Texan mistakenly assumed, but that he has a wife and a son in another country, and that he is cheating on his wife by having an affair with Cecile. The central character is a deceiver. The theme of this story is therefore deception, since character and theme are inseparable in fiction and the theme, the significant human experience or tendency that is explored, always grows organically out of the behaviour of the central character. But please note how skilfully the theme of deception is introduced and sustained throughout this story. It is implicit in the very first line – 'Usually, we don't kiss around other people' – because they are wary of revealing their illicit relationship; and it is explicit in the second sentence – 'Cecile, with her plunging necklines . . . is actually very shy' – since the narrator's mistress seems to be one thing, but is really something else.

Only now can we fully appreciate how the opening paragraph of the story simultaneously presents us with characters, situation and theme, each one indistinguishable from the other two. From there, the development of the story is organic. The opening is the seed; the development is the growth consistent with that. The narrator and Cecile appear to be happily married to each other, an impression that leads to the big Texan's mistaken assumption and that drives the action and the exchanges in the centre of the story. Even the ending remains concerned with exploring the theme of deception. The narrator buys his wife a present, presumably because he is slightly guilty and because he wants to deflect her suspicions. It's not just any old present, however. It's perfume. And the function of perfume, after all, is to disguise or mask what we might refer to as more natural odours; to deceive, in other words. Even though the story itself is not particularly complex, its layers are quite subtle: the narrator is deceiving his wife, and the author is deceiving his reader. As the stewardess says at the end, 'Isn't that a fantastic scent?' The point being that almost everyone has been on the wrong scent.

'On the flight back home, I sat alone . . . I even bought her a present from the duty-free cart in the plane'. There are two things to note about the ending. Firstly, this is a reversal-of-expectations story, a surprise ending. It works very well here, but clearly the limitation of the surprise ending is that it cannot treat a theme with any great depth or subtlety, since something vital must be kept from the reader in order to make the surprise possible. Secondly, note how the future of the characters is dealt with in an accomplished short story. It is *suggested*, not defined. It is contained within the events that have already been described and therefore does not need to be spelled out, but can be left to the reader's imagination. Here, the incident at the core of the story has ended, but the characters clearly go on living, beyond the physical scope of the narrative. What happens to them afterwards? They go on being themselves. A good story captures the essentials of people's personalities, and since we cannot really change our personalities, we know that the characters will not change and that we have seen their futures in the present. Properly understood, the short story is an exploration of the inner life of a character caught in a situation that defines their personality.

The key elements of a successful short story

They are many different types of short story, and there are as many ways of telling a story, as many different styles of writing, as there are individual storytellers, but on the basis of our close critical reading of 'Ironclad Rules', we can identify the following features as the essential requirements of a good short story at Leaving Certificate level.

1. *The opening should plunge the reader into the heart of the incident,* rather than provide informative or explanatory material. The function of an effective opening is to engage the reader's interest in the characters, the situation and the theme. There is always background to be filled in, since the present unavoidably includes the past, but this background can be supplied later, when the reader is already hooked on the story.

2. *The story's time-frame (the duration of the action) should be short and intense* – an hour, an afternoon, a day – rather than extended. The longer a time period the story covers, the more thinly spread the material is. A short period of time gives a depth and intensity that might otherwise be missing. On the other hand, this hour, or day – this short period of time – should encapsulate an entire life, and reveal the essentials of a personality.

3. Properly understood, the short story is an exploration of the inner life of a character caught in a situation that defines their personality and *fictional characters should be revealed through dialogue, appearance, behaviour and reflections,* rather than through surface description of basic actions and physique or through crude analysis. The technique is to show a character in the confused process of living, not to tell the reader what to think about the character.

4. *The story should explore a significant human experience; a theme,* such as love, loss, fulfilment, disappointment, rather than merely present a string of events. This significant human experience is that of the story's central character. For instance, a sensitive portrait of a disappointed man will automatically explore the theme of failure and a profile of a grieving mother will explore loss. The theme therefore grows organically out of the character and should not be imposed in any way. Start with character. However, everything in the story – incidents, locations, images – should then orbit around this theme, keeping it constantly in front of the reader.

5. *The ending of a good short story should suggest, rather than define, the future.* While the particular incident that you have concentrated on should be completed, and the particular crisis that you have created

should be resolved, the question of what happens afterwards should be left to the reader's imagination, guided by the insights that the story has offered.

When you are critically reading a short story in future, you should use it to test the key elements against. If you enjoy the story, if you consider it particularly good, identify which of the elements it most effectively complies with. And then use these techniques to model your own stories on. Imitating the techniques of accomplished writers is how all authors start their careers. Don't think that you're going to be any different. As with drawing the human face, once you have mastered the basic techniques, only then can you go on to create something truly individual.

Homework and tasks

Recommended reading

You now know how to improve your own short story writing techniques by critically reading the stories of accomplished authors. You will find many short story collections in your school library, among them perhaps *The Nimrod Flip-Out* by Etgar Keret, from which 'Ironclad Rules' is taken.

Could I particularly recommend the short stories of the American writer Raymond Carver, 1938–88. Carver never psychoanalyses or morally judges his characters and he is quite a brilliant model for learning how to present and reveal character through speech and movement, dialogue and gesture. His skill is to allow the characters to exist in their own right, without straining to make some sort of point while creating them. Also, Carver has some brilliant openings to his stories, among them the beginning of 'Gazebo':

That morning she pours Teacher's over my belly and licks it off. That afternoon she tries to jump out the window.

I go, 'Holly, This can't continue. This has got to stop.'

and the beginning of 'Mr Coffee and Mr Fixit':

I've seen some things. I was going over to my mother's to stay a few nights. But just as I got to the top of the stairs, I looked and she was on the sofa kissing a man. It was summer. The door was open. The TV was going. That's one of the things I've seen.

My mother is sixty-five.

Class assignment

Using 'The key elements of a successful short story', write a critical analysis of the following piece.

Your choice or mine

Almost everyone in the neighbourhood, apart from his girl friend and the youths whose vocabularies didn't extend to titles that weren't abusive, invariably called him *Mister* Downes. He was only thirty-four, but he dressed severely, didn't practise or invite intimacies, hid behind a strict regime of lifeless habits, and had once studied in London, after leaving school, under a famous composer whose name no one could remember. But people also knew that he was disappointed, that he had once imagined something more accomplished than being a clerk, and so there was a certain amount of compassion in their deference. An arid compassion, like that expended on the dead, because his life simply wasn't exciting enough to reward the curious.

It was characteristic of Downes that he should wait a full year after purchasing a piano before giving his first performance to an audience, and then that he should do so in his own home and invite only Laura Ashwell, whom he intended marrying, someday. This small scale was the one he was most comfortable with. Nevertheless, no one performs for another without the need for acceptance and the hope of applause. It was fifteen years since Downes had last risked it, and this present occasion was a tentative return to a neglected love. For that reason, he was quite nervous about beginning. He drew his chair noisily a little closer to the piano, coughed self-consciously a number of times, flexed the muscles in his right hand and then repeated the exercise with his left, and finally, after returning the chair to its original position, settled into the first item on his programme, Debussy's étude *Pour les sonorités opposées*. His playing was technically correct, as it always had been, even in his teens, but now, in his mid-thirties, it was almost completely devoid of emotion. No more than his name, his music retained nothing that was personal. But even then, if he had performed with less seriousness, he might not have subsequently recoiled with such finality.

Somewhere in the middle of the étude, a youth outside the front window of the house started calling drunkenly to some friend of his in the distance.

'Yammo! Yammo! Yammo!'

It was like a crazed drummer in the background repeatedly hammering the same discordant beat from his instrument.

'Yammo! Yammo! Yammo!'

Downes missed a note, recovered, struggled desperately for a while against the interruption, and then, frustrated and angry, brought both hands violently down on the keys and left them there, inactive. Ironically, the youth simultaneously fell silent on the footpath outside.

'I'm sorry, Laura,' Downes said tensely, without turning to look at her.

'Well,' Laura sympathised, 'you can hardly expect them to appreciate Chopin in this neighbourhood, I suppose.'

'It was Debussy, Laura.'

'What did I say? Did I say Chopin? Debussy, of course. And it was delightful.'

Delightful. The word hurt him, much more deeply than the insensitivity of the youth outside, and so he pretended to ignore it.

'There's nothing wrong with the neighbourhood,' he protested. 'I live here. You live here.'

'They live here, too,' Laura observed.

'No, no,' Downes cried impetuously. 'I don't care who lives here. All I ask is the same consideration in return. But why am I saying this to you? I should be saying it to the lout in the street outside.'

'Except that he seems to be gone now,' Laura pointed out.

Downes listened for a while with a doubtful expression on his tense face, but all he could hear were the faint sounds of traffic and the barking of a dog, both of them far in the distance.

'True,' he said with relief, because, despite his rhetoric, he didn't really want to confront anyone. He simply wanted to be left alone. 'Will we try again?' he suggested.

'Yes,' Laura said eagerly. 'Please.'

But it seemed, that evening, as if there was some conspiracy to sabotage his concert, and perhaps to challenge his aloofness. All through the preliminaries the quietness held outside, but as soon as he had settled seriously again into the étude, someone switched on a ghetto blaster in the street, turned the volume up to an unbearable level, and greeted the blare of music that thundered out with a wild yelp. Downes violently used the keys of his piano with both hands, and then slammed down the lid. His chair toppled and crashed to the floor behind him as he rose suddenly.

'Jack!' Laura cried.

'Excuse me for a moment, Laura,' he said.

'Now, don't go out there, Jack!'

'It's all right, it's all right. I'm only going to look, that's all. I'm only going to look.'

He swept past her and opened the front door. On a patch of grass opposite the house, there was a group of ten or twelve local youths. Some were attempting to dance, others were wrestling with each other, a few were stretched on the ground; all of them seemed already drunk. When they finally noticed Downes and saw that they had disturbed him,

they expressed their delight by shouting derisive obscenities at him and inviting him to do something about it. Realising that his appearance had only intensified their enjoyment, Downes went back inside.

'Cider party,' he said between his teeth.

He went to the telephone and keyed in the six digits of the local Garda station. The line was engaged. His thumb shot out to break the connection and dial again, but it lost its impetus along the way. It had just occurred to him that he did not want to call the police. He had no need of allies, since he had no intention of making or maintaining enemies. Allies, even those who were paid for their services, invariably made counter-claims on your life.

'My name is Downes,' he told the dead instrument, where no one was listening to him. 'I want to complain about a disturbance . . .'

They said nothing to each other, Downes and Laura, while waiting for the policemen who would never come. They simply sat in silence, in separate armchairs, waiting for their separate worlds to fall back into place.

Ten minutes passed. Then twelve. Laura began to glance at her watch, at first surreptitiously, merely to check the time, but then quite openly, as a crude signal, instead of the words she didn't trust.

'I'm sorry, Jack,' she said finally. 'I'll have to get back soon.'

It was a relief, for both of them.

'I'll walk you home.'

Laura paid no attention to the cat-calls and wolf-whistles and obscenities from the youths opposite as they were leaving the house. The jeering infuriated Downes himself, however. He hurried her away from it, forcing

her to walk at a pace she found uncomfortable in her new shoes and dress, both of which she had bought especially for the evening. But when they were finally out of range, mid-way between his own house and the Ashwells', he realised that they were merely in flight, not hastening towards some better objective. He didn't want to visit the Ashwells, but neither did he want to return home and sit a prisoner in his living room. He wanted to continue walking. Alone.
He had known this, without really admitting it to himself, since pretending to have called the police. Laura's presence in his life made him vulnerable. So did the ownership of a piano, and the musical pretensions, and the lingering need for an audience. He saw himself walking alone through the darkness, secretly discarding his burdens as he went, until there was nothing left to be protected any more. It was only then, when he was stripped of them all, that he could see the possibility of comfort once more.

He parted from Laura on the doorstep of her house, projecting, quite cleverly as he thought, a future that would guarantee a return to the past in one or other of its forms, either to their relationship as it had been before that evening, which was how he hoped Laura would interpret it, or to their separate lives before they had met, which was what he really meant.

'I'll have to sort this thing out,' he said. 'There's no point in arranging anything until I've sorted this out.'

'No,' Laura agreed, although she knew, instinctively, that they were saying goodbye.

Writing a short story that is closely relevant to the task that was set

The Chief Examiner's Report in 2005 remarked, 'While the quality of personal response is important for many of the tasks given in the examination, there is also a need to stress close, objective reading of the question so that all its implications are fully recognised.'

But how can you be sure that your short story is an appropriate response to the question on the examination paper? In the past, the instructions given to examiners correcting your Leaving Certificate scripts were encouraging for candidates in one sense and not very helpful in another. Examiners were told to 'reward awareness of narrative shape' and it was stressed that 'an implicit link with the textual prompt given in the title is sufficient' or that 'a tenuous connection with the chosen image/s will suffice.' It seems to suggest that you can write whatever you want. But is that really the case?

There are two problems.

Firstly, encouraged by the belief that any short story would suit any question asking for a story prompted by an image from one of the texts, some candidates learned their stories by heart and reproduced them without alteration in the examination. This led to the criticism in the Chief Examiner's Report in 2005, 'There was some evidence to suggest that a small minority of candidates relied overmuch on prepared material' in the short story option.

Secondly, the terms 'sufficient' and 'suffice' in the instructions to examiners are a little problematic. After all, if your diet is 'sufficient,' then it's enough to keep you alive and healthy, but it surely excludes any treats and definitely falls short of luxuries. In my view, in terms of Leaving Certificate grades, 'treats' are B grades and 'luxuries' are A grades. In other words, if your story has no more than a slight connection with the image that inspired it, then you're in danger of limiting yourself to a C grade, at best. A C grade is 'sufficient', isn't it, to gain you an honour? So, you're on far safer ground if your story has a significant rather than a tenuous connection with the chosen image.

No doubt in response to both problems, more specific guidelines were given to short story writers in the 2008 paper. Essay No. 3 was, 'Write a short story in which the central character is a rebellious teenager (male or female)'. No ambiguity or uncertainty here. If your central character was not a rebellious teenager (male or female) then your story was simply not relevant enough. Essay No. 7 was 'Write a short story in which setting/location is a significant feature. (Your story may be prompted by one or more of the locations depicted in Text 3 or by any other setting of your choice.)'. Not much ambiguity here, either. If location was not a significant feature, then your story was simply not relevant enough.

I expect this trend to continue. What it means is that no candidate can memorise prepared material, and in particular entire stories, and be confident of using this material effectively. It does *not* mean that you cannot use your own original material. If you are interested in writing short stories, you will have written many of them while preparing for the Leaving Certificate. These should not be discarded, but neither should they be relied on. You may well be very lucky and find that one of your stories perfectly suits an examination question. Chances are, however, that you will use and re-shape sections, characters, locales and situations from your own work and mould them into a new story in response to the challenge set by the examination paper.

As the tasks in 2008 indicate, fiction is all about the creation of character and location and the exploration of human experience. There are, therefore, three ways of assuring yourself that your story is an appropriate response to the question on the examination paper. Either your central character is consistent with the character described in the question or presented in the visual text OR your main location is consistent with the location described in the question or presented in the visual text OR the theme of your story is consistent with the theme suggested by the question or the visual text.

To make things clear, particularly if you're working from one or more of the images in the visual text, you should really specify all of this in your title and sub-title. For example, the following heading assures the examiner that you know what you're about:

Your Choice or Mine
A Short Story suggested by Image No. 4
on the theme of Inadequacy.

and the following:

Ironclad Rules
A Short Story suggested by Images 4 and 5
'Home' and 'Abroad'

Assessment sheet – short story

Write a short story prompted by one or more of the images in Text 3.

<table>
<tr><td>P</td><td>While you are free to create whatever material you like, nevertheless you cannot expect a high grade unless your story treats a theme or situation of some substance and significance and depth. Mere anecdotes – the character gets sick after too much booze and promises her parents that she'll take the pledge – are simply too inconsequential. Further, implausible material, depending on accidents of fate – getting knocked down, being stalked by a serial killer – does not make for a very sophisticated story. Similarly, action/adventure stories will not attract the higher grades. Please be aware also that the story must dramatise a life, not merely outline or explain it.
<table>
<tr><td></td><td>The material has depth and significance.</td></tr>
<tr><td></td><td>The material is decent, but not of the highest standard.</td></tr>
<tr><td></td><td>The material is too slight and inconsequential.</td></tr>
<tr><td></td><td>The characters are well drawn and credible.</td></tr>
<tr><td></td><td>The characters are reasonably drawn.</td></tr>
<tr><td></td><td>The characters are poorly drawn and clichéd.</td></tr>
</table></td><td>0–2=NG
3–7=F
8–11=E
12–16=D
17–20=C
21–25=B
26–30=A

/30</td></tr>
<tr><td>C</td><td>You are expected to demonstrate awareness of narrative shape. This means that you must know how to open a short story so that it engages the reader and introduces the theme and situation; that you must know how to develop the story by building tension, by creating a crisis or by increasing conflict within the character, perhaps by use of the character's memories; and that you must know how to end the story by suggesting the remainder of that character's life.
<table>
<tr><td></td><td>Excellent narrative shape.</td></tr>
<tr><td></td><td>Reasonable narrative shape.</td></tr>
<tr><td></td><td>Poor narrative shape.</td></tr>
</table></td><td>0–2=NG
3–7=F
8–11=E
12–16=D
17–20=C
21–25=B
26–30=A

/30</td></tr>
</table>

L	Writing good fiction requires the ability to use dialogue and significant detail to create character, the ability to describe places and people, the ability to capture movement and action, the ability to evoke feelings, and the ability to suggest ideas and thoughts without descending into discussion.	0–2=NG 3–7=F 8–11=E 12–16=D 17–20=C 21–25=B 26–30=A
	Good, creative story-writing techniques.	
	Average, conventional story-writing techniques.	
	Poor story-writing techniques.	/30
M	No problems with spelling and grammar.	4–5=D 6–7=C 8=B 9–10=A
	Problems with spelling.	
	Problems with grammar.	/10
Total		/100

Chapter Seven:

Writing the Composition: The Personal Essay

Introduction

For 100 marks, you are asked to write a personal essay on a given topic. In recent years, only one personal essay option has been set on each examination paper. In 2008, this was '"I have a beautiful view . . ." (Text 3) Write a personal essay in which you describe a place that you consider beautiful.' In 2007, it was '". . . the idealism and tangled passions that raged in my teenage heart." (Text 1) Write a personal essay on the idealism and passions of youth.' And in 2006, '"Let's stop all this pretence! Let's tell each other the unvarnished truth for a change!" (Text 3) Write a personal essay in response to the above statement.'

The examiners correcting your Leaving Certificate compositions are instructed to 'Interpret the term "personal essay" liberally, expecting a wide variety of responses in terms of content and register. Candidates may choose to couch their responses wholly or partly as personal (first person) narratives.' This means that you can treat the Personal Essay either as a *narrative*, in which you give a detailed account of some significant event or sequence of events in your life and allow this story to reveal your feelings on the given topic, or as a *discussion*, in which you offer your reflections and feelings on the given topic and illustrate these with detailed descriptions of your personal experiences. For instance, in 2008 you might have provided a narrative recounting a single visit to a beautiful place or you might have offered an introduction to the varied beauties of a particular place and illustrated each with your own experience of them. In 2006, you could have told a single story exploring the consequences of complete honesty in your personal life or you could have explored the impact of telling the truth in a number of areas in your personal life.

As the name suggests, the Personal Essay asks for *your* feelings, *your* experiences, *your* observations, an exploration of *your* life and *your* take on life. The material is intimate and confessional and therefore more expressive of emotions. Notice the emphasis on feelings in the following remarks from the Chief Examiner's Report in 2005, with reference to the question asking for a personal essay exploring the part that other people's expectations play in our lives: 'Quite a popular choice and many who chose it had good scope to vent their feelings on matters about which they felt strongly.' The danger is that the result can sometimes be sentimental and trivial. People who write about themselves run the risk of being boring, of obsessing about things that are fascinating to themselves, but of no interest to anyone else. To avoid this, deal only with *significant* events, with experiences that changed or moulded your personality, that altered the course of your life and made you what you are. These will be of interest to all readers.

The possible approaches to the Personal Essay are illustrated by the samples provided in the following pages. The first three are *Narrative Personal Essays* and the remaining two are *Discursive Personal Essays*.

Sample 1

I nearly starved to death

Edward Hebden

As a 20-year-old student touring America during my summer holidays in 1989, life seemed endless and full of possibility. I had travelled by Greyhound bus from New York to California. Now I was spending three days walking in the High Sierra mountains; sleeping in a tent, heating corned beef on campfires and drinking from streams.

Most visitors to Yosemite don't venture far from their cars, so after walking for a day and a half I was totally alone. I was enjoying the silence as I descended from Clouds Rest, a peak of more than 9,000 feet, when I lost the path. As I tried to rejoin it, I walked through rough vegetation on a slope that was getting steeper and steeper. Then I stepped on to wet ground and found myself sliding down a rock face. I grabbed at greenery but accelerated until I hit some rocks and knocked myself out.

When I came to, my leg was bent under me so that my right foot was almost touching my

head. Somehow I got into a more natural position, and only then did the full realisation of my situation hit me. My right femur was broken, nobody knew I was there, I had food for another day, I was in an isolated part of the park and was some way from the nearest footpath.

Like the moment after the door shuts and you realise the keys are locked inside, my mind raced around every possible escape route, but found no answers. My leg throbbed and ached. Whenever I moved I could see the skin stretch as the bones shifted underneath, and there were sharp, agonising pains that made me cry out.

I tried to crawl back the way I had come, but my weakened state made this impossible. The route was steep and I dropped my water bottle, which rolled away. As I crawled after it I disturbed a hornets' nest and was stung repeatedly.

I shouted for hours that first day, hoping the occasional person that I had passed on the trail would be close enough to hear me. As night fell, I put up my tent against a tree to stop me slipping down the hillside.

Over the next few days I developed a routine. During the day I crawled on to a rock in the sun to try to signal with my red sleeping bag. There was an amazing view of Half Dome mountain and row after row of distant ranges. If this was where I was to die, it was certainly beautiful. Every minute or so I shouted, giving my location and situation. I lit fires to try to attract planes. I also had a mirror that I used to reflect the sun, but this didn't work like in the movies.

One day I felt something behind me. I turned and saw a black bear running away – he must have been snuffling in my bag before I disturbed him. I knew that black bears were not threatening to people, but my heart raced.

As the days passed I shouted for help less and began to give up hope. The 14th night was the first when I didn't have nightmares. I dreamed of friends and family, and when I awoke, I felt calm. I looked down at my wasting body and realised that if I did nothing, I would be a skeleton before long. I ate the last of my food, filled my reclaimed water bottle and set off up the rock face.

The rocks grazed my legs as I dragged myself backwards over them. At the steepest section I was able to jam my hands into a crevice to hold me as I manoeuvred my good leg to keep pushing me up. A rush of adrenaline got me over and I knew then that I'd make it. I slid back two feet for every three I climbed, but after seven hours I was back on the path.

Two hours later a couple wandered past. Initially they didn't realise I was injured and we exchanged pleasantries for an excruciating few seconds before I abandoned my English reserve and blurted out my story. They left me some chocolate and went for help.

Eight hours later, in the dark, two rangers appeared. They put my leg in a splint and called in a helicopter for first light. I spent two weeks in hospital in America and was back home for the autumn term.

In the 18 years since this happened, those 14 days have become a touchstone to remind me what a privilege it is to be alive. We all know that our time here is temporary and that it can end in a second. With this experience I was reminded of my mortality for two long weeks, and I never feel very far from this knowledge.

A critical reading

'As a 20-year-old student touring America during my summer holidays in 1989, life seemed endless and full of possibility.' The opening illustrates the characteristic perspective of the personal essay, which is looking back on a life that has already been lived, looking back on the past from a position of greater understanding. You know more about yourself now than you did then. This perspective is what creates the reflective element within a personal essay. Without it, the composition would simply be a narrative, wouldn't it? To gain a high grade in the personal essay, you must balance incident and reflection, description and interpretation. This is the essential difference between the short story and the personal essay, by the way. The author never intrudes into the short story to tell the reader what to think, but simply shows the characters in the confused process of living. On the other hand, this type of reflection, where the author steps back from the experiences to consider their impact on his or her life, is essential in the personal essay.

'As a 20-year-old student touring America during my summer holidays in 1989 . . . I was spending three days walking in the High Sierra mountains . . .' The second thing to note about the opening is the amount of detail provided: a specific time, a specific place, a specific situation. Like the short story, the narrative personal essay should plunge the reader into the heart of an incident. Further, you're supposed to be writing about something of great significance in your life, and I guarantee that if you are recalling an event of great importance, then you will vividly remember the day, the time, the weather and every other circumstance. The remembered detail is what gives a feeling of authenticity to a personal essay.

'I was enjoying the silence as I descended from Clouds Rest, a peak of more than 9,000 feet . . .' Again, you will note the impressive detail: not only the name of the mountain, but also its height.

'Then I stepped on to wet ground and found myself sliding down a rock face. I grabbed at greenery but accelerated until I hit some rocks and knocked myself out.' This is quite a dramatic narrative, so all the features of good descriptive writing covered in Chapters Three, Five and Six come into play, specifically the selection of powerful verbs – 'I tried to *crawl* back' – intensifying adverbs – 'stung *repeatedly*' – expressive adjectives – 'my *weakened* state' – and suggestive comparisons – 'Like the moment after the door shuts and you realise the keys are locked inside.'

'In the 18 years since this happened, those 14 days have become a touchstone to remind me what a privilege it is to be alive. We all know that our time here is temporary and that it can end in a second. With this experience I was reminded of my mortality for two long weeks, and I never feel very far from this knowledge.' In a movement characteristic of the personal essay, the piece broadens out from a description of the specific incident to reflect on its consequences, on its impact, on how it changed my life, how it changed my attitude to things, on what it all meant to me. In this sample, the relationship between incident and reflection is quite simple: a lengthy, uninterrupted account of the event is followed by a short passage offering interpretation. This is the most basic form of the narrative personal essay available to you: the description of a single incident opening out onto a reflective ending. It is the easiest to handle, but the approach is unlikely to gain you the highest grades.

A note on length: At 817 words, this is about 200 words too short of the required length of a composition at Leaving Certificate level. The reflective section at the end needs to be expanded to show how what was learned from the experience was afterwards applied to other areas of life, for instance how it changed your attitude to work, to other people, to other situations, and so on.

Sample 2

I never forgot my childhood sweetheart

Jacqueline Hawker

When I was 15, I noticed him noticing me as I walked home from school. We watched each other for a long time. We spoke, we wrote, we started to meet.

My parents were surprised when we started going out – Peter was a popular, good-looking 19-year-old, working at odd jobs before university; I was a shy schoolgirl. But if they didn't exactly approve, they did field his many late-night drunken phone calls with good humour. Our relationship was intense but innocent: we'd hold hands and exchange the odd kiss. One day we raced across the hills on his motorbike, falling off about 20 times. Another time we motorbiked to London to see Talking Heads, but mostly we just walked and talked.

Two years later, Peter went off to university. At Nottingham he was surrounded by new experiences; loads of parties, girls. I missed him, but we both knew that we had a lot of growing up to do. I travelled, worked, dated . . . But we always wrote.

At 21, I got married. Peter was a guest at the wedding. A friend of mine chatted him up and I remember feeling slightly possessive – and guilty for feeling so.

I moved north, he stayed south. I gave birth to a daughter, and another and another. I kept his dusty letters, somewhere, with the bills. They survived every ruthless, frenzied clear-out, every house move. Finally, we lost contact – too many address changes, bedsits, flats. There was no email back then, no text messaging. I moved back south. From time to time I would feel his presence. It wasn't often – I had a busy life – but the fire still smouldered.

In 2000 my marriage ended and I learned to be alone, to be just a mother. I loved it. Men always seemed to be on the periphery, and that was enough. My children spent two nights a week with their father. I worked until 10pm, swam and slept.

A couple of years later, I was working late at the office one night when a colleague introduced me to Friends Reunited. I scorned it. If someone was that good a friend, I told her, you would never lose touch. Curiosity soon had me browsing regardless. Peter was four years older than me, so we were never at school together. I wasn't looking for him, but there was his name, mentioned by an old friend of his. He's out there, I thought, sleeping, eating, talking . . . He's not just in my head.

What I did then was completely out of character. I clicked on his friend's email address and typed, 'Next time you see him, tell him I was asking after him.'

On Monday morning there is a message in my inbox. Not from the friend, but from him. It starts, 'Blimey . . .' and I laugh. I can hear him, see him and feel the chemistry again. We talk fluidly online, laughing at our expanding girths and receding hairlines. I am 35, he is 39. He lives in the north, settled but no family, listens to Radio 2.

We arrange to meet. I spend ages planning what to wear, then end up in my oldest jeans, favourite top and big socks: I need to be myself from the start. I remember him as a clubber, so have a funky bar earmarked for our reunion, but when I mention it he tells me he has already found somewhere he likes the sound of – a quiet old boozer with a roaring fire. It takes about an hour to stop staring at each other, then we just drink all night, laughing at how we've turned out. The 19-year-old stud with the trials motorbike is now a respected counsellor, while I have three kids and a huge mortgage. Months of 4am starts follow, driving up the M1 listening to the shipping forecast. After a year, we know.

In 2003, we sold our houses and together moved into a ramshackle place in the Cotswolds. It is cold and leaky, but it works, because there's space for us all: teenagers, friends, families, toys and dogs. We are both well over 40 now. Our son is four and a joy to his parents, sisters and grandparents.

If we had married young, we would never have stayed together. We both had a lot to do in our different ways. I wanted to be a young mum, he wanted to play the field. Perhaps, subconsciously, we knew we had to wait. Neither of us feels regret, just lucky to get a second bite at the cherry. We were always meant to be; we just needed 20 years to explore and grow up. The years ahead are ours.

A critical reading

'When I was 15, I noticed him noticing me as I walked home from school.' The opening illustrates the characteristic perspective of the personal essay, which is – as noted in the critical reading of Sample 1 – looking back on a life that has already been lived, looking back on the past from a position of greater understanding. Again, the reader is plunged immediately into a specific time, a specific place, a specific situation. However, because this essay will be shaped by the progress of an affair over decades and not by the description of a single incident, there is far less detail and colour in the writing.

'Peter was a popular, good-looking 19-year-old, working at odd jobs before university; I was a shy schoolgirl . . . One day we raced across the hills on his motorbike, falling off about 20 times . . .' Neither character nor incident is developed in any detail, again because this essay is shaped by the outline of a relationship. Both are important, obviously, but each is referred to rather than dwelt on.

'Two years later', 'At 21 I got married', 'In 2000, my marriage ended', 'a couple of years later . . .'. Notice how time is treated in this approach to the narrative personal essay. Entire years, even entire decades, are skipped through.

'Peter was a guest at the wedding. A friend of mine chatted him up and I remember feeling slightly possessive . . .'. Why doesn't the writer mention anything about her own husband? Because the controlling focus of this essay is the relationship between herself and Peter. Nothing else is of relevance. Anything else, even the *name* of the man she married, would be a digression, a distraction. This is an important lesson for you to learn in relation to keeping your material coherent and consistent within a composition. Many, many things are interesting, but if they are not consistent with your chosen approach, they have no business being in your essay.

'If we had married young, we would never have stayed together. We both had a lot to do in our different ways . . . We were always meant to be; we just needed 20 years to explore and grow up. The years ahead are ours.' As noted in the critical reading of Sample 1, the characteristic movement of the personal essay is a broadening out to interpret and reflect on the experiences that have been described. In this sample also, the relationship between incidents and reflections is quite simple: a lengthy, uninterrupted outline of the course of a relationship is followed by a short passage offering interpretation. This is another of the more basic forms of the narrative personal essay available to you: the progress of a relationship through a lifetime. It is easy to handle, but once more, the approach is unlikely to gain you the highest grades.

A note on length: At 793 words this is again 200 words short of the required length of a composition at Leaving Certificate level. More detailed descriptions of characters and selected incidents would solve the problem.

Sample 3

My search for Sophie

Celia Robertson

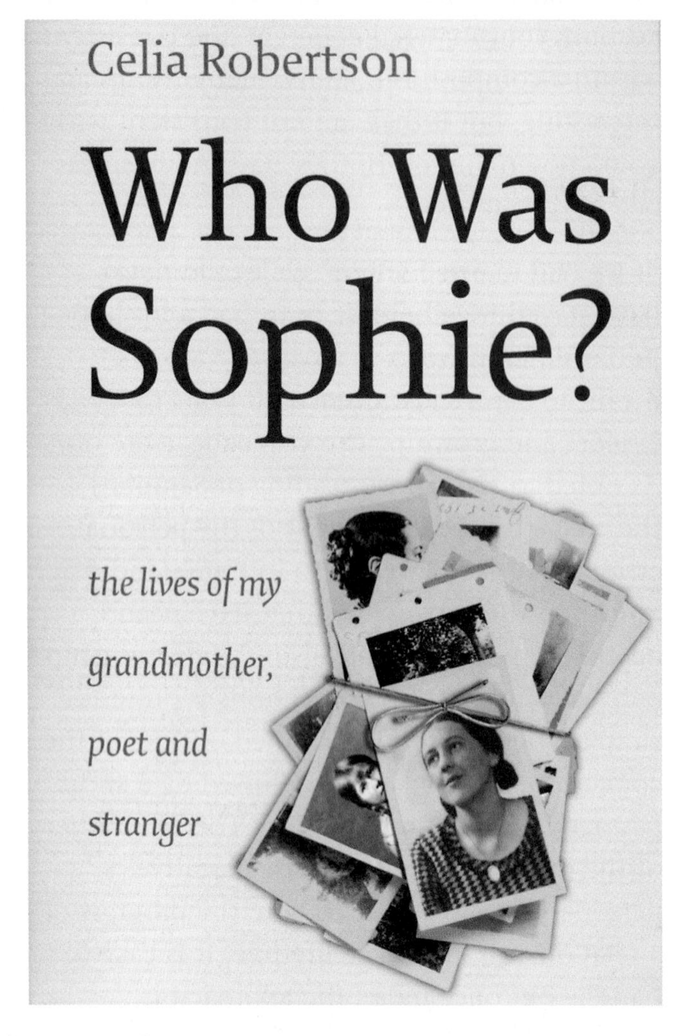

It's 1973. I am swinging on the front gate with my brother, James (me aged six, him four), licking the taste of traffic off the railings. A man walks past and says hello and James tells him that our granny is 'sick in her mind'. Jane, my mother, comes rushing down the stairs to call us indoors.

Sophie was our family secret, like something dark and buzzing kept in a box. Other families did not have mad grandmothers who washed their hair in margarine and cut up their nightgowns. I never told people at school about her, partly because it seemed too complicated to explain and I was sure no one would understand, and partly through a dread of what might happen if I broke the spell. There was another reason, too. In the back of my mind, there was always the fear that I, too, might unravel and spin off into nothing. I did not want to think too much about that.

I first met my grandmother when I was about 17, by which time I was genuinely keen to see her and my mother thought I'd be able to deal with the experience. Sophie was living in a dilapidated council flat and had moved all her belongings into one room. A complicated, web-like arrangement of string snaggled across the windows and was attached to the door with drawing pins. This, she explained, was to catch burglars. She had sprinkled talcum powder on the sills in case intruders got in and left footprints.

She cooked us a cake made of margarine and chocolate in a frying pan and insisted that we filled the kettle very slowly, 'to avoid too much gas coming out of the taps'.

The reality of seeing her was both shocking and a relief; for someone who had loomed so large in my imagination, she was tiny. She came to the door wearing electric pink lipstick, fishnet stockings, complicated shoes that she had made out of cardboard and string, and a nightdress under a coat tied with an old ribbon. She had dyed her hair yellow with turmeric rice and curled it with pipe-cleaners. Despite her disturbing milky eye, she had a dreamy smile that could make her seem suddenly young, and she looked disconcertingly like my mother.

From then on, I would sometimes join my mother on her visits up to Nottingham and, once I had passed my driving test, I would go on my own, or with James, butterflies in my stomach as we headed up the motorway. It was never as bad as I expected. The trick was to live in the moment with her, to walk the tightrope and ignore the drop of her past. If you looked down and recognised the loss, you would go spinning head-first into dizzying sadness.

Because she hadn't always been this person. She was once Joan Adeney Easdale, a teenage girl with two volumes of poetry published by Leonard and Virginia Woolf, reviewed in the national newspapers and invited to tea by Vita Sackville-West. But how had the slightly self-conscious, glossy-haired girl, photographed dancing round a birdbath for the *Book Society News* in 1931, become the old woman who ranted about sex and politics, cut up Christmas presents in case they hid a listening device in the lining, and approached the manager of the local Marks & Spencer with her own hand-stitched prototype for what she called a 'freedom bra'?

Joan was born in 1913. Brought up by her mother, Ellen, she and her older brother, Brian, shared a somewhat bizarre childhood. Ellen was highly strung and self-dramatising, and focused all her energies on the creative imagination of her children. One of her most disturbing theories was that she had conceived Joan through some mysterious process, whereby a poetic being had 'pressed' her in her sleep, inseminating her with the Spirit of Genius. Under Ellen's eagle eye, Joan and Brian spent their evenings inventing games, putting on puppet shows in the sitting room or the garden shed, and giving concerts and dramatic performances to whoever would come along. They were genuinely talented (Brian would go on to win an Oscar for writing the score to Powell and Pressburger's film *The Red Shoes*), but the pressure of constant maternal surveillance did little for their personal development.

When Joan sent a few poems off to the Woolfs in 1930, they were immediately intrigued. Virginia Woolf wrote of her to Hugh Walpole and in his review of Joan's *A Collection of Poems*, published by the Hogarth Press in 1931, Walpole described her work as 'astonishingly adroit, acute, accomplished'. Her second volume, *Clemence and Clare*, was published in 1932.

After this bright beginning, Joan fell in love with my grandfather, Jim Rendel – a young geneticist with a pet chameleon and a passion for ballet – and they married in 1938. She threw herself enthusiastically into her new life, believing that she could combine writing with domesticity. But pressure to be competent at domestic things sat in direct opposition to Joan's desire to write. She had her first baby – my mother – in 1940 and, as the strains of the war took their toll, she struggled to find the space, time and focus for her poetry. Two further children, Polly and Sandy, followed. They shared meals and living space with other scientific families.

Joan became more chaotic and unhappy and finally sought psychiatric help in the late 40s, in the hope that it might save her marriage. Her analyst told her that she should give up writing altogether and concentrate on being a good wife and mother. She took this advice so completely to heart that she burned every piece of work she had ever kept, every diary, notebook and poem, in a big bonfire in 1951.

Then Jim was offered an exciting research post in Australia, and she reluctantly agreed to join him. Her mental health deteriorated quickly. Some days, the children would come home from school to find her still sitting at the uncleared breakfast table where they had left her that morning. She became convinced that there were spies in the roof. She saw Jesus Christ in the living room. It was eventually decided that she would go back to England for a holiday and return to Sydney when she felt stronger. She said goodbye to Jane (then aged 13), Polly (10) and Sandy (six) and caught a plane.

She never came back.

After a few weeks of relative sanity, Joan suffered a full-blown psychotic breakdown in the autumn of 1954 and was admitted to Holloway Sanatorium at Virginia Water, Surrey. She would remain there for several years. Schizophrenia, treatment (drugs and hefty bouts of ECT), loneliness and living in an institution all combined to dismantle the person she had once been.

She missed her children terribly, but gave up on the idea of ever returning to Australia. Jim couldn't cope with her illness and divorced her. By the time she discharged herself in 1961, she no longer wanted anything to do with the past. She attacked her mother and denounced art and culture. By the end of the 60s, she was calling herself Sophie – or Sophia – Curly.

In some ways, it's amazing my grandmother's story didn't end here, but she had a strong instinct for survival. Thus her decision to make Nottingham her home seems to have been both arbitrary and sound; the city absorbed her and for 20 years allowed her to be 'her own person'. She lived to 85.

I can't join all the pieces up, but in writing my version of her several lives, I hope I have shown her to be a remarkable woman.

A critical reading

'It's 1973. I am swinging on the front gate with my brother, James (me aged six, him four), licking the taste of traffic off the railings.' As with Samples 1 and 2, this piece opens on a specific moment in time, in a specific place, in a specific situation. It's an incident that has stuck in the author's mind and has become significant and representative for her. Once more, the opening illustrates the characteristic perspective of the personal essay, which is – as noted in the critical readings of Samples 1 and 2 – looking back on a life that has already been lived, looking back on the past from a position of greater understanding.

'Sophie was our family secret, like something dark and buzzing kept in a box.' Very quickly, the essay broadens into a profile of the author's grandmother. Interpretation is added to the description of events, reflection immediately follows the depiction of incident. Notice how this essay moves smoothly and consistently back and forth between the two styles.

'In the back of my mind, there was always the fear that I, too, might unravel and spin off into nothing. I did not want to think too much about that.' Although this is a profile of the author's grandmother, it is for the moment a personal, not an objective portrait; a profile of Sophie *as experienced by the writer*. Since the author was a child or a girl at the time, this gives rise to a sense of wonder, mingled with anxiety, ultimately leading to the question: What was she *really* like, this grandmother of mine? In turn, this leads to the second part of the essay, a more objective portrait of Sophie.

'Because she hadn't always been this person. She was once Joan Adeney Easdale, a teenage girl with two volumes of poetry published . . .'. Here, the essay moves from personal experiences of the grandmother – the woman that *I* knew, the strange person that *I* encountered, with my limited perspective – to a more objective profile. And so it continues from there, into a biographical sketch of Sophie *without* the presence and perspective of the author. It is, obviously, drifting into slightly dangerous territory for the personal essayist. Although the grandmother is a close relative and therefore the material will always remain personalised, nonetheless the style, the approach, is becoming increasingly impersonal, something the Chief Examiner's Report in 2005 cautioned against with the observation, 'Examiners noted that some candidates demonstrated confusion between the genre of the personal essay and the third person narrative.'

'I can't join all the pieces up, but in writing my version of her several lives, I hope I have shown her to be a remarkable woman.' As noted in the critical readings of Samples 1 and 2, the characteristic movement of the personal essay is a broadening out to interpret and reflect on the experiences that have been described. 'My Search for Sophie', which is the profile of a character very close to the author, a biographical approach to the personal essay, is an attractive alternative to the other two narrative samples. Firstly, it combines incident and reflection much more smoothly and consistently than either of the other two and it doesn't wait until the final paragraph to broaden into interpretation. Secondly, its structure is far more sophisticated. It opens impressively on a single incident, expands into a personalised profile of the subject, further expands into a more rounded, objective portrait, and finally gathers everything neatly back together in the concluding paragraphs.

A note on length: At 1,280 words this may be a little longer than you can comfortably manage in the examination. The obvious place to trim is within the objective profile of Sophie.

The key elements of a successful narrative personal essay

1. As with the Short Story, the *opening should plunge the reader into the heart of an incident*, rather than provide informative or explanatory material. The function of an effective opening is to engage the reader's interest in the characters, the situation and the topic.

2. *The time-frame of a narrative personal essay may be very brief*, as in Sample 1, *or quite stretched*, as in Samples 2 and 3. The management of time is controlled by your choice of approach. Your focus must be on something clear and specific: an incident (Sample 1), a relationship (Sample 2) or an individual (Sample 3). Each works very well, but mixing them does not.

3. Like fictional characters, *real people should be revealed through dialogue, appearance, behaviour and reflections, although the personal essayist has the added advantage of discussion and interpretation in the presentation of all characters, including the character of the essayist themselves*. This is because the personal essay does not watch people stumbling through life in real time. It looks back, with greater understanding, on a time now past and on incidents long completed.

4. *The narrative should provide a consistent and comprehensive exploration of the given topic.* The potential problem with a story is that it may be too narrow an illustration of a theme. This makes the narrative approach to the personal essay slightly more risky than the discursive approach. Please understand that you must provide a first-person narrative. There is no other perspective from which to write a narrative personal essay. As observed in the Chief Examiner's Report in 2005, third-person narratives are not appropriate and risk heavy penalties.

5. The ending of a good narrative personal essay should broaden out to reflect on the significance and the impact of the events that have been described. Without this reflective dimension, your narrative risks becoming merely a tale that no one can quite see the point of.

Sample 4

Being obese made me a social outcast

Madeleine White

We were on the ferry, returning from a break in Ireland, queuing for food. When I saw my husband's fish and chips, I decided I fancied some, too. But instead of the generous portion Evan received, I got a handful of chips and a piece of fish half the size. I didn't put the plate on my tray because I assumed the man at the counter hadn't finished dishing up. But instead of supplementing my chips, he told me, in an 'all mates together' kind of way, that I shouldn't expect any more, as, by the looks of things, I'd had quite enough already. As those waiting to be served looked on with interest, I stood rooted to the spot, red-faced and deeply humiliated.

Today, I'm 38, 5ft 8in and weigh around 11 stone. I run 15 miles a week, as well as ride, swim and cycle, and I watch what I eat. But seven and a half years ago, things were different. I weighed around 21 stone and was barely able to get up stairs. I felt ill most of the time and the effort of heaving my bulk around and trying to catch my breath made normal activities a test of endurance.

I had battled with my weight – and the ensuing eating disorders – since my teens. However, it was only after meeting Evan at 21 that obesity started strangling my life. I'd had a contraceptive injection that, while protecting me from unwanted pregnancy, had the side-effect of helping me gain seven stone in 18 months. I won't pretend I didn't overeat, but the effect was to turn me from a normal young woman into a non-person.

Assistants on beauty counters would tell me that, although the product was designed to be toning, on my surfeit of flesh it would be a waste of time. Prospective employers, delighted by my CV and enthusiastic on the phone, would in person eye the straining buttons on my size 24 dress and say they didn't think I fitted the company culture.

When I went to the doctor with chronic pain in my shoulder, rosacea, eczema and bouts of nausea and vomiting – clear symptoms of a diseased gall bladder – my GP simply Googled the nearest Weight Watchers class and gave me the time and date of the next meeting.

The sad thing was that I believed I deserved it all. I regarded being obese as a sign of personal failure.

However, the mockery and dismissals didn't help with my dieting. What they did was feed an ever-growing obsession with food. The less a member of society I felt, the more I stuffed into myself. I was no longer validated as Madeleine, so I used the process of foraging for food in bins, and eating it behind locked doors or in toilets, in order to exist.

It wasn't all bad, of course. I did eventually

get a job and, in 1994, I got married, but overridingly the memories of these years are dark. After having my second child, my self-esteem had sunk so low that I felt unable to return to work.

The tone of the government's new Healthy Weight, Healthy Lives strategy smacks of explaining something very simple to a slightly backward child. What it ignores is that most obese people have already tried and failed any number of diets, and know only too well what the extra weight they are carrying means for their health and personal lives.

Obesity is not the result of a lack of information or self-control; it stems from not valuing sufficiently yourself and the food you eat. Turning overweight people into national whipping boys will only drive further into the biscuit barrel those who already have little self-confidence.

It was after dieting unsuccessfully for several months that I came across an article about the gastric bypass operation. Despite evidence that morbid obesity is almost untreatable without surgery, the NHS was not prepared to fund this life-saving operation, so I remortgaged our house and paid the £8,000 myself.

It's amazing what losing 10 stones can do. Within a year I went from comic curiosity to real person again. I started an exercise regime and, as my skin and muscle tone improved, so did my confidence. Surgery had revealed the undiagnosed problem with my gall bladder and I won compensation from my health insurer for the treatment I received. I took on a senior role at work and, in 2005, started my own PR agency.

What I've achieved in the past few years shows I've always had drive, determination and self-discipline. It's just that in a society that excludes on the basis of body fat, none of that was recognised.

A critical reading

'We were on the ferry, returning from a break in Ireland, queuing for food.' Although this discursive essay deals quite explicitly with the theme of obesity, it begins, as all personal essays should, in a specific moment in time, with a specific incident. The anecdote lasts for the opening paragraph and, although treated in some detail, does not extend beyond that. As in all discussions, it does not exist merely for its own sake, but is used as a lead-in to a more general treatment of a topic.

'. . . seven and a half years ago, things were different. I weighed around 21 stone'. The essay immediately broadens into a profile of the author as she was then, demonstrating once again that the opening anecdote functions only as a specific illustration of a general point and that the characteristic perspective of the personal essay is one of looking backwards on a life that has already been lived, looking back on the past from a position of greater understanding. In this case, the profile extends over two paragraphs.

'Assistants on beauty counters', 'Prospective employers', 'When I went to the doctor'. Having completed the profile of herself as she was then, the author illustrates her point by applying it to three areas of her personal life: shopping, work and health. Each is mentioned only in passing and none is developed in any detail. Nonetheless, the passages demonstrate the correct technique.

'It wasn't all bad, of course. I did eventually get a job'. The author returns to complete the personal profile after the various illustrations.

'The tone of the government's new Healthy Weight, Healthy Lives strategy smacks of explaining something very simple to a slightly backward child.' Something very interesting now happens in this essay. Up to this, obesity has been treated as a personal issue. Now for two paragraphs the essay expands a little bit more to treat obesity as a social issue; as an issue impacting not only on the writer, but on many other lives, an issue ultimately of concern to everybody.

'It was after dieting unsuccessfully for several months that I came across an article about the gastric bypass operation.' The treatment of obesity as a social topic having been completed, the essay returns to the personal story. The backbone of any personal essay is the profile of the individual and no author can risk staying away from it for very long.

'What I've achieved in the past few years shows I've always had drive, determination and self-discipline. It's just that in a society that excludes on the basis of body fat, none of that was recognised.' A brief concluding paragraph, but characteristic again of the personal essay. What have I learned? Looking back on it all now, what impact has it had on my life? How has it all changed my life? The final paragraph contains the point the author wishes to make. Although she is writing a personal profile, she does have a point of view that she fervently wants to express and to share. However, you will note that the point is made in the concluding paragraph and is not part of the introduction. It is what the essay develops *towards*; the expression of that opinion.

'We were on the ferry, returning from a break in Ireland', 'in a society that excludes on the basis of body fat, none of that was recognised.' See how the essay develops from a specific point in time to an abstract moral point, without ever losing touch with the personal? This is the most sophisticated of all the personal essay samples and the approach that is most likely to gain the highest grades. Structurally, it is far more complex and satisfying, opening on a relevant anecdote, developing a personal profile from this, applying that profile to three areas of personal life, expanding the scope of the treatment to consider the topic as a social issue, completing the personal story, and gathering everything together in a concluding paragraph that returns to the opening anecdote. Purely in terms of content, it's far more varied and impressive than any of the other samples. And finally, because it displays all the skills in the use of language that you're supposed to be studying at Leaving Certificate level – narrative and descriptive, informative and argumentative and persuasive – it's also going to score highly in terms of 'Efficiency of language use'. So, this – taking an issue and examining it in relation to your own and other people's experiences – is the recommended approach for those of you who are hoping to get an A grade for your Personal Essay.

A note on length: At 793 words, this is 200 words short of the required length for a Leaving Certificate composition. By devoting a separate paragraph to the difficulties caused by obesity in each of the personal areas that the author merely refers to – shopping, work and health – the piece would be vastly improved, not only in terms of length, but with regard to content and structure also.

Key elements of a successful discursive personal essay

1. *The opening should plunge the reader into the heart of an incident,* which will be used as a specific illustration to introduce a personal point of view on the given topic. At this stage, informative and explanatory material should be avoided. Regardless of whether the approach is narrative or discursive, the function of an effective opening is to engage the reader's interest.
2. The second paragraph, organically developed from the opening anecdote, should be used to *express and explain the writer's point of view on the given topic.*
3. *That point should then be applied in detail to two or three of the layers of your personal life,* which are the same for everybody, really; namely, family, friends and socialising, romantic relationships, education, career, sport, politics and social affairs, entertainment, hobbies, habits, possessions.
4. Whether employing narrative, argumentative or informative techniques, *the style throughout should be intimate and confidential,* since it is not otherwise possible to be personal.
5. The ending should return to recycle or complete the opening anecdote and to re-state the writer's point of view on the given topic.

Using the key elements to plan a discursive personal essay

When planning a discursive personal essay, you should organise the material in the centre of the essay first and only then turn to the introductory anecdote. Otherwise, you do not know what you're introducing. The story at the beginning has to lead into the first of the central sections.

For example, '"Image is everything in today's world." Write a Personal Essay using the above quotation as your title.'

Firstly, I decide what layers of my personal life I'm going to apply this topic to, I decide in what order I'm going to treat these and I outline my approach to each:

- **Part One: Sport.** How important is image in sport? Very important in marketing, but not at all important in performance. Personal stories to illustrate this.
- **Part Two: Romantic relationships.** How important is image in romantic relationships? Maybe important in the beginning, not much afterwards. Personal stories to illustrate this.
- **Part Three: Family.** How important is image to the family? Not at all important within the family itself, but maybe parents worry about how the family is perceived from outside. Personal stories to illustrate this.

Secondly, I consider my opening anecdote, which now has to be sport-related, since it must lead naturally into my opening section on the importance of image in sport:

- **Introduction:** What's the most memorable sports story I can recall about someone posing? I want it to illustrate the point I'm about to make, that image loses its relevance when it comes to performance.

And finally, I consider the ending, which must be a summary, in one form or another, of everything that has gone before.

- **Conclusion:** The quotation I was given was, 'Image is everything in today's world.' Based on what I've provided, what is my final response to this? That image may be important in every area of life, but that it certainly isn't *everything* in any of them.

Class assignment

Using the guidelines already introduced, write a short critical analysis of the following discursive personal essay, written in response to composition No. 1 on the 2006 Leaving Certificate paper: '"Let's stop all this pretence! Let's tell each other the unvarnished truth for a change!" (Text 3) Write a personal essay in response to the above statement.'

Sample 5

Let's tell each other the unvarnished truth for a change!

Although I would never admit it to the wife, I am now, and have been for some time, an unhappily married man. I accept, of course, that there is nothing particularly unique about my troubles. Millions of deluded fools have wandered into the same cul-de-sac long before I did. But still . . .

It doesn't help to realise that there was a time when I might've ended up with a different mother-in-law. Her name was Mrs Cynthia Catterstairs, a lonely, disappointed, middle-class widow, whose only daughter, Ruth, was on the point of abandoning her studies in university in order to marry a bricklayer and devote her life to bearing his children. 'I don't like him,' Mrs Catterstairs confided in me when the engagement was announced. 'He can't look you in the face, you know, when he's talking to you. Unlike yourself. I don't suppose you get on with him, either.'

Should I have told her the truth? Should I have told her that she was lonely and depressed after her husband's death, that she was terrified of losing her daughter and being abandoned, that she had always considered Ruth too good for anyone less than a god, that she looked down on manual labourers, that in reality she was a snob? Don't ask what good it would have done. Ask instead if my description of it as the 'truth' is at all accurate. Mrs Catterstairs was all of these things that I've mentioned, but she was also a resilient and independent woman, a survivor, a selfless mother, a tireless volunteer who dedicated much of her spare time to helping the underprivileged. In other words, like the rest of us, a complex mass of contradictions.

So the issue is hardly whether or not to tell the truth. Mrs Catterstairs was right. Ruth's future husband never did look you in the eye when he was talking to you. And Mrs Catterstairs was wrong. I rather liked the guy. The issue, really, is the sheer *impossibility* of telling the truth, which is so vast, so complicated, and so fluid – changing from one moment to the next – that it simply can't be contained by language. Telling the truth is not an option, you see. Even *knowing* the truth is not really an option.

As an example, let's take a closer look at this whole area of body language and facial expression that Mrs Catterstairs was so hung up about. She had convinced herself that her future son-in-law was shifty and spineless, because – and this *is* the truth – he couldn't stand the sight of her, couldn't bear looking at her. She had also persuaded herself that, by contrast, I was honest and open, simply because I found her very beautiful – she was only about forty-two at this stage, and I couldn't take my eyes off her. (I never told her that, either, by the way. Another 'unvarnished' truth that lay buried for years.)

But let's be honest. Don't we all, to some extent, share in the conviction that those who look us straight in the eye are sincere and trustworthy? Don't we have the considerable authority of the CIA and the FBI to support our view? Criminals, the cops and the cops-and-robbers serials on television keep reminding us, are shifty and unable to maintain eye contact. And who would suggest that the CIA would manufacture evidence simply to mislead the rest of us? Well, the Iraqis, of course, and the Iranians, and the Venezuelans, and the Russians, and the Chinese, and the Afghans . . . but nobody you can really trust. In any case, we have an even more popular authority on our side in this argument. Writing about the plainclothes detectives in the newly reformed London Metropolitan Police Force in the late nineteenth century, Charles Dickens said of them admiringly, 'they all can, and they all do, look full at whomsoever they speak to'. The implication, of course, was that they were therefore frank, upright and truthful.

We have other pointers to character, each one as foolproof and as indispensable as the other. We all know people who reluctantly offer us a dead hand when introduced and who then leave it hanging there limply like a dead fish. We accept that this is a sign of coldness, perhaps of sneakiness, just as we accept that the complete stranger who crushes our knuckles and dislocates our shoulder while pumping our hand in hearty greeting is open and warm and sincere. And whatever about the *medical* benefits of an erect posture, morally it still characterises the upright

individual. Dickens, on the Metropolitan Police Force again, said of them that they were all men of good deportment and unusual intelligence, never lounging or slinking about. Not contemporary teenagers, in other words.

It will hardly come as a surprise to anyone that these quotations are from a Victorian. They seem to have started this business of being uncomfortable with the complexities of truth, of searching desperately for a truth that's plain and simple, that's 'unvarnished', in other words. We have only inherited their uneasiness. They, too, liked to reduce life to simplicity with labels, with one set of gestures, like the warm handshake, expressing honesty, and another, like the sneer, expressing deception. Like ourselves, they were very fond of comparisons with animals. Dogs, as we all know, wag their tails only when they're being friendly. Birds have one signal for danger and another for mating, and never confuse the two. If only humans were that straightforward! If only mating and danger were that distinct from each other! A once noted psychologist, B. F. Skinner, actually wasted his entire life drawing conclusions about men's activities by studying the behaviour of albino rats that he'd locked in cages. But we all know, in our hearts, that the comparisons don't hold. If humans had tails, some would undoubtedly wag them while they were preparing to bite you. And no ornithologist has yet come across a complete messer of a bird who gave a warning signal to his own species just for the heck of it when there was no danger, unlike the boy in the fairy tale who kept crying wolf.

We're liars, aren't we? Natural born liars. For our own purposes, we mislead each other, not only by words, but by gestures, by facial expressions, even by postures. We desperately want to believe, of course, that appearances can be trusted. Not always trusted. Not automatically trusted. But 'oft', as Polonius says in Shakespeare's *Hamlet*, when he is praising what we now refer to as power dressing: 'For the apparel oft proclaims the man.' And the 'ofter' the better, obviously. How else can we live without driving ourselves crazy with cynicism? We even have a recurring ritual to express and sustain our eternal optimism. No, it's not marriage, despite my earlier confession. It's this . . . Once every four years or so hordes of well-dressed men and women descend on the rest of us with outrageous promises. They look us steadily in the eye. They shake our hands vigorously. And you'll never catch them lounging or slinking about. They're called politicians, they control a large part of our lives, and they're voted into power by the rest of us. But what chance would they have of getting elected if they told us nothing but the truth?

No. As Algernon in Oscar Wilde's *The Importance of Being Earnest* pointed out, 'The truth is rarely pure and never simple. Modern life would be very tedious if it were either, and modern literature a complete impossibility.' There's no such thing as 'the unvarnished truth'. It doesn't exist, I'm afraid. And encouraging us to pretend to something that doesn't exist is encouraging us to tell a lie.

As for Mrs Catterstairs . . . The last time I saw her, a few years ago, she was a nervous grandmother. 'Ruth's little boy,' she complained to me. 'He stares at me all the time, without even blinking. It makes me very uneasy. I wish he wouldn't do it.'

Homework and tasks

Preparing yourself for writing the personal essay

If you are strongly considering the Personal Essay as your composition option, you should now decide on which approach suits you better, the narrative or the discursive. Your choice will allow you to prepare relevant material. For example, without composing a full-length essay, you could write descriptions of several significant events in your life. You could also outline the progress of several significant relationships in your life or sketch the biographies of some interesting people close to you. Finally, you could set down your views on some issues that touch you personally and indicate what stories you might use to illustrate your views. Not all of this material will suit every composition title, but I guarantee you that you will use a good deal of it in your Leaving Certificate Personal Essay.

Assessment sheet – Composition 1

'. . . the idealism and tangled passions that raged in my teenage heart.' Write a personal essay on the idealism and passions of youth.

<table>
<tr>
<td>P</td>
<td>The title invites reflections or a story, either serious or humorous, illustrating the passionate idealism/idealistic passions of young people, exploring their dreams of a better world, their optimism, their dedication to causes. In a discursive treatment, you are expected to clearly present your own interpretation and to provide a generous number of ideas and illustrations with reference to your chosen interpretation. In a narrative treatment, while you are free to create whatever relevant material you like, nevertheless you cannot expect a high grade unless your narrative treats a personal situation of some substance and significance and depth.
<table>
<tr><td></td><td>You offer a variety of relevant, interesting discursive material and score highly with regard to content.</td></tr>
<tr><td></td><td>The discursive material is decent, but not of the highest standard.</td></tr>
<tr><td></td><td>You fail to provide sufficient discursive material that is relevant to this topic and you lose marks for poor content.</td></tr>
<tr><td></td><td>Your narrative is an interesting exploration of the topic and therefore you score highly with regard to content.</td></tr>
<tr><td></td><td>Your narrative is an exploration of the topic, although it doesn't cover quite enough relevant ground, and you score only reasonably on content.</td></tr>
<tr><td></td><td>I'm not convinced that your narrative properly illustrates this topic. For that reason, you lose marks for poor content.</td></tr>
</table>
</td>
<td>0–2=NG
3–7=F
8–11=E
12–16=D
17–20=C
21–25=B
26–30=A

/30</td>
</tr>
<tr>
<td>C</td>
<td>You are expected to provide an engaging and relevant opening, a coherent development of the topic, and an ending that offers your final reflections on the issue or on your experiences.
<table>
<tr><td></td><td>The opening is strong and effectively draws the reader into your essay.</td></tr>
<tr><td></td><td>The opening is weak and fails to engage the reader.</td></tr>
<tr><td></td><td>A nice, fluid movement between anecdotes and your reflections, and between different aspects of the topic, so a well organised discursive personal essay.</td></tr>
</table>
</td>
<td>0–2=NG
3–7=F
8–11=E
12–16=D
17–20=C
21–25=B
26–30=A</td>
</tr>
</table>

	You have structural problems in managing a *discursive* approach. Excellent *narrative* shape. Reasonable *narrative* shape. Poor *narrative* shape. The ending is strong and effective. The ending is weak and fails.	/30
L	The style of the personal essay should be intimate and confidential. You succeed in striking and maintaining the appropriate tone. The style of the personal essay should be intimate and confidential. You fail to strike and maintain the appropriate tone. It is not permitted to write a *narrative* personal essay as a third person narrative. Good written expression. There are examples of careless, thoughtless, sloppy or otherwise poor writing and the standard of your expression is a cause for concern.	0–2=NG 3–7=F 8–11=E 12–16=D 17–20=C 21–25=B 26–30=A /30
M	No problems with spelling and grammar. Problems with spelling. Problems with grammar.	4–5=D 6–7=C 8=B 9–10=A /10
Total		/100

Assessment sheet – Composition 2

'"I guarantee . . . he will reply in a tongue you simply will not understand." Write a personal essay about the problems one can have when communicating.'

P	The title invites reflections or a story, either serious or humorous, illustrating the problems of communicating, with parents, friends, lovers, officials, foreigners, etc. In a discursive treatment, you are expected to clearly present your own ideas on the causes and consequences of such problems in a number of scenarios and to provide a generous amount of illustrations. In a narrative treatment, while you are free to create whatever relevant material you like, nevertheless you cannot expect a high grade unless your narrative treats a personal situation of some substance and significance and depth.	0–2=NG 3–7=F 8–11=E 12–16=D 17–20=C 21–25=B 26–30=A
	You offer a variety of relevant, interesting *discursive* material and score highly with regard to content.	
	The *discursive* material is decent, but not of the highest standard.	
	You fail to provide sufficient *discursive* material that is relevant to this topic and you lose marks for poor content.	
	Your *narrative* is an interesting exploration of the topic and therefore you score highly with regard to content.	
	Your *narrative* is an exploration of the topic, although it doesn't cover quite enough relevant ground, and you score only reasonably on content.	
	I'm not convinced that your *narrative* properly illustrates this topic. For that reason, you lose marks for poor content.	/30
C	You are expected to provide an engaging and relevant opening, a coherent development of the topic, and an ending that offers your final reflections on the issue or on your experiences.	0–2=NG 3–7=F 8–11=E 12–16=D 17–20=C 21–25=B 26–30=A
	The opening is strong and effectively draws the reader into your essay.	
	The opening is weak and fails to engage the reader.	
	A nice, fluid movement between anecdotes and your reflections, and between different aspects of the topic, so a well organised discursive personal essay.	

		You have structural problems in managing a *discursive* approach.	
		Excellent *narrative* shape.	
		Reasonable *narrative* shape.	
		Poor *narrative* shape.	
		The ending is strong and effective.	
		The ending is weak and fails.	/30
L		The style of the personal essay should be intimate and confidential. You succeed in striking and maintaining the appropriate tone.	0–2=NG 3–7=F 8–11=E 12–16=D 17–20=C 21–25=B 26–30=A
		The style of the personal essay should be intimate and confidential. You fail to strike and maintain the appropriate tone.	
		It is not permitted to write a *narrative* personal essay as a third person narrative.	
		Good written expression.	
		There are examples of careless, thoughtless, sloppy or otherwise poor writing and the standard of your expression is a cause for concern.	/30
M		No problems with spelling and grammar.	4–5=D 6–7=C 8=B 9–10=A
		Problems with spelling.	
		Problems with grammar.	/10
Total			/100

Chapter Eight:

Writing the Composition: The Discussion Essay

Introduction

For 100 marks, you are asked to write a discussion on a given topic. What is a discussion? Well, any composition that does not identify itself as either a Short Story or a Personal Essay is treated here as a Discussion Essay.

Unlike the other two genres, the discussion always implies a *public* audience. This may be the readers of a newspaper or magazine, as in 2008, 1: 'Write a magazine article (serious and/or light-hearted) in which you give advice to adults on how to help teenagers cope with the "storm and stress" of adolescence' and 2008, 6: 'Write an article for a school magazine in which you explore aspects of life that make you happy.' Or it may be a live audience sitting in front of you as you speak, as in 2008, 2: 'Write a speech in which you argue for or against the necessity to protect national culture and identity' and 2008, 5: 'Write the text of a talk you would deliver to your classmates on the topic: Appearances can be deceptive.' Awareness of audience is therefore vitally important while writing the discussion, something that was repeatedly stressed in the Chief Examiner's Report in 2005: 'A good sense of audience was often achieved and many candidates seemed to enjoy this task and demonstrated a keen awareness of audience.'

The presence of a *public* audience influences both the type of material you use and the manner in which you present it, something that was again stressed in the Chief Examiner's Report of 2005 when it observed approvingly that 'Rhetorical elements and persuasive techniques were features of many attempts.' Some topics, such as 'the necessity to protect national culture and identity', require well-informed views and factual evidence. Other topics, such as 'How to help teenagers cope with the "storm and stress" of adolescence' and 'Appearances can be deceptive', require no more than general knowledge. A few topics, such as 'aspects of life that make you happy', which is very close to the discursive personal essay treated in the previous chapter, can rely on personal experience. However, because you are always addressing a public audience, regardless of the topic, you must master the literary devices used in public debate and in the public expression of opinion and you must learn how to shape a discussion for maximum effect.

Sample 1 illustrates all these requirements.

Sample 1

Worshipping at a new altar

Joe Humphreys

On February 13th, 80 million Pakistanis were getting ready to vote in their country's parliamentary elections, 60,000 families were confirmed to have been affected by major flooding in Bolivia, and roughly 26,500 children died of preventable diseases in the developing world (as they do every day, according to UN estimates).

Oh, and a 68-year-old Italian working for a professional football club in Austria was named manager of the Irish soccer team.

Needless to say, only one of these stories made the front pages of our national newspapers (including this one) the next day. And only one drew extensive comment from a western head of government. Within minutes of news breaking of Giovanni Trapattoni's appointment, Bertie Ahern was on RTÉ Radio's *Drivetime*, speaking with a rare sense of purpose.

'Okay, the Austrian league may not be Europe's strongest league, but still it's a formidable league and with Red Bull in Salzburg up to last season he did very well . . . He was with AC for over a decade – a long time ago, admittedly. He was a defensive midfielder, always known – that I recall – in his European days is that his teams mightn't get many goals but you sure didn't get many past him.' So the Taoiseach continued for seven (yes, I counted them) minutes, going on to accurately rattle off the win-lose-draw stats of 'Stevie' (as Ahern insisted on calling him) Staunton, and conveying an intimate knowledge of the Republic of Ireland's Group Eight opponents in the 2010 Fifa World Cup qualifying tournament. 'I have to say, we have to be realistic. If anyone thinks that Georgia, or Montenegro, or Bulgaria, or Cyprus – again – or any of these matches, are going to be easy matches, I tell you they won't. We are in a tough group, of course not to mention Italy . . .'

It is hard to think of an occasion down the years where Mr Ahern spoke with more verve and conviction. Just where does he get the time to keep up with developments in the Austrian Bundesliga? By so playing up his sporting credentials, the Taoiseach was following a long political tradition. Since the dawn of mass-spectator sports, political leaders from Benito Mussolini to Kim Jong-Il have sought to exploit public fervour surrounding popular games for their benefit. Adolf Hitler used the 1936 Olympics to rehabilitate his public image.

Thaksin Shinawatra bought Manchester City last year to boost his chances of regaining power in his native Thailand. George W. Bush cultivated an 'Ordinary Joe' persona by religiously watching *Monday Night Football* on ESPN (occasionally while eating/choking on pretzels). And, during his term of office as British prime minister, Tony Blair hammed up his 'common man' credentials by advertising his love for Newcastle FC – once memorably as a panellist on the BBC's *Football Focus* (not unlike the Taoiseach, who once showed up on RTÉ's *The Premiership*).

Atheist philosopher Richard Dawkins has argued – with a hint of despair – that someone who doesn't believe in God has little chance nowadays of being elected to high office.
But what of someone who doesn't support a

Premier League team? Or, God forbid, someone who fails to possess a set of golf clubs? The comparison here between sport and religion is deliberate – sport is increasingly resembling a faith-based system of worship. This is especially true in Ireland, where the sports bar has largely replaced the sacristy, and the post-match analyst the priest.

Since the late 1980s, Mass attendances in 'Catholic' Ireland have been decreasing almost in direct proportion to the rising demand for Dubs tickets. In 2005, a World Cup qualifying game between the Republic of Ireland and Switzerland attracted almost twice as many Irish viewers as the Pope's funeral. Is no one else shocked by the €1.35 billion price-tag recently put on Setanta Sports? It must be worth more now than RTÉ. Global figures indicate that one in five people watched some of the last Fifa World Cup – which means football alone has more recorded followers than either Christianity or Islam today.

As well as muscling in on traditional worshipping patterns, sport is increasingly appropriating the language of religion. Without irony, athletes are spoken of as gods, and golf shots as miracles. The Olympics, and other such international sporting events, are imbued with a supposed power to unite the peoples of the earth, and bring peace and harmony and goodwill, in a way only the man above used to be able to do.

'What is soccer if not everything that religion should be,' wrote one sports journalist on the eve of the 2006 Fifa World Cup. Rhetoric like this is as commonplace today as grace-before-meal was 20 years ago.

The truth is, there is little to celebrate in sport. And I say this as someone who strongly held the faith for many years. I've spent some of my formative days in dimly lit snooker halls, and some of my happiest ones on a river, rowing for my college team. I retain sporting moments that mark out the chapters of my life better than any biography, from a school sports-day relay medal (courtesy of a courageous last leg in the 4x50m) to a photo of myself standing next to the Red Rum statue at Aintree, which was taken by my late father during a precious bonding trip to the races.

I know, in other words, that sport can be great fun. It can bring people together and even give meaning to people's lives. But is it especially equipped to do so? And are those lives that depend on sport full or satisfying ones? The main problem with sport is that it is sustained by a series of myths, including the legend that sport was born of Corinthian purity and has since been sullied by 'unsporting' professionalism (a theory that is quickly debunked when you compare the levels of violence, and especially the frequency of punch-ups, in rugby and soccer during the amateur era compared to the present one).

Perhaps the greatest myth in sport is that it 'builds character', turning waifs and delinquents into pillars of society. This theory is sustained by countless anecdotes of the 'sport made me a man' variety. But research in the area shows that competitive game-playing is actually bad for your morals, not good. In the words of pioneering sports psychologists Brenda Jo Bredemeier and David L. Shields, serious sport creates 'lower level moral reasoning in both sport and life'.

But don't just take their word for it. Nor indeed mine. 'It's a fairly mythical idea that sport develops traditional virtues like fair play, social cohesion, and respect for opponents,' says Prof.

Aidan Moran, a leading Irish sports psychologist and an occasional mind-coach to golfer Padraig Harrington. 'Even in amateur sports, we can give lots of examples of cheating, distortion of the rules and disrespect.' Prof. Moran argues that sport can only play a role in character development if it is accompanied by a rigorous process of self-examination, or philosophical and moral instruction. He suggests parents in particular have unrealistic expectations about the value of sport, believing 'something magical happens in between the time [their children] are dropped off and collected from training'.

A further myth relating to sport is that it is somehow helping to ease conflict or 'break down barriers' between different people. The International Olympic Committee is partly responsible for sustaining this myth, proclaiming its role to be one of 'helping to build a peaceful and better world'. The world footballing body Fifa similarly claims to be 'making the world a better place through football'.

In truth, sporting fervour has triggered more conflicts than it has ended. Sport has sometimes directly caused bloodshed, and frequently acted as a safe haven for forms of intolerance and hatred long since dispatched from other realms of society. In fact, it could be argued that sport is a last refuge for racism, sexism, homophobia, animal cruelty, and perhaps bad language too.

It is also a refuge for stupidity, the sort of unashamed, primeval stupidity that sees grown men dancing around in silly costumes and falling down drunk. (I should know, I have done it myself on occasion.)

Worst of all, perhaps, is sport's propensity to distract us from the things that really matter. A bit of escapism is fine. Even taoisigh are entitled to some time out. But, judging by the way in which sport – and especially spectator sport – has become so ubiquitous, you have to wonder whether we have escaped reality altogether.

Ironically, one of the few organisations in the State to question our addiction to sport has been the Catholic Church. Conscious of the growing competition for hearts and minds on the Sabbath, Catholic bishops recently urged the GAA to reschedule Sunday matches and training to avoid clashes with religious services. The public response was entirely predictable: some gentle coughing and then back to business as usual.

Where, indeed, can one find serious reflection about sport? Hardly within the ranks of sporting pundits. TV 'analysts' and other professional commentators, with a few rare exceptions, tend to trade in platitudes. Most of them misleadingly depict phenomena such as doping, greed and excessive violence as aberrations in high-level sport whereas, in fact, they are inherent to it.

The result is that we have difficulty seeing the wood for the trees. We think it is great, for example, that 20,000 people turn up to watch a schools rugby match in Donnybrook. Great? It is completely obscene to have such a mob screaming and yelping at a bunch of kids. Let's face it, schools sport – at a competitive level – is mainly about parents living out their fantasies through their children.

We also fail to ask just what it is we trade off for the time we spend watching, talking about, gambling upon or otherwise engaging in sport. We fail to ask, for example, whether there is any downside to the proliferation of what Umberto Eco calls 'sports chatter'? Eco, a

native of sports-mad Italy, certainly has his concerns, suggesting that talking about sport is a way of feigning engagement with politics.

Addressing the typical fan, he says: 'Instead of judging the job done by the minister of finance (for which you have to know about economics, among other things), you discuss the job done by the coach; instead of criticising the record of parliament you criticise the record of athletes . . .'

Which brings us back to the Taoiseach, media hysteria over the Trapattoni appointment, and the way in which sport is generally encroaching further and further on the public consciousness.

Sport, like any religion, has the potential to make the world a better place – but perhaps only if we stop taking it so seriously.

From *Foul Play: What's Wrong With Sport* by Joe Humphreys, published by Icon Books.

Courtesy of The Irish Times

A critical reading

'On February 13th . . .'. An anecdotal opening. That is, the article begins, not with a statement of the author's opinion, but with the description of specific events on a specific day. Two things to note. This is a compound anecdote, referring to a number of separate things that happened on a particular day. And it's a news item, using something reported in the news, something currently occupying people's attention. This is an example of factual evidence, of material in the public domain, that can be independently checked and verified. In a serious discussion, it is obviously much more impressive than the personal anecdote, which may well illustrate a point, but can never prove it.

'Oh, and a 68-year-old Italian . . .'. Note the ironic, slightly derisive tone, which is introduced early and maintained throughout the article. Humour is one of the weapons that the discussion essayist must master. Properly used, it makes your own position more appealing and simultaneously mocks the opposition.

'We are in a tough group, of course, not to mention Italy'. This is the end of the extensive opening anecdote, which recounts in some detail the relevant events that happened on a particular day. Now, an extremely important observation. In a discussion essay, stories are not told for the information of the audience; stories are not told for the entertainment of the audience; stories are told to make a point. And there are two aspects to the development of a point.

'It is hard to think of an occasion down the years when Mr Ahern spoke with more verve and conviction.' Firstly, the author provides an interpretation of the opening anecdote, stepping back from the description and offering his reflections on it, his considered views on it. He is no longer telling the story, but explaining *why* he has told it.

'Just where does he get the time to keep up with developments in the Austrian Bundesliga?' A rhetorical question, and the first of many in this article. Along with satirical humour, the discussion essayist must develop the skilful use of the rhetorical question. It is an amazingly versatile device, since it can be used to effectively introduce a new point, to clarify a point, to more forcefully express a point and to invite the audience's engagement with and support of your position.

'Mr Ahern . . . Benito Mussolini . . . Kim Jung-Il . . . Adolf Hitler . . .'. In a single paragraph, we have gone from Bertie Ahern, the Irish Taoiseach up to 2008, through Italian and Korean dictators, and on to Adolf Hitler. Not our historical experience in Ireland,

luckily, but it does demonstrate the shape of the discussion essay, starting with a specific incident and expanding outwards with many examples and illustrations.

'Thaksin Shinawatra . . . George W. Bush . . . Tony Blair . . .'. Further examples, none developed in any detail, because they are not important in themselves, but each adding a little more weight to the argument. Illustrations are provided to *support* an argument; for no other reason. Shinawatra was the disgraced premier of Thailand; George Bush an American president who served two terms in office and was noted for his verbal gaffes ('I'm honoured to shake the hand of a brave Iraqi who had his hand cut off by Saddam Hussain'); and Tony Blair was Prime Minister of England. Note also the agreeable variations in expression, from the formality of 'boost his chances' through the satire of 'occasionally while eating/choking on pretzels' to the colloquial 'hammed up'.

'But what of someone who doesn't support a Premier League team? Or, God forbid, someone who fails to possess a set of golf clubs?' Two rhetorical questions together, powerfully gathering momentum. When that occurs, they are usually building towards something. But then, the entire opening section of the article – anecdote, examples, illustrations, rhetorical questions – has been building towards something. What?

'. . . sport is increasingly resembling a faith-based system of worship'. This is what we have been led towards. This is the central point that the writer wants to make. This is the controlling focus of the article. It is essential that you study its placement and its expression. Note where it occurs, at the conclusion of the introductory session, following the anecdote and the interpretation and expansion of the anecdote. Note also how it is expressed with great clarity, simplicity and conviction. And please, please observe that in a discussion article or essay, you have only *one* point to make and that if you try to make any more than one, then you will create terrible difficulties for yourself in terms of structure. This writer has *one* point, that sport is replacing religion in our culture. Notice finally how that point is immediately repeated and clarified by way of a specific illustration: 'This is especially true in Ireland, where the sports bar has largely replaced the sacristy'.

'Since the late 1980s, Mass attendances in "Catholic" Ireland have been decreasing almost in direct proportion to the rising demand for Dubs tickets.' Having clearly made his point, the author now applies it to a number of areas of public life. This is the first. In terms of social behaviour, sport has replaced religion in Ireland. As the dominant means of socialising, of meeting and interacting with others, sport has replaced religion. Once more, a number of examples and illustrations follow. The last two-part sentence in this paragraph – 'Global figures indicate that one in five people watched some part of the last Fifa World Cup – which means football alone has more recorded followers than either Christianity or Islam today' – is a perfect example of the balance between evidence and opinion in a discussion. The first part is a fact; the second is an interpretation of that fact.

'As well as muscling in on traditional worshipping patterns, sport is increasingly appropriating the language of religion.' The second area that the author's point will be applied to. In terms of language use and communication, of a shared vocabulary that

we rely on, sport is replacing religion. Again, examples and illustrations are provided to support this, aptly described by means of metaphors drawn from religion, such as 'gods' and 'miracles'. Of course, if you have a number of different aspects to cover when discussing a topic, you must be able to move smoothly between one and the next. The other thing to note here is the technique of linking one section to another by using the opening sentence in each paragraph to refer back before moving forward. In the current paragraph, *as well as* refers back to the previous material, while *the language of religion* introduces the next topic.

'The truth is, there is little to celebrate in sport. And I say this as someone who strongly held the faith for many years'. The point being discussed, that sport has replaced religion, is treated here from a personal perspective. You should not banish the personal from a serious discussion – the personal humanises everything and adds colour and intimacy – but you should pay careful attention to just how much of the material is personal in a serious discussion (about one-tenth in this article) and precisely where the personal perspective is introduced (well into the development section in this article, when the point has already been extensively explored). You should avoid *starting* a serious discussion with a personal perspective; always a temptation for Leaving Certificate essayists. If you do so, you will find it incredibly awkward to move away from. In this paragraph, a number of anecdotes follow, but as always none is described in any detail. Events are noted or referred to, never extensively treated. You never describe incidents at great length in a discussion, because this would over-balance the essay by slowing up the development of the argument.

'I know, in other words, that sport can be great fun. It can bring people together . . . But is it especially equipped to do so?' Here we have an interesting technical problem. As mentioned above, it is always difficult moving from the personal to the objective perspective. How does this writer manage it? The opening sentence – 'I know . . . that sport can be great fun' – again refers back to the material from the previous section, and then two rhetorical questions – 'But is it especially equipped to do so? And are those lives that depend on sport full or satisfying ones?' – are used as the bridge, introducing the more general question that this paragraph will move forward to. Yet another valuable function of the very versatile rhetorical question. 'That was my experience. But is it the same for everyone? And is it good enough?' It offers an easy transition from the personal to the objective, the individual to the universal.

'The main problem with sport is that it is sustained by a series of myths.' The author has applied his point, that sport is replacing religion, to socialising, language use and his own experience. This is the fourth aspect, that sport is supplying the myths that religion once provided us with and that these new myths are hollow. Specifically, he deals with two sports-related myths: that sport improves the moral fibre of individuals and that sport brings people together in harmony. Various effective and colourful examples are given over this and the next five paragraphs, ending, you will notice, with a re-introduction of the personal perspective, which remains an important but not dominant feature throughout the article: 'grown men dancing around in silly costumes and falling down drunk (I should know. I have done it myself on occasion.)'

'Worst of all, perhaps, is sport's propensity to distract us from the things that really matter. A bit of escapism is fine . . . but . . .' Sport as escapism, the last of the areas that the author applies his point to; that sport has disastrously replaced religion in our culture. Religion provided meaning, sport does not. Over six paragraphs, the author expands on and illustrates this aspect. Note again how the opening sentence refers back before moving forward. 'Worst of all' means, 'all those things that I've already mentioned are bad enough, but this that is to follow is the worst of all'.

'. . . the proliferation of what Umberto Eco calls "sports chatter"'. This article has skilfully used news items, historical events, personal experiences and quotations as supporting material. As with everything else, when a quotation is used, it must be provided with a context, it must be commented on and interpreted, and it must be expanded on.

'Which brings us back to the Taoiseach, media hysteria and the Trapattoni appointment'. The second-last paragraph refers back to and recycles the opening anecdote, thereby creating a nicely closed, circular and self-contained structure. Notice that nothing more complex or elaborate than the simple phrase 'Which brings us back' is required.

'Sport, like any religion, has the potential to make the world a better place – but perhaps only if we stop taking it so seriously.' The final paragraph re-states the author's central point, that sport has replaced religion in our culture and that the shift, so far, has damaged us.

Key elements of a successful discussion essay

1. Since the function of an effective opening is to engage the reader's interest, the beginning should avoid abstract points and expressions of opinion and instead use a colourful anecdote or collection of related anecdotes that will illustrate and introduce the central point of the essay. There are four types of anecdotal opening available to the discussion essayist: a news item, a historical event, a quotation and a personal experience. For a serious discussion, the news item is strongest, followed closely by the historical event; the quotation is a decent alternative, but the personal anecdote is the weakest. In a lighter discussion, all four are of equal value.

2. The second section, organically developed from the opening anecdote, should be used to express and explain the writer's point of view on the given topic.

3. That point should then be applied in detail to three or four areas, one of which may be the author's personal life. Essentially, the author is demonstrating the validity of the central point by showing a number of contexts in which it holds true.

4. Whether approaching the topic in a serious or lighter vein, the style throughout should be rhetorical, employing the techniques essential to the public expression of opinion, including emphasis, repetition, irony, exaggeration, humour, rhetorical questions, colourful description.

5. The ending should return to recycle or complete the opening anecdote and to re-state the writer's point of view on the given topic. Most effectively, the author is hoping to present an incident or an image that *clinches* the argument.

Using the key elements to plan a discussion essay

When planning a discussion essay, you should organise the material in the centre of the essay first and only then turn to the introductory anecdote. Otherwise, you do not know what you're introducing. The story at the beginning has to lead into the first of the central sections.

For example, 2007, 6: '". . . the first and most important stage in encouraging viewers to imagine . . ." (Text 1) Write an article for a popular magazine on the importance of the imagination.

Firstly, I note how inadequate the exclusively personal perspective would be, although this is an article for 'a popular magazine'. If, as many candidates did, you open this essay with something like, 'When I was four, I had a vivid imagination', you immediately, and tediously, narrow its range. Everyone has a vivid imagination when they're four. No one is particularly interested in yours. The essay title does not ask you to explore the importance of the imagination to you, but, more broadly, 'the importance of the imagination'. To human life, to people in general, to everyone.

Secondly, I decide what areas of life I'm going to explore the importance of the imagination in relation to. I decide in what order I'm going to treat these and I outline my approach to each:

Part One: Science. The importance of the imagination in science, particularly in inventions. An invention, after all, is something that didn't exist previously, something that had to be imagined before being realised. Most scientists will tell you that the imagination is as powerful an instrument in their discipline as it is in the arts. Examples and references required.

Part Two: Art and literature. An obvious, but vital area, allowing for personal preferences within the arts, exploring the imagination in fiction, film, music, painting, and so on. Examples and references required.

Part Three: Personal life. Perhaps developed from considering in the previous section how great works of the imagination enrich one's life. How important is the imagination in the identity of the individual? Personalised anecdotes required.

Part Four: Politics. From the beginning of time, human beings have imagined a better world. Utopia. Some have even attempted to create in reality such an imagined perfection. The results have been disastrous. An exploration of the darker side of the imagination, which might also have been touched on in Art and Literature.

Next, I consider my opening anecdote, which now has to be science-related, since it must lead naturally into my opening section on the importance of the imagination in scientific invention. I opt for a historical event.

Introduction: Leonardo da Vinci was the first to think of a machine for vertical flight, the 'airscrew', as he called it, although it would be known as a helicopter today. The plans are dated 1493, long before the actual creation of such a machine.

And finally, I consider the ending, which must be a summary, in one form or another, of everything that has gone before.

Conclusion: Envisage a grey world in which the imagination is either banned, as in George Orwell's *1984*, or non-existent, as a final means of demonstrating its importance in life.

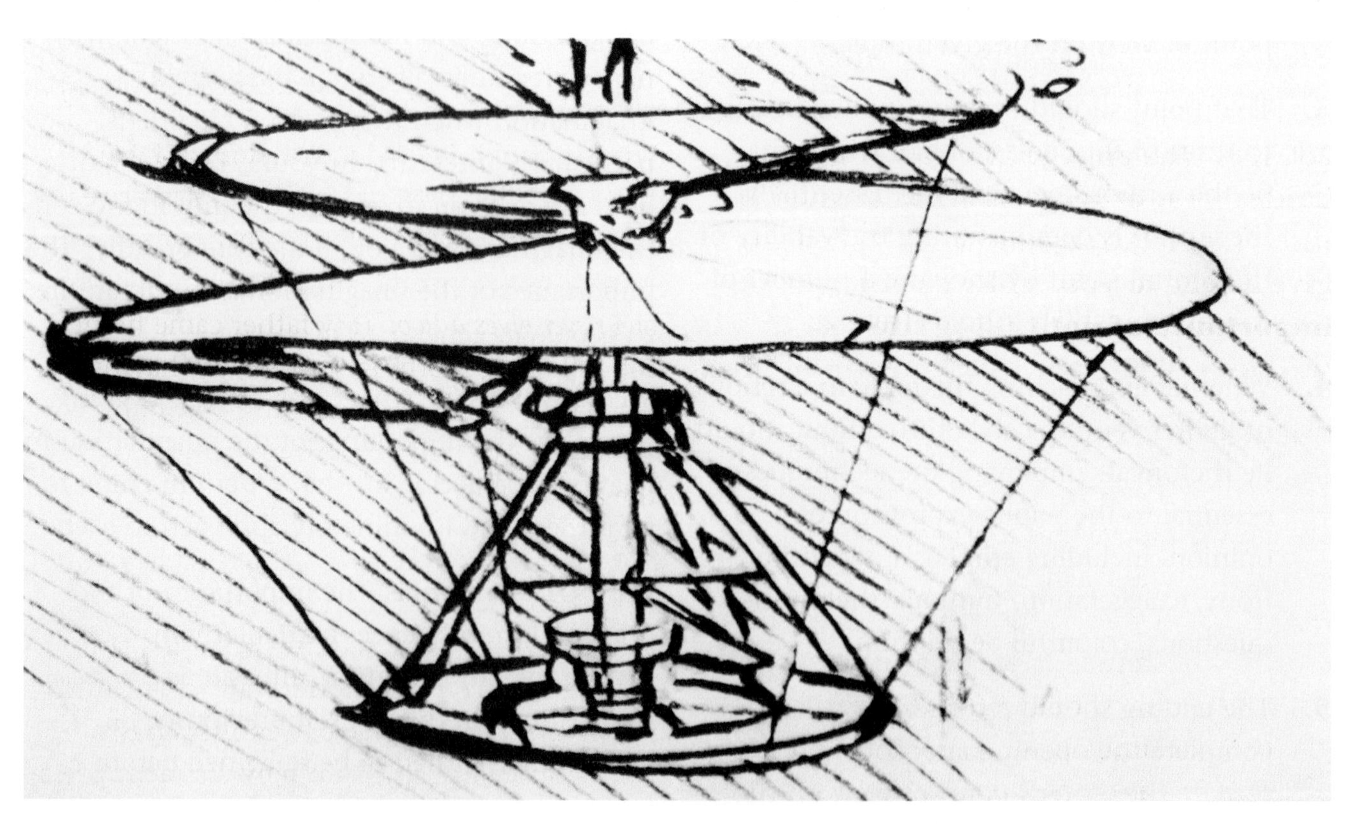

Sample 2

The importance of not taking life too seriously

2005, 6: 'She engaged in none of the banter that other customers seemed to like.' (Text 1) You have been asked to give a talk to your class on the importance of not taking life too seriously. Write the talk you would give.

Sample answer

The wise owl never gives a hoot. Four weeks, to the day, before we take our Leaving Certificate examination, and having just watched our English teacher being escorted from the class room by two muscular psychiatric nurses, the last thing you want to hear is a light-hearted platitude from my lips. I realise that. But the principal has asked me, as Head Boy, to address you on recent developments, and all I can think of at the moment is the last sentence my father spoke on the night he abandoned us to join a hippy commune in Kafiristan. *The wise owl never gives a hoot.* (My father came home the following morning, by the way, having sobered up on the back seat of the number 16 bus, where he fell asleep on his way to the airport.)

We all know that for several months now, Mr Keen, our recently departed English teacher, has been engaged in an obsessive war against the use of slack expression in our essays. And we all know that we have been mercilessly baiting him, and entertainingly distracting him

– in all senses of that word, obviously – by deliberately throwing out clichés during class discussions. Well, last night, apparently, in the midst of a passionate kiss that was promising to lead to even greater intimacy, and to even more burning excitement, a young woman suddenly withdrew from the embrace and anxiously enquired of Mr Keen, 'You're not only after the one thing, are you?' Which explains why he appeared in front of us this morning in a rather trance-like state, and why Cooper's unhappy choice of cliché for today – 'A man has more respect for a girl who says No!' – provoked him into lashing out so viciously with the umbrella he was mysteriously carrying.

What can we learn from Mr Keen – or 'Mustard', as we affectionately knew him – now that he is no longer with us? No, no, no, not to avoid girls who talk while you're kissing them. Don't be silly. What can we learn that will help us with our preparations for the examination? No matter how enthusiastic we are about something – and Mr Keen was wildly enthusiastic about English, you have to admit – obsession, preoccupation, grimness and mania will all spoil our enjoyment of it. A hang-up is a hang-up, even if the object of it is good in itself. Life, that gift we get only one attempt at – for unlike the Leaving Certificate that we are all currently so anxious about, we cannot repeat it – is too precious and too important to be taken as seriously as Mr Keen took written expression in English Composition.

No matter how important something is, obsession will destroy the benefit of it. Work, for instance, is vitally important. Work, as we all realise now, and possibly too late for some of us, is essential. There's an inseparable relationship between it and success, it and achievement. And yet, taken *too* seriously, it becomes a drug; and you turn into that commonplace addict known as the workaholic. I remember reading an essay by the great nineteenth-century English writer, Robert Louis Stevenson, author of *Treasure Island* and *Dr Jekyll and Mr Hyde*. It's called *An Apology for Idlers*, and in it he describes 'a sort of dead-alive' person who has no pleasure in life because he 'pines for his desk'. The image has always stayed with me. Although the essay was written more than a hundred years ago, the type of zombie Stevenson describes is now much more recognisable, and much more common, I suggest, that it was then. The student who is impatient in class because they must get to the Study Hall to prepare for

the next class, impatient in the Study Hall because they must get home to revise, impatient at home because they must get to school to learn more. The company executive on the way home with her briefcase and laptop, resenting the amount of time wasted by the city's traffic jams, by the family dinner, by the child's high spirits. The friend who sits across from you at lunch, not really listening to what you're saying, because their mobile phone lies on the table between the two of you and they are expecting an important call from . . . well, from somebody more important than you, obviously. 'Let it go,' you want to scream. 'Forget about it for an hour. Give it a rest.'

Rest. For a sense of balance in life, relaxation is as vital as labour, rest as essential as activity. You can't be too careful about relaxation, can you? Ah, but you can, you can. Sport, the most popular form of relaxation in the contemporary world, and as important as academic pursuits in most schools – including our own, as you know – is as open as anything else to the corruptions of obsessiveness. For sport, taken too seriously, becomes more than a game. And sadly, with the possible exception of eleven-year-olds scampering around the local park, sport is now more than a game for almost everyone. After the 1994 World Cup in America, a Colombian soccer player named Escobar, who had conceded an own goal to knock his country out of the tournament, returned home and was promptly murdered. Prior to the 1994 USA ice skating championships, the favourite Nancy Kerrigan was attacked by a man wielding a baseball bat, who had been employed by Kerrigan's rival Tanya Harding to get the main competition out of her way. Attend any soccer derby between Glasgow Rangers and Glasgow Celtic and savour the bitter sectarian hatred between the two sets of fans. Look at the unnatural physical development of almost any Olympic champion in athletics and swimming. And nearer home, take a close, careful look at the rivalry, on and off the rugby pitch, between this school and several others like it in our city. Only a game? How we wish we could return to the innocence of that claim. But we can't. Money, greed, nationalism, obsession and fanaticism have all played their grubby parts in making modern sport a serious business, although it's quite difficult to decide which of these two words – 'serious' or 'business' – is the more repulsive.

Am I striking too grim a note in a talk which the principal asked me to devote to the importance of not taking things too seriously, even the very serious occurrence of losing your English teacher four weeks before the Leaving Certificate? Probably. In which case, I'll merely mention, rather than develop, the other topics I had in mind. Hobbies – and we all have them – if taken too seriously become obsessions and transform us from humans into geeks. Relationships – and we all have *them*, too, although some more successfully than others – relationships, taken too seriously, become entanglements. And English, taken too seriously, becomes a chore. Which brings me neatly back to our recently departed teacher, and to the Get Well card that Templetire here, in an admirable gesture of forgiveness, passed among you to be signed. I'm afraid it will not do, lads. In his current fragile state, under psychiatric observation, and presumably under arrest as well, Mr Keen is unlikely to appreciate any of the following: 'No one said life was supposed to be fair', 'Happiness is a choice', 'You need to get out more', 'You're just looking for attention' and 'Have you ever tried camomile tea?'.

A critical reading

'. . . having just watched our English teacher being escorted from the class room by two muscular psychiatric nurses'. This is an example of the lighter, more humorous approach to the discussion, as befits a response to the suggestion that we should not take life too seriously. It opens anecdotally, as do all the other samples, but uses a comic incident rather than factual material. The fact that the audience is known to me also encourages this more personalised approach.

'. . . the last thing you want to hear is a light-hearted platitude from my lips'. Please note the consistent awareness of the audience throughout this composition. It is written as a speech and therefore addresses a live audience. In a speech, it is not sufficient merely to refer to the audience at the beginning – ladies and gentlemen – and afterwards ignore them. You must relate to them at all times. The repeated use of the second person plural pronoun – you – is one device for maintaining this relationship. I'll be pointing out some of the others along the way.

'We all know that . . .'. The use of the first person plural pronoun – we – is another device for relating to the audience. It suggests a shared experience, a shared perspective.

'. . . for several months now, Mr Keen, our recently departed English teacher, has been engaged in an obsessive war against the use of slack expression in our essays.' The anecdote referred to in the opening paragraph is here developed in some detail, assisted by some familiar features of descriptive writing, such as the creation of character, the use of dialogue, the effective selection of images, adjectives and verbs.

'What can we learn from Mr Keen – or "Mustard", as we affectionately knew him – now that he is no longer with us?' The central point of the speech must be developed from the opening anecdote and employing a rhetorical question, as here – What can we learn? – is one of the simplest and most effective means of setting this up.

'No matter how enthusiastic we are about something . . . obsession, preoccupation, grimness and mania will all spoil our enjoyment of it.' The central point, the focus of the entire speech. Everything else is preparation for this, illustration of this or clarification of this. Notice that I do not simply parrot the phrasing of the title – not taking life too seriously – but find instead a new way of expressing it. Notice also that to add emphasis, various synonyms of 'seriousness' – obsession, preoccupation, mania – are used.

Robert Louis Stevenson

'A hang-up is a hang-up . . . Life . . . is too precious to be taken as seriously'. The remaining sentences in this paragraph are merely repetitions through variation of the central point. They add clarification, explanation and emphasis to its expression.

'No matter how important something is, obsession will destroy the benefit of it.' The opening sentence of a new paragraph, indeed of a new section of the speech, the development following the introduction, is linked to the previous material by a re-statement, with slight variations, of the central point. This is another of the techniques used to ensure smooth movement from one topic to another and to create a coherent structure.

'Work, for instance, is vitally important'. The first area that the central point will be applied to, demonstrating its validity by showing a context in which it holds true.

'Work, as we all realise now, and possibly too late for some of us, is essential.' Note again the awareness of the audience. A point is made – Work is essential – and might be expressed as simply as that in a newspaper article, but in a speech to a live audience little tags like 'as we all realise now' are simple, but necessary insertions.

'I remember reading an essay', 'The student', 'The company executive', 'The friend'. Notice how much of any argument relies on examples and illustrations. A paragraph contains one assertion – in this case, that if work is taken too seriously it becomes an obsession – but multiple instances supporting that assertion.

'Rest.' In this case, the paragraphs are linked by a single word. The final word in the previous paragraph becomes the opening word in this. It refers back, obviously, but also moves forward, because it has a number of different meanings.

'Sport . . . is as open as anything else to the corruptions of obsessiveness.' The second area that the central point will be applied to, further demonstrating its validity by showing another context in which it holds true.

'the 1994 World Cup', 'the 1994 USA ice skating championships', 'any soccer derby between Glasgow Rangers and Glasgow Celtic'. Note again how the one general assertion, that sport can be taken too seriously, is again supported by many examples within the one paragraph. No illustration is developed or described in any detail, of course. All exist only as evidence to support the central point. Even though this is a light, mostly humorous approach to a topic, the examples used here are factual. A speech consisting entirely of anecdotal and personal material would be far weaker in its impact than one combining factual and anecdotal evidence.

'Am I striking too grim a note in a talk which the principal asked me to devote to the importance of not taking things too seriously, even the very serious occurrence of losing your English teacher four weeks before the Leaving Certificate?' A rhetorical question sets up the final paragraph and, by the way, maintains contact with the audience, yet another function of the versatile device.

'In which case, I'll merely mention, rather than develop, the other topics I had in mind.' Here's an interesting technique. I've run out of time and I simply won't have an opportunity to apply my central point to all the areas I had in mind. Rather than throwing them all away, I devote a sentence rather than a paragraph to each. It's a little trick that adds substance to a discussion without too much additional work.

'And English, taken too seriously, becomes a chore. Which brings me neatly back to our recently departed teacher . . .'. A return to the opening anecdote, accomplished, as in the previous essay, by simply mentioning that I'm doing it. As always, this return gives a nice rounded, finished shape to an essay or a speech.

Class assignment 1

Using the guidelines already introduced, write a short critical analysis of the following serious discussion essay, written in response to composition No. 5 on the 2006 Leaving Certificate paper: '"What seems to be the problem . . .". Write the speech you would deliver to a group of world leaders in which you persuade them to deal with one or more of the world's problems.'

Sample 3

A problem we cannot ignore

Mr Chairman, ladies and gentlemen . . . as the spokesperson for the Irish Youth Delegation, charged with the task of addressing you and conveying the concerns of my peers, I feel honoured and privileged to be afforded this unique opportunity. I also feel extremely humbled. Of all the problems confronting the world today, which one has the greatest claim to be heard in this forum? What right do I have to select one and ignore the others? How can such neglect be justified?

But of course, as politicians and leaders, you all know that nothing can be resolved all at once, that every journey, as the Chinese philosopher Confucius pointed out, must begin with the first step. I have to start somewhere.

May I begin then by confirming your worst suspicions about the frivolity of young people in the developed world and mentioning the famous pop singer Madonna. Many of you may already be familiar with her music. Many of you, like myself, may consider it slight and uninteresting, depending on mild controversy and low-level sensationalism to make an impact. Some of you, because you employ very efficient secretaries to keep you up to date, may even be aware that Madonna was in Malawi, in Africa, this week. According to some reports, she was there so that her adopted Malawian son could visit his father. According to others, she was quoted as saying that she was seeking a 'sister' for David and had found the little girl she was looking for: three-year-old Grace, whom she had seen in a video taken in conjunction with the work of her charity organisation, Raising Malawi. Perhaps, like many others, you privately disapprove of her 'baby-shopping' trips to Africa.

Malawi, as you know, is one of the most impoverished countries in Africa, among the poorest places on earth. Like many African countries, it is riddled with AIDS. Average life-expectancy is about thirty-five and the average income less than one euro a day.

With his mother dead, and his father unable to cope, David Banda ended up, like hundreds of thousands of Malawian children, in an orphanage. I'm sure you'll agree, at least, that being adopted by Madonna means David has multiplied his chances of surviving to middle-age. His father says he agreed to the adoption for precisely this reason. At thirty-two, a great deal younger, I notice, that any of you listening to me, he is himself a senior citizen in Malawi.

Africa haunts all of us in wealthy countries. It raises questions about the West's past history of colonialism and exploitation, about continuing inequality and about the denial of human dignity in a world capable of conferring vast wealth or abject poverty as the result of an accident of birth. In Malawi, if we were there now instead of sitting here in comfort, in your case, or shuffling anxiously, in mine, then we might download a Madonna song while someone a little up the road is dying from a disease caused by the widespread incapacity to obtain clean drinking water and while the rain pours down outside. The 'immorality' of this is not the most shocking thing about it. Don't you agree that what is truly appalling, despair-making and absurd, is that it is a reversible catastrophe.

Many of us in the West, through our involvement in missionary bodies, aid organisations sponsored by your governments and voluntary activities, are doing our best to help; but despite these immense efforts, I think you'll have to concede that the situation gets no better. Aren't you beset by the suspicion, as I am, that much of this activity exists more for the purpose of expressing western good intentions than achieving real change?

At the moment, my own country, Ireland, acquits itself well in terms of its contribution to the international aid effort. I cannot speak in the same detail, of course, for the other nations you represent, but I'm sure that their contributions are equally impressive.
However, there are a number of difficulties in this area. I don't have to tell you, for instance, that aid channelled through African governments is highly subject to corruption. As well as that, this aid is seen by us, primarily, as a way of discharging some vaguely felt moral duty to the underdeveloped world, a way of salving our consciences to enable us to get on with our own very different lives. What I want to convince you of, is that we need to find a new way of giving, beyond charity, beyond compassion, and certainly beyond morality.

In this context, Madonna's adoption of an African child becomes significant as a concrete action transcending guilt, posturing and empty rhetoric. The solution she offered David Banda belonged to the now, to the actually existing circumstances of his life.
It did not seek to maintain him within his

problematic situation in a way that allowed Madonna to feel better. It was transformative. Madonna appears to have gone to Africa and addressed both the sense of bewilderment in herself that many of us share, and pursued a radical solution for one African that has almost certainty saved him.

This is not to propose that we all go out and adopt African children, that you world leaders immediately abandon your duties at this summit, fly to Malawi, and grab the nearest available orphan. However, as I'm sure you cannot deny, there *is* a need here for more concrete, practical responses. Why should such initiatives come only from famous pop stars? Why should pop singers set the trend in social action? Is it not the duty of leaders, such as yourselves, to lead, preferably by example? None of us alone can solve the problem of Africa, but together, with the right approach and focus, with the right leadership, we might surprise ourselves. For this we need to be prepared, like Madonna, to change our own lives a little. But each little matters hugely. Or, as the Chinese philosopher Confucius pointed out, every journey must begin with the first step.

(**Note:** Apart from a few alterations to fit in with the task of addressing world leaders, this is the text of an article by the journalist John Waters, 'Saluting Madonna's African Aid', published in *The Irish Times* in 2007.)

Class assignment 2

Using the guidelines already introduced, write a short critical analysis of the following discussion essay, written in response to composition No. 6 on the 2007 Leaving Certificate paper: '"Imagine it's St Valentine's Day . . ." Write an article for a popular magazine on the importance of romance in our lives.'

This essay uses a quotation rather than an anecdote for its opening, although its central point – *why* is romance so important? – is developed and expressed as usual. In another departure from the previous essays, that question is then applied to the experiences of a single woman and the experiences of a long-married couple. In other words, two contrasting human-interest stories are used as illustrations. This is an approach that works particularly well with an article for a popular magazine, since such articles, in reality, are always filled out with human interest stories. See what you think of it, in any case.

Sample 4

The importance of romance

'Love is the answer,' the American comic and film maker, Woody Allen, once declared passionately. And if we accept that romance is more than just candlelit dinners, boxes of chocolates and bunches of flowers, and is instead, in the words of one hopeful subscriber to an online dating site, 'a meaningful and fulfilling relationship', then clearly romance is also the answer. Nobody is quite certain what the original question was, of course, but it's reassuring to have one certainty at least in life. On this issue, there is universal agreement. Romance is not merely important, but vital. Without it we would be deprived of the Mills & Boon novels, teenage magazines containing articles with such titles as *He Trod on My Ugg Boots and I Didn't Care*, several hundred movies starring Hugh Grant as a bumbling but endearingly romantic Englishman, and such poetic gems as this online effort by an American chap who seems to have lost slightly more than his heart: 'You are the most precious thing,/in my life today./You mean more to me than anyone else/and I hope you're here to stay.'

All right, all right . . . there are a few things here that we could gladly struggle on without, if we had to, and while I'm in the mood for concessions, let me admit that the quotation by Woody Allen is not exactly accurate, either. What the man actually said was, 'Love is the answer, but while you're waiting for the answer, sex raises some pretty interesting questions,' which seems to suggest that romance is unattainable and we need to keep ourselves otherwise entertained. On the other hand, Allen married at least three times, and marriage, I suggest, is an attempt to preserve the romance and not merely to legitimise the sex. The fact that it destroys both is neither here nor there, since it's the motivation rather than the result that matters here. Marriage is a testimony to man's desperate search for the secret of eternal romance. A doomed search, I'm afraid. For even though we are all agreed that romance is vitally important, none of us seems to know *why* it is so important.

In an effort to answer this question, let's consider the case of a young professional woman whose life is utterly devoid of romance. Kate Millicet, a successful 31-year-old business woman who lives in London, actually dates men, but if what we mean by romance is the heart ruling the head, the giddy sensation of being overwhelmed by intense emotion, then clearly she deliberately steers well clear of it. 'I never date people thinking I will only see this person for a set amount of time,' she explains. 'But after a couple of months I just inevitably find that I start to feel things have run their course. The guys that I go out with know from the outset that I have a very full life and that they're not my priority.' She enjoys spending time on her own and doesn't feel any pressure to be with someone. Occasionally, she has to put up with accusations of sleeping around – men who do the same, she notes, are affectionately labelled 'players' – but she's indifferent to these. She doesn't worry about ageing, about being 'left on the shelf', as some of her male colleagues sneer. She reckons that the most important part of her – her personality – isn't going to change just because she ages a few years. For Kate, the absence of romance in her life, and its replacement by controlled, calculated dating, is, as she puts it, 'an important lifestyle statement'. Is she missing out on anything? Not according to herself, she isn't. And who are we to contradict her judgement from outside?

Hmnnn . . . Not very conclusive, is it? If a young professional woman like Kate can eliminate romance from her life and still confidently describe herself as 'never happier', then just how vital can romance possibly be? Well, you may say, she doesn't appreciate romance simply because she has never actually experienced romance. And despite her claims that getting older will make no difference to her, the alternative to romance for an elderly person is not independence, as it is for Kate now, but loneliness. For surely this is the true importance of romance, that it is the first, necessary stage of a relationship that will hopefully blossom into something so wonderful, so fulfilling and so complete that it will . . . well, always retain the romance, I suppose.

One such relationship is that between the co-founders of the famous Sher System skincare studio, Willer, who is 78, and Helen, who is 72. They have been married to each other for fifty-five years. A quick little calculation will confirm that Helen was only seventeen when she married. 'I was very young,' she recalls, 'and although my parents adored Willer, they weren't too thrilled when things got serious. I remember my mum saying that he'd never be a millionaire. But I would have lived in a barn if it meant being with him. When I turned sixteen we got engaged and married in June 1951.' Willer has similarly warm, and similarly sharp, recollections of their early years together. 'We didn't earn much. We had each other, and unlike the high expectations couples have now, that was enough.' *We had each other, and that was enough*. Isn't that the perfect definition of romance, really? No chocolates needed. No flowers. No candlelit dinner. No Valentine cards. Just two individuals who both agree that they're 'better people' when they're together.

And perhaps because they never relied on anything outside themselves to either express or sustain their romance, they're still together, and still as romantic as ever. 'Our relationship improves all the time,' Helen explains. And Willer is just as enthusiastic. 'I could kiss Helen a hundred times a day. Fifty-five years together has passed in the blink of an eye.'

But while the Shers are living testimony to the importance of romance – it has clearly been the key to their obvious happiness – even they are at a loss to explain precisely *how* it works. 'Everybody wants this kind of relationship,' Helen points out, 'and if I could tell you the secret, I'd have millions. Truth is, it just works.' Funnily enough, an academic called David Pennett at the University of St Andrews in Scotland, who is – wouldn't you know it – a 'cognitive psychologist', recently conducted a study to discover what makes one individual feel romantic towards another individual. Pennett morphed a digital photo of his subjects' faces into one of the opposite sex and them showed them a variety of portraits. When asked who they found most attractive, subjects invariably chose the morphed version of themselves.

It couldn't possibly be true, could it, that romance is so important simply because it's another form of self-love? What did Oscar Wilde, that enjoyable old cynic, have to say on the matter? Ah, yes . . . 'To love oneself is the beginning of a lifelong romance.' And I always thought he was joking.

Homework and tasks

Preparing yourself for writing the discussion essay

If you are strongly considering the Discussion Essay as your composition option, you should now decide on which approach suits you better, the lighter or the more serious. Your choice will allow you to prepare relevant material. For the lighter approach, written for a popular magazine, delivered to an audience of students or intended for a young audience, you can prepare in much the same way as for a Personal Essay. That is, without composing a full-length composition, you could write descriptions of several significant events in your life, you could outline the progress of several significant relationships in your life, you could sketch the biographies of some interesting people close to you and you could set down your views on some issues that touch you personally and indicate what stories you might use to illustrate your views. Not all of this material will suit every composition title, but it may encourage you to note that much of it would have been directly relevant to three of the titles given in 2008: 'Write a magazine article (serious and/or light-hearted) in which you give advice to adults on how to help teenagers cope with the "storm and stress" of adolescence' and 'Write the text of a talk you would deliver to your classmates on the topic: Appearances can be deceptive' and 'Write an article for a school magazine in which you explore aspects of life that make you happy'.

For the more serious discussion, usually written for a serious newspaper or journal or delivered to an educated, knowledgeable audience, you need to be well-informed on the topic. Since you cannot anticipate the topic, although the range is predictable enough – in 2008 it was 'The necessity to protect national culture and identity' – it means that you must have a natural interest in current affairs and be up to date with what is happening in the world. If you are not interested in current affairs, you should not attempt the serious discussion. It's as simple as that. Why bother? There are plenty of other choices available to you.

Assessment sheet – Composition 1

2007, 2. 'And yet what romance existed in the old cloth-capped world . . .' (Text 2) Write a speech in which you attempt to persuade an audience that the past should not be glorified.

<table>
<tr>
<td>P</td>
<td>The title invites a speech to an audience of your choice, attempting to persuade them that the past should not be glorified. You must explore the negative aspects of such glorification – the dangers, the drawbacks, the limitations. You must supply convincing examples and illustrations to support your view and not rely merely on assertion. These examples and illustrations must have historical relevance and significance. In other words, this is a serious topic and demands serious content.
<table>
<tr><td></td><td>You offer a variety of relevant, interesting material and score highly with regard to content.</td></tr>
<tr><td></td><td>You fail to provide sufficient material that is relevant to the title and you lose marks for poor content.</td></tr>
<tr><td></td><td>You consistently address the negative features of glorification.</td></tr>
<tr><td></td><td>You fail to consistently address the negative features of glorification.</td></tr>
</table>
</td>
<td>0–2=NG
3–7=F
8–11=E
12–16=D
17–20=C
21–25=B
26–30=A

/30</td>
</tr>
<tr>
<td>C</td>
<td>You are expected to provide an engaging and relevant opening and a coherent development of the topic. The subject is broad and you must impose a shape on your material. In particular, simply hopping from one example to another is not good enough, so you must have smooth links between one section of your speech and another to create the sense of an ordered progression.
<table>
<tr><td></td><td>The opening is strong and effectively draws the audience in.</td></tr>
<tr><td></td><td>The opening is weak and fails to engage the audience.</td></tr>
<tr><td></td><td>You devote separate sections to separate aspects of the topic and establish smooth links between them so a decent grasp of the basic structural requirements of a discussion.</td></tr>
<tr><td></td><td>You seem to jot down points as they come into your head, without being aware of the need to construct a logical, coherent presentation.</td></tr>
</table>
</td>
<td>0–2=NG
3–7=F
8–11=E
12–16=D
17–20=C
21–25=B
26–30=A

/30</td>
</tr>
</table>

<table>
<tr><td rowspan="5">L</td><td colspan="2">At all times you must be aware of the audience you are addressing and advising. Language may be formal or informal, depending on your chosen approach, whether serious or light-hearted, but it must be consistently maintained and it must always demonstrate an awareness of your target audience.</td><td rowspan="5">0–2=NG
3–7=F
8–11=E
12–16=D
17–20=C
21–25=B
26–30=A
/30</td></tr>
<tr><td></td><td>Good rhetorical techniques in addressing an audience.</td></tr>
<tr><td></td><td>Poor rhetorical techniques.</td></tr>
<tr><td></td><td>Good standard of expression.</td></tr>
<tr><td></td><td>There are examples of careless, thoughtless, sloppy or otherwise poor expression and the standard is a cause for concern.</td></tr>
<tr><td rowspan="3">M</td><td></td><td>No problems with spelling and grammar.</td><td rowspan="3">4–5=D
6–7=C
8=B
9–10=A
/10</td></tr>
<tr><td></td><td>Problems with spelling.</td></tr>
<tr><td></td><td>Problems with grammar.</td></tr>
<tr><td>Total</td><td colspan="2"></td><td>/100</td></tr>
</table>

Assessment sheet – Composition 2

2007, 5. '. . . make us want to change the world.' (Text 1) Write the text of a talk, serious or humorous, to be given to your peers, entitled: 'How I intend to change the world!'

<table>
<tr><td>P</td><td>The title invites a speech to an audience of your peers (teenagers, in your case) in which you present your schemes, serious or not, for changing the world. It follows that you must identify what is currently wrong with the world, that you must advance many examples and illustrations of your concerns, and that you must address remedies for each problem. These examples and illustrations must have contemporary relevance and significance. In other words, whether you're humorous or not, you cannot simply invent the world's problems.
<table>
<tr><td></td><td>You offer a variety of relevant, interesting material and score highly with regard to content.</td></tr>
<tr><td></td><td>You fail to provide sufficient material that is relevant to the title and you lose marks for poor content.</td></tr>
<tr><td></td><td>You consistently address the world's problems and their remedies.</td></tr>
<tr><td></td><td>You fail to consistently address the world's problems and their remedies.</td></tr>
</table></td><td>0–2=NG
3–7=F
8–11=E
12–16=D
17–20=C
21–25=B
26–30=A

/30</td></tr>
<tr><td>C</td><td>You are expected to provide an engaging and relevant opening and a coherent development of the topic. The subject is broad and you must impose a shape on your material. In particular, simply hopping from one unrelated point to another is not good enough, so you must have smooth links between one section of your speech and another to create the sense of an ordered progression.
<table>
<tr><td></td><td>The opening is strong and effectively draws the audience in.</td></tr>
<tr><td></td><td>The opening is weak and fails to engage the audience.</td></tr>
<tr><td></td><td>You devote separate sections to separate aspects of the topic and establish smooth links between them so a decent grasp of the basic structural requirements of a discussion.</td></tr>
<tr><td></td><td>You seem to jot down points as they come into your head, without being aware of the need to construct a logical, coherent presentation.</td></tr>
</table></td><td>0–2=NG
3–7=F
8–11=E
12–16=D
17–20=C
21–25=B
26–30=A

/30</td></tr>
</table>

<table>
<tr><td>L</td><td>At all times you must be aware of the audience you are addressing and advising. Language may be formal or informal, depending on your chosen approach, whether serious or light-hearted, but it must be consistently maintained and it must always demonstrate an awareness of your target audience.<table><tr><td></td><td>Good rhetorical techniques in addressing an audience.</td></tr><tr><td></td><td>Poor rhetorical techniques.</td></tr><tr><td></td><td>Good standard of expression.</td></tr><tr><td></td><td>There are examples of careless, thoughtless, sloppy or otherwise poor expression and the standard is a cause for concern.</td></tr></table></td><td>0–2=NG
3–7=F
8–11=E
12–16=D
17–20=C
21–25=B
26–30=A
/30</td></tr>
<tr><td>M</td><td><table><tr><td></td><td>No problems with spelling and grammar.</td></tr><tr><td></td><td>Problems with spelling.</td></tr><tr><td></td><td>Problems with grammar.</td></tr></table></td><td>4–5=D
6–7=C
8=B
9–10=A
/10</td></tr>
<tr><td>Total</td><td></td><td>/100</td></tr>
</table>

Appendix 1: Some questions answered

Can I make up evidence to support my points?

In a serious discussion, where you are presenting material as objective fact – statistics and events – you can't get away with inventing evidence. The exposure of your material as unreliable will undermine your argument. In a lighter discussion, you can, however, cleverly invent a certain amount of evidence and get away with it simply by introducing the material with something like 'In our Transition Year we actually did a survey on this very issue and found that 25 per cent of Irish people . . .'. Where you are presenting personal experience to support a point of view, you can invent as much as you like, since no one will ever be any the wiser.

Can I use swear words?

Ordinary cursing is the lowest form of language. The words are overused, over familiar, devoid of any real meaning and childishly intent on drawing attention to themselves. Generally, the use of swear words at Leaving Certificate level is taken as an indication that your vocabulary is so poor that you can find no better alternative than the first sound that pops into the murky brains of the uneducated: it exposes the poverty of your written expression. Occasionally, the use of coarse language may be consistent with a fictional character, but even here you should exercise restraint and caution.

Will I get marked down if the examiner disagrees with my opinions?

No. It's your literary skills that are being tested, not your opinions.

So I can be racist and anti–everything, then?

All forms of racism are simply irrational rants, and you can't construct a subtle argument while ranting irrationally. The same applies to being 'anti–everything'. It's just a rant. And what we're really looking for is a combination of assertion and control. Outside pure prejudice, which is not acceptable, aesthetically or politically, you can make a case for any opinion – even a controversial one, such as preventing foreign nationals from working and settling in this country – provided that case is presented in a rational, logical manner and is supported, as any opinion must be, by evidence and personal experience.

The Composition questions often give a quotation from one of the texts and then quite separate instructions, as in Composition No. 2 on the 2004 paper. The quotation 'Everyone knows the sounds of rejection' seems to suggest that I could write exclusively about some personal experience of rejection, but the instruction 'Write an article for publication in a serious newspaper or journal in which you draw attention to the plight of a person or group of people whom society has rejected' indicates quite different material. Which should I work from?

The instruction. Write about what you are told to write about, which is the phrase following the instruction *Write*, in this case about 'the plight of a person or group of people whom society has rejected'. Unless you are specifically told to do so, you never use the quotation from the text as your essay title. In fact, you ignore the quotation from the text. In the present case, the title of your essay is 'The plight of a group of people whom society has rejected' or 'The plight of a person whom society has rejected'.

Appendix 2: Time management and other issues on the day of the examination

Use any past Leaving Certificate English Paper as a sample.

Imagine that you have never seen it before and that it is placed in front of you.

You have two hours and fifty minutes to complete it.

What do you do?

First, turn to Section II, Composing. You should already know which composition type you prefer, Short Story, Personal Essay or Discussion. You should know what your fall–back option is. The Short Story and the narrative Personal Essay are similar and one is available to you as an alternative to the other. The Discussion and the discursive Personal Essay are also similar and one is available to you as an alternative to the other. Select your essay.

Next, turn to the Question B tasks. Read all three. You should already know which type you prefer and what your fall–back option is. Grade them in order of preference, 1, 2 and 3.

Next, turn to the Question A tasks. Read the titles and introductions to each text and all the set questions. On the basis of how comfortable you are with the *questions*, grade the texts in order of preference, 1, 2 and 3.

On the basis of your preferences, select the combination of Question A and Question B that you will attempt, keeping in mind that you cannot answer Question A and Question B from the same text.

Return to your chosen essay and jot down a preliminary plan. This will consist of an outline of its structure and some indication of what material you intend using and where the material will be placed.

Return to your chosen Question B and jot down a preliminary plan. This will consist of an outline of its structure and some indication of what material you intend using and where the material will be placed.

Return to your chosen Question A text, re–read the questions, read the text twice and on each occasion note or jot down the words or phrases from the text that you will use to answer the questions.

Fifteen to twenty minutes have now passed.

It is recommended that you devote at least fifteen minutes to this type of rigorous reading, planning and preparation. At the end of the process, you know exactly what you're about. Further, while you are writing, your subconscious can work away happily refining and adding to the material you have settled on.

You now have 150 to 155 minutes remaining.

Divide the time as follows:
Question A (50 marks) – thirty-five minutes;
Question B (50 marks) – thirty-five minutes;

Composition (100 marks) – eighty minutes; five minutes, if available, to be allocated where required. Note that time is allocated strictly on the basis of the marks available for each section.

Start with the section that you are most comfortable with, the one that you find the easiest to handle. This will boost your confidence and allow your subconscious further time to improve your treatment of the more difficult sections. Continue with the section that you find next easiest. End with the section you find the most difficult.

Never run over the allocated time for any section. If time has expired, stop and move on to the next section. Failure to do so will cause you to panic about running out of time and severely damage your performance. Usually, you will find that time is saved on one section that can then be re–allocated to another.

With the Composition, refine your preliminary outline and then write the essay. Hopefully, you will have time afterwards to re–read and make adjustments. Keep handwriting legible and well–spaced to allow for alterations.

With Question B, refine your preliminary outline and then write the piece. Hopefully, you will have time afterwards to re–read and make adjustments. Keep your handwriting legible and well–spaced to allow for alterations.

With Question A, quickly re–read the questions, scan the text again if necessary, and start answering, allowing eleven minutes for a 15–mark question and thirteen minutes for a 20–mark question.

Acknowledgments

The author and publisher are grateful to the following for permission to reproduce copyrighted material:

'Carnage at Harvey Nicks' reproduced by kind permission from the *Sun*; 'Store gunman "had stalked victim"' © Guardian News & Media Ltd 2007; 'Films to Change Your Life' taken from *1000 Films to Change Your Life* (Time Out Guides); 'An Irishman's Diary' by Kevin Myers reproduced courtesy of *The Irish Times*; 'Headscarves' © Guardian News & Media Ltd 2007: Catherine Johnson; 'Baby, this just isn't working for me' © Guardian News & Media Ltd 2007: Madeleine Bunting; Extract from *Tenderwire* by Claire Kilroy reproduced by kind permission of Faber and Faber Ltd; Extract from *Hidden Lives – A Family Memoir* by Margaret Foster (Viking 1995, Penguin Books, 1996). © Margaret Forster 1995; 'Hidden Lives' from *The Golden Horde, Travels from the Himalaya to Karpathos*, Sheila Paine (© *The Golden Horde, Travels from the Himalaya to Karpathos* 2005) is reproduced by permission of PFD (www.pfd.co.uk) on behalf of Sheila Paine; *Teenage: the Creation of Youth Culture* by Jon Savage, published by Chatto & Windus. Reprinted by permission of The Random House Group Ltd; 'Web Safety' by Rachel D. Greenville from www. teenink.com; 'Celebrity Obsession' by Camryn R. Pascoag from www.teenlink.com; 'Prison Diaries' © Guardian News & Media Ltd 2007; 'Ironclad Rules' from *Nimrod Flip-Out* by Etgar Keret, published by Chatto & Windus. Reprinted by permission of The Random House Group Ltd; 'I nearly starved to death' © Guardian News & Media Ltd 2008: Edward Hebden; 'I never forgot my childhood sweetheart' © Guardian News & Media Ltd 2008: Jacqueline Hawker; *Who Was Sophie? The lives of my grandmother, poet and stranger* by Cecilia Robertson reproduced by permission of Virago Books, an imprint of Little, Brown Book Group; 'Being obese made me a social outcast' © Guardian News & Media Ltd 2008: Madeleine White; 'Worshipping at a New Altar' by Joe Humphries courtesy of *The Irish Times*; 'A Problem we Cannot Ignore' adapted from the *Irish Times* article 'Saluting Madonna's African Aid' by John Waters; 'A night in Sundance' from *The Lost Continent* by Bill Bryson, published by Black Swan. Reprinted by permission of The Random House Group Ltd.